Emerging Voices, Urgent Choices

Religion in the Americas Series

VOLUME 4

Emerging Voices, Urgent Choices

Essays on Latino/a Religious Leadership

by

Edwin I. Hernández, Milagros Peña,
Kenneth G. Davis and Elizabeth Station

BRILL
LEIDEN • BOSTON
2006

This book is printed on acid-free paper.

Library of Congress Cataloging-in-Publication Data

Hernandez, Edwin I.
    Emerging voices, urgent choices : Essays on Latino/a religious leadership / by
Edwin I. Hernandez, Milagros Peña, Kenneth G. Davis and Elizabeth Station.
       p. cm.—(Religion in the Americas series, ISSN 1542-1279 ; v. 4)
    Includes bibliographical references (p.) and index.
    ISBN 90-04-14816-7 (pbk. : alk. paper)
       1. Church work with Hispanic Americans. 2. Christian leadership. 3. Leadership—
Religious aspects—Christianity. I. Peña, Milagros, 1955- II. Davis, Kenneth G., 1957-
III. Title. IV. Series.

    BV4468.2.H57H47 2006
    253.089'68073—dc22

                                                                                2005054247

ISSN 1542-1279
ISBN 90 04 14816 7

PRINTED IN THE NETHERLANDS

CONTENTS

ACKNOWLEDGEMENTS

This volume is only possible because of the hard work of numerous people. Besides thanking the contributors, we also wish to extend our appreciation to:

The Lilly Endowment, Inc., which provided partial funding for this research as part of the Pulpit & Pew Project;

The Pew Charitable Trusts, which provided partial funding for this research;

Jack Carroll, Becky McMillan and Bob Wells from Duke Divinity School, who provided the support and hospitality for us to convene and consider these papers;

The Center for the Study of Latino Religion at the University of Notre Dame's Institute for Latino Studies, which contracted the contributors and prepared the preliminary manuscript with the help of Maria Thomson and Rocio Melendez Bardales;

The *Journal of Hispanic/Latino Theology*, from which the chapter "Hispanic Catholic Leadership: Key to the Future" is gratefully reprinted with adaptations;

America Press, Inc., which gave us permission to reprint portions of the introduction that were originally published in *America* magazine;

The National Catholic Council for Hispanic Ministry, whose members initiated the title of this book;

Graduate students Catesby Clay Jr., who compiled the supplemental bibliography, and Karen Boyd, who proofed footnotes, references and the bibliography;

To all of them and to the faith traditions that informed this work we are grateful, and hopeful that our work will help develop strategies to strengthen Hispanic ministry.

Edwin I. Hernández, Milagros Peña, Kenneth G. Davis
and Elizabeth Station
May 2005

FOREWORD

Pulpit & Pew, a project of Duke University Divinity School with funding from the Lilly Endowment, Inc., has supported a variety of research initiatives on pastoral leadership in the United States. A guiding principle of the project is that pastoral leadership will be strengthened through better understanding of changes affecting ministry in recent years and by identifying policies and practices that support creative leadership and vital congregations in response to these changes. Nowhere is this more evident than in Latino religious life in the United States. As this book makes clear, Latinos or Hispanics are transforming life in the United States. They have become the nation's second largest ethnic group, with a population of over forty million. Latinos are also deeply religious—traditionally Catholic but increasingly Protestant as well. The need, however, for trained, effective Latino pastoral leadership has not kept pace with the population's growth. The authors of the chapters in this volume address this need from various perspectives and offer important practical proposals.

Their analyses were originally prepared for a national summit on Latino pastoral leadership that brought together Catholic and Protestant leaders for a three-day meeting at Duke University under the auspices of *Pulpit & Pew*. *Pulpit & Pew* has been pleased to collaborate with the Center for the Study of Latino Religion, part of the Institute for Latino Studies at the University of Notre Dame, in sponsoring the summit and supporting the research and reflection reported in this volume. The summit's purposes fit well the goals of *Pulpit & Pew*, which aims at addressing three related sets of questions:

- What is the state of pastoral leadership at the new century's beginning, and what do current trends portend for the next generation?
- What is "good ministry?" Can we describe it? How does it come into being? Do its characteristics vary by denominational tradition? By congregational context?
- What can be done to help "good ministry" to come into being more frequently, and how can it be nurtured and supported more directly?

This volume addresses these questions in important ways. Denominational leaders and theological educators will find them of special
relevance as they contemplate ways of understanding and strengthening Latino pastoral leadership. I commend the book and express
deep appreciation to its editors, Edwin I. Hernández, Ph.D., Milagros
Peña, Ph.D., Kenneth G. Davis, O.F.M., Conv., and Elizabeth
Station. I thank all to all the authors, including the editors, for their
careful, thoughtful and stimulating research and interpretation of
their findings. I am also grateful to my colleague Becky R. McMillan,
Ph.D., Senior Research Associate of *Pulpit & Pew*, who was our principal representative in planning the pastoral summit.

Jackson W. Carroll, Ph.D.

INTRODUCTION

ORIGINS OF THIS BOOK

"Hispanic Ministry in the 21st Century: A National Gathering to Develop Strategies to Strengthen Hispanic Ministry," was an historic, multi-denominational summit of Christian leaders held at Duke Divinity School in October 2003. The event was a unique attempt to improve the quality of Hispanic pastoral leadership in so many faith communities across the United States.

On that momentous occasion, thirty-four women and men from nineteen denominations came together for several days of intensive discussion, deliberation, brainstorming and worship. Their goal was to create "progress in work"—that is, to build and begin advancing an agenda for greater multi-denominational cooperation among Hispanic church leaders. Summit participants represented an impressive cadre of the "emerging voices" calling for "urgent choices" to strengthen Latino/a religious leadership. Like the authors of this book, they are deeply committed to this task and intimately acquainted with the diverse contexts in which Hispanic faith leaders struggle, contribute and flourish.

The *Pulpit & Pew: Research on Pastoral Leadership* project, funded by the Lilly Endowment, Inc. in collaboration with the Center for the Study of Latino Religion at the University of Notre Dame, sponsored and organized the summit.[1] The majority of the research in this volume was prepared as background reading for summit participants. In conversations at the gathering, it became apparent that the research themes and findings had resonated among leaders across denominations. "I received my first impression about the depth of the dialogue and quality of the academic research of this summit when I read the papers assigned in preparation for the meeting," said

---

[1] Additional information about Pulpit and Pew is available at www.pulpitand-pew.duke.edu. Further information about the Center for the Study of Latino Religion and the Institute for Latino Studies at the University of Notre Dame can be found at www.nd.edu/~cslr and www.nd.edu/~latino.

participant José Daniel Montañez. Another participant, Alicia C. Marill, hailed the chapters as "excellent material, which render the grounding contextual reality for the serious discussion of Hispanic ministry in the twenty-first century."

As summit participants developed an agenda for improving the quality of Hispanic pastoral leadership in faith communities across the U.S., they confirmed the accuracy of the conclusions that our contributors present in this volume. Each chapter was written independently of the others, which means styles and methodologies differ. In some collections of essays, that is a weakness. In this case, however, the authors worked separately but arrived at parallel conclusions, which is a surprising but stupendous strength. Approaching the topic from diverse disciplines, denominations and locations, these independent scholars obtained very similar results, a fact that adds significant weight to their findings.

Earlier Scholarship on Hispanic Religion

This volume critiques much of the wisdom received from previous scholarship on the U.S. Hispanic experience, which either tends to ignore the role of religion, downplay its importance, or presume that organized Christianity was generally an oppressive force in the lives of U.S. Latinos/as.[2] Cuban-focused scholarship represents an example of this problem. One of the best and most recent treatments of Cubans is María Cristina Garcia's *Havana USA: Cuban Exiles and Cuban Americans in South Florida 1959–1994*. However, it treats religion only in a cursory fashion. Religion is not mentioned in *On Becoming Cuban: Identity, Nationality, and Culture* (University of North Carolina Press, 1999) by Louis A. Perez and son. Finally, the influential volume by Gustavo Perez Firmat, *The Cuban Condition* (Cambridge University Press, 1989) almost wholly neglects religion as well.

Robert E. Wright alone laments the neglect Chicano scholars have shown toward religion. They have tended to follow the lead of pres-

---

[2] For an example of this disconnect by Puerto Rican scholars see José O. Díaz's "Gender, Ethnicity, and Power: Recent Studies on Puerto Rican History," *Latin American Research Review* 37 (1) 2002: 215–229. Only one book in the bibliography deals with religion (in a single chapter) and even that paucity was ignored in this review article.

tigious intellectuals such as David J. Weber (*The Spanish Frontier in North America.* Yale University Press, 1992) and deal only with Franciscan missions or themes repeated regularly but without profundity (e.g., *penitents* or the controversy between Pedro Martínez and Bishop Lamy). Until recently, no biography of the late labor leader César Chávez has dealt with his religious faith (see *The Moral Vision of César Chávez* by Frederick John Dalton). Yet ignoring such a fundamental element leaves out a critical part of the story, and would be tantamount to ignoring Martin Luther King's spirituality in a "definitive" biography of the African American leader.

Not only secular scholars have failed to attend to the religion of Hispanics. Scholars of religion also continue to ignore or misunderstand this growing and very religious population. Peter W. Williams' *America's Religions: From Their Origins to the Twenty-First Century* (Urbana: University of Illinois, 2002) and Catherine L. Albanese's *America: Religions and Religion*, 3rd ed. (Belmont, CA: Wadsworth, 1999) are just two recent examples of religious scholars who are content to repeat clichés about Hispanics. Invariably, permanent religious structures of enduring importance are described as beginning in the thirteen colonies and moving west. Meanwhile, the few exceptions are either limited in scope (e.g., Michael J. McNally and Philip Gleason's *Catholicism in South Florida: 1868–1968.* University of Florida Press, 1984) or are brief works written by non-professional historians (*On The Move* by Moises Sandoval).

In the United States, the faith and language of Hispanics is undergoing profound changes. To understand the broader social consequences of this transformation, the gulf between religious scholars and Hispanic scholars must be bridged. This volume begins the task. In diverse ways, the contributors to this volume book allow us to listen to the emerging voices in the U.S. Latino church and as a result, a more complex picture emerges. Notably, almost all the authors reported difficulties in gathering data on the religion of U.S. Hispanics. Future studies may solve some of those problems, but in the meantime the book includes an extensive supplementary bibliography as an immediate resource for researchers.

ORGANIZATION OF THE BOOK

The following essays are arranged like an hourglass, that is, moving from a broad view to more narrow foci, and then back to the broader outlook. Hence the first and last chapters both take a multi-denominational view of Hispanic social and community activism while the five chapters between focus on specific denominations or locations.

Chapter One, "Latino/a Good Ministry as Community Work," explicates what is implicit throughout the book: that Hispanics are very religious and that their churches are particularly important to them since churches are frequently the only strong, stable, Latino-owned institutions in the *barrios*. Chapter One is also frank about how little literature exists on the civic engagement of those Latino Christian churches, and the difficulties inherent in research seeking to fill that gap. It explains across denominations what other chapters explore with specifically Protestant or Catholic congregations, namely, that Latinos consider good ministry to be a practical as well as spiritual service, and that most religious leaders and their churches put faith into practice through social services. "Latino/a Good Ministry" notes that Hispanic ministers and churches are expanding their influence through strong personal relationships and institutional networks. At the same time, this chapter also highlights the financial and educational barriers facing Hispanic religious leaders that compromise the potential social capital of Hispanic churches.

The book's focus begins to narrow with Chapter Two, "Hispanic Catholic Leadership: Key to the Future," the first essay to examine the denomination that is home to the largest number of Hispanics. It too concludes that the Church has not invested in building the capacity of its Hispanic leaders despite their growing numbers, obvious youthfulness, and desire to serve. Chapter Three, "Latino/a Catholic Leaders in the United States," surveys specific kinds of lay and ordained Catholic leadership. It also highlights how educational and financial barriers stymie Hispanics who wish to serve as religious leaders.

The next two chapters continue the narrower focus by examining Protestant denominations, and although each was developed independently of the other, readers will find clear parallels. Chapter Four, "Hispanic Ministry in Fourteen Protestant Denominations," signals both the difficulty of gathering data and the need to do so to address glaring research gaps. The chapter also quite boldly states that churches seem to face one of two dilemmas in relation to the barriers to Hispanic leadership: either to accept Hispanics who do not have advanced degrees in leadership positions, or hold to higher standards of formal education that exclude too many Hispanics. One sees yet again how few denominations seem able to attract and retain large numbers of highly educated Latinos in their leadership ranks. Chapter Five, "The Community Serving Activities of Hispanic Protestant Congregations," is more concerned with civic engagement and its consequence for Hispanic churches. It also looks at leadership issues, since congregations normally engage the broader community only when led by convinced and convincing leaders. The author notes that Hispanic religious leaders are rarely trained for the more practical, social service-oriented aspects of pastoring, and that this is the main obstacle churches face in providing those services.

In Chapter Six, "Hispanic Clergy and Churches in Political and Social Action in the United States," the author again looks across denominations and candidly admits that his research findings rebutted his own initial presumptions, which had been shaped by such influential scholars as Rodolfo Acuña. Echoing the other contributors to this volume, he argues that ". . . Hispanic clergy, churches, and religious organizations are actively engaged in political and social action and have the widespread support of both the Hispanic population in general and civic leaders in particular."

With the provocative title "If The Pastor Says 'Let's Do It,' It Gets Done: Success Stories in Latino Ministry," Chapter Seven looks at the role that churches play in building social capital. Through case studies of two socially engaged churches—a mainline Protestant and a Catholic parish in the city of Chicago—and a Latino owned-and-operated faith-based organization in Florida, the chapter shares best practices of successful leaders. It also provides a list of action steps and recommendations that, if implemented, can significantly help Latino churches and faith-based organizations to more effectively serve vulnerable populations.

While offering richly diverse perspectives, the essays thus make very similar observations across denominations. Like the summit of Hispanic religious leaders, they offer readers a collective "state-of-the-communion" address. The research was essential because developing strategies for strengthening Hispanic ministry (the goal of the summit) first requires study of the actual resources and limitations of that ministry. As we will see, the chapters take different routes to end up with similar reflections on the limitations and resources of Hispanic Christian churches. Limitations include economic and educational factors, which are often interrelated. Resources include interdenominational dialogue and cross-ethnic alliances, as well as Latino/a church leaders' strong desire to serve.

LIMITATIONS FOR HISPANIC PASTORAL LEADERS

Understanding the context in which Latino pastoral leaders work is essential to understanding what both inspires and limits their action and reflection. To begin with, Hispanic church leaders and their congregation members face economic limitations; the median family income for U.S. Latinos is between $25,000 and $35,000. This is particularly distressing since Hispanic households tend to be larger than those of non-Hispanic Whites. Hispanics are also more likely than non-Hispanic Whites to be unemployed, underemployed and earn less when employed. They are more likely to live in poverty. This data indicates that the economic situation of the average Latino or Latina, including clergy and other religious leaders, is often precarious. If they are undocumented or particularly dark-skinned, they face additional difficulties and discrimination. And Latinas generally fare worse than Latinos.

Since poor congregations find it more difficult to pay a full-time pastor, Hispanic religious leaders are often bivocational; that is, they work part time in their church and part time or full time elsewhere in order to earn a living. Such fragmentation can distract them from their pastoral responsibilities, as well as limit their service and availability to their congregation. Therefore, in Hispanic churches volunteers must do much more of the church's work than among wealthier Christian congregations, a factor also contributing to their growth.

Limited disposable income can limit one's educational opportunities. The most prestigious schools and seminaries are often the most expensive. However, paying even modest tuition may be difficult for persons who must balance one or more jobs, especially if they have family responsibilities or debt. These problems begin early—43 percent of Hispanics do not even complete high school. As a result, only a tiny number of Latino and Latina religious leaders have both the academic credentials and the economic means to enter accredited seminaries. Consequently, in a nation that is nearly 14 percent Hispanic, just 2.5 percent of students in institutions accredited by the Association of Theological Schools are Latino/a. Once Hispanics

enter seminaries and schools of theology, graduation remains economically difficult. Financial difficulties are sometimes exacerbated
by indifference or prejudice, particularly for Hispanic women.

Although an accredited seminary education often does not prepare religious leaders well for the reality of ministry in the *barrio*,
such credentials are frequently needed for ordination, certification
and advancement to regional and national offices. Because educational limitations often result in depressed incomes and depressed
incomes limit educational opportunities, the cycle is repeated. Limited
income can have a negative affect on educational opportunities, and
a poor education in turn limits income. Both Hispanic congregants
and their religious leaders share this dilemma, making it difficult for
them to exercise leadership in the wider church.

Ironically, in virtually all the Christian churches in the United
States, the segment of the population that is youthful and growing
is Hispanic. Meanwhile, virtually all those same denominations continue to invest hugely disproportionate resources in those segments
of their populations that are aged and shrinking. Both the research
presented here and previous, independent analyses indicate that when
churches invest in their Hispanic members, those same members in
turn donate their time, talent and treasure to such supportive churches.
Nonetheless, most churches do not make that investment, but instead
direct their assets to serving White non-Hispanics.

Despite this almost universal situation, Hispanics remain among
the most religious people in the country. Our authors tell us that
interdenominational and cross-ethnic alliances and a strong desire to
serve are among the resources that make this possible.

RESOURCES

Like the churches, social service agencies are trying to meet the
needs of the Latino/a population, whose growing numbers can place
heavy demands on the local social safety net. In Raleigh, North
Carolina, for instance, the Hispanic population grew seven times
faster than the rest of the country between 1990 and 2000, a sce-
nario repeated in other cities, towns and rural areas around the
United States.

Hispanic churches help to mend the social safety net in various ways. Many offer direct services such as food pantries, clothing

distribution, English classes, immigration counseling, tutoring and youth programs. Others create alliances with secular and religious agencies that have the resources but not the language skills or cultural awareness to assist Hispanics. Still other Latino congregations advocate for their constituents through education, voter registration, community organization and other strategies aimed at institutional change.

Our authors note that these efforts are quite often interdenominational and cross ethnic; that is, alliances are formed between Hispanics and non-Hispanics to serve the needs of Latinos and Latinas of all faith traditions. This kind of collaboration is frequent and widespread. When it does not occur, the authors found, it is usually because of leaders' lack of know-how rather than their indifference or ill will.

What factors contribute to this lack of know-how among church leaders? First, as noted above, Hispanic religious leaders have not had equal access to education. Second, even those with a seminary education do not necessarily have the savvy to navigate secular social service agencies or negotiate political and business relationships. Third, areas of the country such as Raleigh that have experienced a relatively recent influx of Latinos do not have a tradition of strong, local Hispanic churches, media, political leaders or neighborhood organizations that communities such as San Antonio, Texas have built over decades or centuries.

Yet despite the fact that they have less formal education, economic clout, practical experience and political access than White, non-Hispanic congregations, Hispanic churches are more likely to actively mend the social safety net than other institutions, according to our authors. They do so through direct service, cross-ethnic and interdenominational alliances and advocacy. Such tremendous resources grow out of a religiously inspired desire to serve.

Latino/a religious leaders say that their inspiration comes from both a divine call and human mentors. Many have experienced conversions but also relied on role models. And although leaders differ by doctrine, they exhibit remarkable similarities in their approach to ministry.

For most Hispanics, ministerial leadership is not just professional but personal. It is personal because it requires not only formal education but qualities such as honesty and integrity. And it is personal because it is expressed not only through purely spiritual means but through incarnational leadership to real persons who need services that the church can provide directly or facilitate access to. Whether paid—or more likely—unpaid, whether full or part-time, whether Catholic or Protestant, Hispanic religious leaders express their spiritual call through somatic service.

Hispanic churches are typically the only strong organizations in the *barrio* that actually belong to Latino/as themselves. Such churches are frequently the only anchors in turbulent waters, and effective Hispanic religious leadership is the chain linking that anchor to surrounding neighborhoods.

Years of work with common limitations and similar resources made it possible to organize the historic, multi-denominational summit meeting of Hispanic religious leaders. Reading these chapters one hears their voices clamoring across denominations for remarkably similar, and urgent choices. The discovery of that surprising commonality was the main achievement of the summit; this book helps map the way for leaders to reach it. *¡Arriba!*

LATINO/A GOOD MINISTRY AS COMMUNITY WORK

Milagros Peña, Edwin I. Hernández and Melissa Mauldin

INTRODUCTION

On a gray Sunday morning, the Iglesia Cristiana Wesleyana in Kernersville, North Carolina, is filled with families sitting on blue-cushioned pews under the glare of fluorescent lights. At the pulpit, with a small wooden cross adorning the wall behind him, Pastor Fermín Bocanegra, a small man who speaks with big, passionate gestures, greets his congregation in Spanish. Bocanegra, who came to North Carolina from his native Peru in 1968 to attend college, was once lonesome for the sound of Spanish-speaking voices. Today, he ministers to more than 300 families, a small section of North Carolina's growing Hispanic population . . .

Back at the basement of the Iglesia Cristiana Wesleyana, Pastor Bocanegra holds free dental clinics after Sunday services. He got a good deal on dental chairs and equipment from a retiring dentist, turned a former women's restroom into an x-ray room, and found local dentists to donate their time. But because none of the volunteering dentists speak Spanish, Bocanegra often runs back and forth, translating for the patients. Last week, he says, they saw 43 patients, and he translated for all of them . . . Bocanegra doesn't plan to stop there. He hopes to open a daycare center, build a soccer field, provide prenatal and pediatric care, and start a family resource center for the area's Hispanics. His vision, he says, "is not just to preach, but to change their life."[1]

The resourcefulness and commitment illustrated in this snapshot of Pastor Bocanegra's ministry, and the life-changing scope of his pastoral vision, are remarkably representative of Hispanic ministry in the United States. Laboring on the frontlines of immigrant and urban neighborhoods, Hispanic religious leaders must constantly adapt their efforts to meet the immediate needs of their community members, even while they advocate for community-wide efforts that can address those needs in the long term.

As many have observed, the dramatic growth in the Hispanic[2] population has accelerated the social transformation of the United

---

[1] From "The Hispanic Boom," by Jane Kitchen in the January–February 2002 edition of *Hispanicmagazine.com*.

[2] The terms "Hispanic" and "Latino" will be used interchangeably throughout this report. As Fernando Segovia (1996) points out, these terms have been a source

States and prompted much debate over how to adapt civic and social structures to reflect the needs and contributions of all who live within our borders. According to recent U.S. census data, there are close to 40 million Hispanics in the United States—approximately 3 million more, in 2000, than the Census Bureau had predicted there would be. Given the demonstrably religious character of the Hispanic community in general, churches are often the first institutions that immigrants seek out as they adjust to life in the United States. In responding to these requests, Hispanic ministers like Pastor Bocanegra often become conduits between their community members and the social and economic structures of the broader society.

Yet while Latino/a clergy are doing much of the work of caring and advocating for what is the fastest growing community in the U.S., little research has been dedicated to the exclusive study of Hispanic religious leaders. This chapter seeks to address this gap through its examination of the complex role that Latino/a ministers play and of the myriad ways they mobilize resources on behalf of their communities. By exploring how these leaders define "good ministry" and by identifying the barriers they face in efforts to live up to their own standards, we hope to help deepen understanding of how Hispanics in the U.S. are faring. We also hope to illuminate some of the resources and supports that could help strengthen these leaders' efforts to meet the spiritual and social needs of their communities.

LITERATURE REVIEW

Our research builds upon the work of others, adding to a growing body of work that investigates the role of churches and religious institutions in immigrant communities. In her book *Congregation and Community* (1997), Nancy Ammerman highlights how once small or dwindling faith communities throughout the U.S. are being reinvigorated by recent immigration, while others are seeing their pews and communities transformed by the cultures and social needs of new

---

of much unresolved debate within various disciplines. We use the terms to encompass a community that shares a language, history, and culture embedded in the Americas.

immigrants. Stephen Warner and Judith Wittner's *Gatherings in Diaspora: Religious Communities and the New Immigration* (1998), with Helen Rose Ebaugh and Janet Chafetz's *Religion and the New Immigrants: Continuities and Adaptations in Immigrant Congregations* (2000), provide a context for detailed discussions on changes in the U.S. religious landscape occasioned by previously established and recent immigrants. Paula Nesbitt and those who contributed to her volume *Religion and Social Policy* (2001) further add to the discussion by focusing on the impact of demographic shifts and religion on social policy. Ram Cnaan's *The Invisible Caring Hand: American Congregations and the Provision of Welfare* (2002) explores how civically engaged faith communities throughout the U.S. are providing social services to their local communities. Michael Mata's report "Protestant Hispanics Serving the Community" (1999) highlights the findings from his study of Hispanic Protestant ministry in southern California. And Helene Slessarev-Jamir's report *Sustaining Hope, Creating Opportunities: The Challenge of Ministry among Hispanic Immigrants* (2003) provides a broadly helpful overview of the economic and social situation of Latino/a immigrants, as well as profiles of several religiously based efforts to serve new immigrants.

Yet more remains to be learned about the social and civic engagement of Latino churches and their leadership, and about what fosters and what hinders good ministry in these communities. As Amy L. Sherman, author of one of the chapters in this book, has observed, "we know much more about the community servicing activities of African American congregations than we do about the work of predominantly Hispanic/Latino congregations" (2003: 4). Sherman notes how, in broad studies of congregational outreach, "almost always, data specific to the Hispanic congregations is not disaggregated and analyzed" (2003, 4). This chapter aims to help narrow this gap, and to prompt further inquiries into the critical service Hispanic ministers are providing to their communities as well as to the broader society.

METHODOLOGY AND DATA SOURCES

The findings discussed in this chapter are derived from two sources: a series of focus-group interviews with Latino/a pastoral leaders that the Center for the Study of Latino Religion at the University of Notre Dame conducted, and the National Survey of Leadership in

Latino Parishes and Congregations (NSLLPC) that was done by the Program for the Analysis of Religion Among Latino/as (PARAL).[3] Although, as we have noted, no fully representative study of Latino/a clergy has yet been conducted, the information supplied by the PARAL study provides a useful window into the reality of Hispanic ministry in the U.S., and offers preliminary themes and insights for further investigation.

The PARAL results reflect the responses of 883 Roman Catholic and mainline Protestant religious leaders, and thus supply important information on the major religious denominations, with the notable exception of Pentecostals. To compensate for the absence of non-mainline participants in the PARAL study, we intentionally sought Pentecostal and independent ministers to participate with Roman Catholic and mainline Protestants in our focus groups. The two sources provided the desired depth and breadth, and allowed us to balance the more elaborate observations of the focus group participants with the quantitative information supplied by the survey respondents.

Nine focus groups were conducted in all, with the participants selected by Hispanic seminary faculty in collaboration with the research team. Each group was comprised of 6 or 7 participants, and altogether 24 women and 36 men were interviewed, representing the following traditions: 26 percent Pentecostal, 21 percent Roman Catholic, 16 percent Methodist, 13 percent from Independent Churches, 10 percent Southern Baptist, 5 percent Disciples of Christ, 5 percent Presbyterian, 2 percent United Church of Christ, and 2 percent Mennonite.

---

[3] The PARAL study was conducted with heads of Latino faith communities who were drawn from nationwide databases provided by leaders from the following denominations: American Baptist Church; Christian Reformed Church; Disciples of Christ; Evangelical Lutheran Church in America; Pentecostal Church of God; Presbyterian Church, USA; Roman Catholic; Seventh-day Adventist; Southern Baptist; United Church of Christ; and United Methodist Church. The survey involved two phases of data collection: a "mail out" conducted between December 2000 and February 2001; and a phone survey conducted by the firm Blum and Weprin during March and April 2001. In all, 497 records (52%) were collected by mail and 463 (48%) by phone, yielding 960 records in the original data file. Data cleaning and removal of denominations that were non-representative produced 883 valid cases for analysis. While this data is not representative of the total population of Latino/a clergy, it does supply an important portrait of general trends among this growing and elusive population. At the time of this writing, more information on the study was available at www.religionsociety.org/national_survey.

The Latino/a pastors and lay leaders who participated in the focus groups were all actively serving as designated ministers in their communities at the time of the interviews. Since the terms "pastor" and "ordained" designate different meanings in the denominations represented, and signify in some traditions distinct sacramental and ecclesiastical roles, we use the term "minister" in this chapter to refer to the participating pastors and lay leaders. This functional title appropriately reflects the nature of the work they do in their churches and surrounding communities.[4]

The focus groups were conducted in Boston, Massachusetts; Chicago, Illinois; Fort Worth, Texas; Los Angeles, California; New York City; Raleigh, North Carolina; and San Antonio, Texas. These cities were chosen because they represent the ethnic diversity of Hispanics in the U.S., and the shifting demographic trends in both long-standing Latino communities (e.g., San Antonio and Los Angeles), and in areas of the country that have only recently experienced rapid growth in their Latino populations (e.g., North Carolina).

How Latino/a Ministers Define "Good Ministry"

Focus group conversations centered on the question of what the participating ministers consider as "good ministry." To help launch these discussions, we used as a starting point the attributes identified in Adair T. Lummis' survey of what congregants from across the denominational spectrum look for when hiring or evaluating a new pastor or lay leader (Lummis 2003: 2, 7). The key characteristics cited in her study were: demonstrated competence and religious authenticity; good preaching and leading of worship; strong spiritual leadership that inspires others; an air of approachability and caring; and the ability to combine "head and heart" in ministry (Lummis 2003: 2).

In discussing the characteristics and challenges of good ministry, the focus group participants talked about the variety of strategies they adopt to minister in congregations that serve monolingual and bilingual Spanish populations who come from different countries and

---

[4] The distinction between ordained and un-ordained is taken up later, when we address the relationship between formal education and ordination. When citing particular remarks that were made in the focus groups, we do designate the speaker as a pastor or lay person in the interest of narrating the diversity of the groups.

cultures of origin. They also discussed the challenges of serving communities on the economic fringe, and of the ongoing socioeconomic challenges that even long-landed Latino/as confront as minorities.

Latino/a ministers describe good ministry in much the same terms as their non-Latino counterparts. Several focus group participants spoke of good ministry as "providing leadership" and "being practical" while nurturing a community's spiritual life. A Southern Baptist pastor from Fort Worth, Texas, whom we name Gabriel,[5] stated that good ministry is "being faithful to God and the Bible's revelation, but faithful also to the community out of which we come." Pastor Miguel of Los Angeles said that good ministry is "living how Jesus lived. I would not examine the ministry by the number of people that I have, but by the true impact that the teachings of Christ in a world of suffering have." Gloria, a Catholic lay leader in San Antonio, Texas, reflected, "For me the words that come to mind are 'enabler,' 'catalyst'."

When asked about influences on their ministry, focus group participants most often cited other pastors and lay ministers who had been crucial mentors in their lives. For Pastor Nestor of Chicago "a priest from a religious community," and a Latina head of a youth conference in Los Angeles where he grew up, were pivotal in his choice to go into ministry. The head of the youth conference, he said, "made me believe and helped me realize that there was something good in me. It was there where I started to think, well, I am good for something better than wandering around in the streets."

Several participants noted that they had started on the path to ministry in contexts where spiritual concerns were linked with commitments to social ministry. Yet as important as this link was to the ministers we interviewed, the connection between spiritual and social needs "causes great confusion in the churches," Pastor Juan of Los Angeles noted, "because many do not understand that social work is the mission of the church and say that . . . the most important [work] is saving souls. But we are not solely spirit; we also have material and other needs and the church has to provide the individual with those necessities, like Christ did."

---

[5] The names used in direct quotes throughout the document were changed to protect the anonymity of participants.

The Importance of Social Ministry

Pastor Juan's commitment to meeting people's spiritual and material needs was echoed frequently in the focus groups, and social ministry was repeatedly named as a hallmark of good ministry. A pastor from Los Angeles insisted that concrete outreach is essential so that "we do not remain in the plane of context and theory and are able to attend to the needs of the people."

Thus, it was not surprising to find that many of the represented congregations strive to meet a variety of needs at once. Pastor Enrique of Los Angeles conveyed this in listing his church's extensive offerings of individual and group counseling; seminars about immigration issues; ESL, computer learning and after-school tutoring; food distribution, baby baskets, feeding the homeless; and organizing and advocating for schools, housing, and other needs.

The PARAL survey revealed a remarkable breadth of social ministries, illustrating that Latino churches are most active in distributing food, clothing, and money. Over 50 percent of Latino/a ministers in seven out of the nine denominations surveyed said that their churches offer these services. The Seventh-day Adventists led in this category (75 percent), followed by Roman Catholics (69.6 percent), Lutherans (65.3 percent), and Disciples of Christ (61.1 percent). Fully 40 percent of the remaining churches indicated that they are highly involved in such distribution.

Latino/a ministers also demonstrate significant concern for providing services to the elderly and preschool children. According to the PARAL survey, 55 percent of Seventh-day Adventists said their churches provided services for senior citizens, followed by Catholics (39.9 percent), Presbyterians (31.3 percent), and Disciples of Christ (30.6 percent). Young people emerged as a particular priority, as demonstrated by the number of congregations offering conferences, youth groups or sports activities.

Focus group participants echoed this concern for young people, and several expressed particular commitments to reaching out to youth who are at risk of falling into drugs or gangs. Pastor Eleanora noted the "Sanctuary for Youth" project her church developed in Chicago to provide at-risk youth with "a variety of services . . . legal, educational, medical, whatever, especially if they wanted to unlink themselves from gangs or they needed some particular help to make a transition into another place."

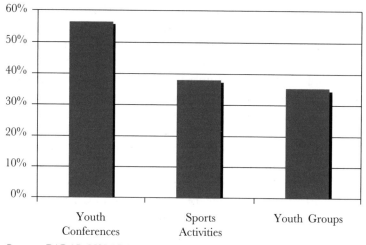

Source: PARAL NSLLPC data

Figure 1. Youth Programs Offered by Churches

In describing the importance of youth programs, many ministers mentioned their own experiences with pastors and programs that had reached out to them when they were young. For some, this outreach strengthened or awakened their connection to a faith community, and helped shape their sense of the Church's role within the larger community. A pastor in Los Angeles recalled the impact that a pastor from his youth had on him and others in his community:

> He started to organize a group at church . . . with the youth that were not from the church, and he started with some sports groups . . . and he soon started to provide health services . . . clothes and food. As a result, his movement allowed many people to start searching for the Lord, and from a small church it grew to one of tremendous magnitude . . . He caused a profound impression that made me think of my vocation and what to do with my life in the future, and it was in this way that God started to talk to me. In those times it was called church mission, not social work. There was no division between the social and the spiritual. The church encompassed an integral, complete mission.

According to the PARAL study, Latino churches and congregations are also active in providing services to the homeless and others affected by housing needs. Further, although fewer churches offer on-site health services, many serve as conduits to health clinics (57

percent), family violence programs (49 percent), rehabilitation programs (58 percent), and AIDS programs (53 percent).

It is important to note that when providing referrals to external
agencies and service providers, churches do much more than hand
out pamphlets or phone numbers. Many of the focus group ministers described how they frequently drive community members to the
necessary agencies and then stay with them to serve as a translator.

The complicating role of language barriers was frequently discussed in the focus groups. Participants noted how this both makes
it difficult for Latino/as to gain access to social services, and discourages people from learning that such services exist. Several participants also identified how problematic it is when an immigrant
who does not speak English encounters a social service provider who
does not speak Spanish. This is particularly pronounced in areas of
the country where Hispanics have arrived more recently and social
service agencies are often unprepared to serve a primarily Spanish-
speaking population. Pastor Sergio, now serving in Fort Worth,
described the culture shock of the new immigrants he worked with
in Atlanta, who "immigrated from rural communities that did not
even have electricity [and] were dropped in the middle of Atlanta,
without knowing the language, the culture ... [and] little knowledge
of what the North American system is." The situation is even worse
for immigrants who arrive with little formal education, Pastor Sergio
continued, since "they often knew little even of how the system
worked in the countries they came from."

Pastor Naomi of Boston, who ministers in a community of "many,
many ethnic groups" that is "constantly receiving dozens of new
immigrants," talked about members whose "families are fragmented"
because of immigration, and who struggle with balancing the need
to work with the desire to learn English:

> They have to survive in this country, but also they have to feed their
> families—wherever they have left them ... They're always constantly
> in the tension between immigration, housing, and education. Many of
> the parents would love to learn English, but they have to keep at least
> two jobs in order to survive and do something—even pay the money
> they have borrowed to come.

In response to this need, Latino churches and congregations often
offer English classes, despite limited resources. In seven of the nine
denominations included in the PARAL study, over 30 percent offered

English classes themselves. In all nine denominations, if congregations did not offer English or literacy classes on site, they referred people to other religious or public agencies. These numbers are in keeping with recent findings that "congregations with higher percentages of Latinos are more likely to report that they have a group meeting in the church for educational purposes other than religious education" (Sikkink and Hernández 2003: 13).

SURVIVING THE FIELD:
THE SUSTAINING IMPORTANCE OF NETWORKS

The ministers we interviewed expressed enormous commitment to their work, but also talked of the exhaustion that comes from trying to meet so many needs with such limited resources. Pastor Cristina of Los Angeles talked about the "burnout" she and her colleagues struggle with, and Pastor Angelica of Raleigh, North Carolina noted how she suffers from stress because of all that she is supposed to be accomplishing due to "the need for pastors to be a jack-of-all trades."

When asked what sustains them in their work, the focus group participants consistently identified the networks and collaborative efforts they have forged with other ministers, community members, and their own religious institutions. The PARAL data also demonstrates the importance of such relationships for Hispanic ministers, which more frequently occur between Protestants and Protestants, and Catholics and Catholics, with considerably less interaction between Protestants and Catholics. As the table below indicates, except for the Roman Catholic and Seventh-day Adventist ministers, nearly two-thirds of the other ministers surveyed indicated that they are involved in such alliances, with 72 percent of the Presbyterians and 67 percent of the United Church of Christ pastors associating with other Protestants (Respondents could check as many of the three collaborative groups as applied, and so the percentages for each denomination in Tables 1, 2, and 3 do not add up to 100. For example, of the 84 percent of Presbyterians in Table 1 who participate in councils of churches or ministerial associations, 41 percent collaborate with Catholics, 72 percent with Protestants, and 16 percent with non-Christians).

Table 1. Participate in Councils of Churches or Ministerial Associations

	N = 883	No	With Catholics	With Protestants	With non-Christians
American Baptist	88	22%	30%	60%	11%
Christian Reformed	11	36%	18%	64%	27%
Disciples of Christ	36	28%	31%	58%	8%
Evangelical Lutheran Church in America	75	37%	39%	55%	16%
Presbyterian Church, USA	32	16%	41%	72%	16%
Roman Catholic	496	65%	29%	18%	4%
Seventh-day Adventist	20	60%	35%	30%	20%
United Church of Christ	6	33%	17%	67%	33%
United Methodist Church	119	35%	39%	53%	13%
Total		50%	32%	35%	9%

Source: PARAL NSLLPC data

This tendency to collaborate with other religious groups and leaders extends to worshipping with other communities, illustrated in Table 2 below. 82 percent of Christian Reformed, 72 percent of Disciples of Christ, and 65 percent of American Baptist Hispanic ministers said that they participate in such joint services, and more than 50 percent of most of the other ministers do likewise. The relatively low number of Roman Catholics who share worship services with Protestants (19 percent) is likely influenced by how Catholic sacramental beliefs discourage shared communion with non-Catholics.

Table 2. Joint Worship Services

	N = 883	No	With Catholics	With Protestants	With non-Christians
American Baptist	88	19%	25%	65%	13%
Christian Reformed	11	18%	9%	82%	18%
Disciples of Christ	36	11%	42%	72%	11%
Evangelical Lutheran Church in America	75	33%	43%	53%	16%
Presbyterian Church, USA	32	28%	44%	53%	28%
Roman Catholic	496	53%	40%	19%	4%
Seventh-day Adventist	20	65%	30%	20%	10%
United Church of Christ	6	33%	17%	50%	17%
United Methodist Church	119	25%	37%	57%	13%
Total		42%	37%	36%	9%

Source: PARAL NSLLPC data

Similarly, with few exceptions, Latino/a ministers and their congregations collaborate with groups outside of their particular faith community on social outreach and service projects. As Table 3 indicates, only 38 percent of ministers said they do not participate in such efforts compared to the 50 percent who are not involved in ministerial councils, and the 42 percent who do not participate in joint worship services. Not surprisingly this outreach-related cooperation involved more participation with non-Christians than was indicated for shared worship or church councils. Overall, 18 percent of Hispanic ministers collaborate with non-Christians on such efforts, and a full 45 percent of Christian Reformed, 33 percent of United Church of Christ, 30 percent of Seventh-day Adventist, and 28 percent of Disciples of Christ ministers indicated that they work with non-Christians on such efforts. Interestingly, more than 50 percent of Lutheran, Presbyterian, and Seventh-day Adventist ministers indicated that they work with Catholics on such projects, while only 28 percent of Catholic ministers said they work with Protestants on such initiatives. Even so, this is a notably higher percentage of collaboration with Protestants than the Catholic respondents gave in Table 1 (18 percent) or Table 2 (19 percent).

Discussing the impact of these collaborative exchanges, focus group participants noted how they bolster the spirits of Latino/a ministers and help increase the efficacy of their efforts. Addressing how fel-

Table 3. Joint Social Outreach, Services, and Projects

	N = 883	No	With Catholics	With Protestants	With non-Christians
American Baptist	88	39%	23%	47%	13%
Christian Reformed	11	18%	18%	73%	45%
Disciples of Christ	36	33%	33%	42%	28%
Evangelical Lutheran Church in America	75	25%	51%	61%	21%
Presbyterian Church, USA	32	31%	53%	50%	25%
Roman Catholic	496	42%	51%	28%	14%
Seventh-day Adventist	20	40%	55%	35%	30%
United Church of Christ	6	50%	17%	33%	33%
United Methodist Church	119	32%	42%	51%	24%
Total		38%	46%	38%	18%

Source: PARAL NSLLPC data

lowship with other area religious leaders sustains him, Pastor Antonio of Fort Worth said, "I personally have a small group of pastors that are friends and are very successful in the ministry. And we nurture each other, because of our experience, because of our education, because of our relationships, because of our knowledge."

This networking occurs with non-Latino groups and religious leaders, as well as in specifically Hispanic circles. Pastor Lydia of Fort Worth noted that for her, coming together with other Latino/a ministers was particularly helpful, because building from a "common framework" allows for the kind of conversation that she described as "life-giving." Having opportunities to be with other local pastors and lay leaders, Pastor María of Boston insisted, is sustaining even if just for "getting together, praying together and getting to know each other, to be a support for each other." She named the ministerial association "Cofraternal de Pastores Hispanos de Nueva Inglaterra" (Confraternity of Hispanic Pastors of New England), and another group called La Iglesia Hispana a la Luz de Septiembre 11 (The Hispanic Church in Light of September 11th) as being particularly helpful in her work in Boston's predominantly Latino community of Chelsea.

Francisco, a pastor in Los Angeles, observed how informal networking "pollinates ministerial alliances [and] coalitions of pastors," that in turn serve as a forum for encouraging churches not currently active in social ministry to become more involved in meeting the social needs of the community. Pastor Johnny in New York noted how prayer meetings of local pastors also serve as a catalyst for inviting people to get involved with groups like the Urban Youth Alliance— an indigenous, community-based, multicultural, cross-denominational urban youth ministry serving the Bronx.[6] Several other New York ministers cited the Latino Pastoral Action Center (LPAC)[7] in the Bronx as a model of collaboration. LPAC works with the Urban Youth Alliance to support BronxConnect, a faith-based alternative to incarceration program for Bronx court-involved youth, ages 12–18, and sponsors other projects including counseling services, a leadership

---

[6] More information on the Urban Youth Alliance/BronxConnect is available at www.uyai.org.

[7] The Latino Pastoral Action Center (LPAC) has multiple sites in the Bronx and South Florida. For more information, see www.lpacministries.com.

school, Latina-led programs for emerging female leadership, and collaborative efforts with AmeriCorps.

Pastor Eleanora of Chicago noted that ministerial organizations allow pastors and lay leaders to initiate community action projects that offer critical and effective organizing campaigns on behalf of their neighborhoods. She particularly praised the clergy caucus of the Near Northwest Neighborhood Network, and noted how it "is very much involved in the socioeconomic development of the community [and has] taken on the issue of gentrification . . . [and] done the best job I've seen. . . . trying to root people back in the community; instead of having them flee, [helping them] find jobs, and deal with housing."

Thus, along with being involved with church-based groups, some focus group participants are also active in cultivating relationships with non-religious coalitions. They view both kinds of networks as essential for finding out what local groups and services are available in one's neighborhood. Pastor María shared how being "better acquainted with all the programs [and] social services already in existence . . . things that the families maybe don't need to pay for, things that the teenagers may get involved with . . . helps make my work easier." Other organizations mentioned include COPS (Communities Organized for Public Service)[8] in Texas and the Mexican American Cultural Center in San Antonio,[9] which Minister Martín praised for providing "training specifically for social ministry to farm workers." Pastor Naomi of Boston noted a youth program called Roca, Inc.[10] that reaches out to teenage mothers and gang members with "after-school programs, meetings, and opportunities for them to see that they can get out of that kind of level of thinking and behaving," and which has formed significant relationships with "the city manager and the police department." She went on to note the

---

[8] A profile of this organization can be found at www.iisd.org/50comm/commdb/desc/d19.htm.

[9] More information is available at www.maccsa.org.

[10] More information is available at www.rocainc.com.

[11] This high number of Latino clergy with formal education reflects this sample's overrepresentation of Catholic and mainline Protestant ministers, since those denominations tend to both require and encourage formal education for their clergy. The percentage would be lower had independent and Pentecostal ministers been adequately represented in the sample.

importance of "churches and a city manager and other people [being] willing to sit down and negotiate to find ways to help out." These networks not only support Latino/a ministers and their congregations' efforts, but also help develop the social capital beyond the Latino community that is critical for these communities to thrive.

Along with community networks, Latino/a ministers also seek out connections within their particular denominations. Pastor Eleanora of Chicago described how her community and others in the Lutheran context reach out to one another through "a group of . . . about eleven congregations [that] collaborate. We worship together in Lent [and] we're right now looking at a process by which we can determine . . . what kind of structural ways we should be connected." Some focus group participants expressed frustration with their denominations' lack of support. A Catholic lay leader in Chicago noted how little his church does to support Latino/a leadership:

> We are not taken seriously as leaders and ministers. We have to work very hard in order for people to believe in us . . . It's worrisome to see how the Hispanic community is growing in Chicago and at the national level at a time when Hispanic faces are not available in the positions where we should be. So, people who do not understand our reality are still making the decisions for us . . . It worries me to see how many parishes and archdioceses are functioning with programs that are translated from English. These programs are not saying a lot to our community . . . We need to be given wings, so that we can fly in our community and create, from our own experience, and the experience that our Hispanic community has of God.

Pastor Juan of New York, reflecting on how much his faith had changed his life, also spoke of "how much people need ministers . . . to be from my community—not only from my church but part of the entire community."

On a more hopeful note, as Table 4 indicates, many of the PARAL survey ministers consider their denominations to be supportive of their work. Overall, 46 percent of the ministers rated their denominations as "very supportive," and 39 percent as "somewhat supportive." Notably, 75 percent of the Seventh-day Adventist ministers, and nearly 64 percent of the Roman Catholic and Christian Reformed ministers rated their denominations as very supportive, while 33 percent of United Church of Christ ministers indicated that their denomination is unsupportive.

Table 4. Perceived Level of Denominational Support for Latino/a Ministers

	N = 883	Very Supportive	Somewhat Supportive	No Special Attention	Not Very Supportive	Not Reported
American Baptist	88	43%	33%	7%	17%	0%
Christian Reformed	11	64%	36%	0%	0%	0%
Disciples of Christ	36	39%	50%	0%	11%	0%
Evangelical Lutheran Church in America	75	40%	45%	0%	15%	0%
Presbyterian Church, USA	32	34%	47%	0%	19%	0%
Roman Catholic	496	64%	28%	3%	3%	3%
Seventh-day Adventist	20	75%	15%	0%	5%	5%
United Church of Christ	6	0%	67%	0%	33%	0%
United Methodist Church	119	46%	39%	3%	9%	3%

Source: PARAL NSLLPC data

Yet while support is being offered to Hispanic ministry on an institutional level, the testimonies and data on the extensive civic engagement of Latino/a ministers underscores how many Latino communities in the U.S. primarily rely upon individuals who have answered the call to serve. As we explore in the next section, the burden on these ministers is decidedly increased by the need to secure the very resources, training, and support that they and their ministries need to survive.

The Dilemma of Low Incomes and Poor Communities

A very concrete barrier that Latino/a ministers confront daily is the lack of financial assets within and available to their communities. Personal income, though not the only manifestation of this, does have an impact on the sustainability of many ministries. As Table 5 shows, church leaders' median family income (that is, the pastor's salary plus the earnings of others contributing to household income) is just $25,000 to $34,999. Of the ministers who responded to the PARAL survey, 85 percent have family incomes of less than $50,000.

Table 5. Family Incomes of Latino/a Pastors and Lay Leaders

Family Income	Number	Percentage
< $5,000	18	2.0%
$5,000–$9,999	39	4.4%
$10,000–$14,999	111	12.6%
$15,000–$24,999	209	23.7%
$25,000–$34,999	141	16.0%
$35,000–$49,999	133	15.1%
$50,000–$74,999	100	11.3%
$75,000 +	39	4.4%
No answer	93	10.4%
TOTAL	883	100%

Source: PARAL NSLLPC data

Low incomes also can impede ministers from pursuing the education and training that would help them better serve their communities, and in some cases this lack of education conversely impedes access to full-time positions in their churches or congregations. Francisco, a Catholic lay leader in Chicago, spoke of this cycle of low financial resources limiting access to formal education, and the lack of formal education making someone less effective for ministry:

> A lot of the leaders that are up front have not completed or passed to do their master's degree. And when we notice that it's a need, no resources are available. First, our salary is not enough for us to say, "I am going to go study and go to a Catholic institution." For example, if both my wife and I work, financial aid is not going to be enough, or it may be nothing.

Along with affecting future ministerial prospects, focus group participants emphasized how their relatively low incomes can make remaining in ministry stressful, and dampen their enthusiasm for encouraging people who are considering ministry. A lay leader in San Antonio, Nilda, shared her frustration:

> . . . I am discouraged. I have a discouraged family. And I am thinking of another [minister] . . . who has three children . . . He's very gifted in computers, but he wanted to leave it all to come do ministry. . . . "Don't do that!" That's my gut reaction, because . . . the reality is you can be making twenty-three, twenty-four, or maybe twenty-five [thousand dollars] raising a family. He did it anyway. For a short period of time he was able to do it, but then it came to a point where he had to choose again–but he loved the work. He loved the ministry.

The lack of available resources to help strengthen pastoral leadership extends beyond the scarcity of personal income. While increasing family income would ease some of the pressure on Latino/a ministers, many Latino congregations can barely afford to maintain their churches at their current levels. A pastor from Chicago noted:

> I once calculated that if everybody in the congregation were employed at minimum wage and they were all tithing, then we could support our ministry if we had 2,000 members. But you know, we weren't going to have 2,000 members, and we had a lot of students and kids and underemployed people. So, that is obviously not a model that's going to work for our ministry in a poor community.

Another pastor from Chicago talked about how in communities that are too poor to support their social ministries, some Latino/a ministers see no other option than to create "a business or something that will produce income so you can support your ministry." Pastor Johnny of the South Bronx in New York City also talked about the challenge of serving a community whose meager resources are perpetuated by the "cycle of poverty" that he observes. Exacerbating the situation, he says, "we have people coming in [where] there's three generations and no one has been married . . . So everyone has been born out of wedlock. Or no one has graduated high school."

THE NEED FOR GREATER EDUCATIONAL RESOURCES

As stated earlier, the pastors and lay leaders in our focus groups insist that good ministry serves not just people's spiritual but material needs. Related to this, many in our focus groups talked about personal conversion and a call to strengthen marginalized Latino communities resisting racism, poverty and inequality. As Pastor José from New York put it, "I had a passion and a mercy particularly for those who, to use a buzzword, were 'marginalized.' And I felt that God was all the more important to get that love to communities that have been ostracized, even at times by the church."

At the same time, many of the Latino/a ministers interviewed observed that a lack of education and/or practical skills often hindered people from answering this call. Further, while seminary degrees are not alone sufficient for good ministry, the average experience of both pastors and lay leaders suggests that such credentials are helpful.

The PARAL data show that 85 percent of Latino/a ministers have a Bachelor's or professional degree, or higher.[11] Latino/a leaders (men and women) who receive credentials from a graduate or post-graduate program account for a higher percentage of the ministers who hold the highest ranking position in their local faith community, and who work in full-time ministry, as well as comprising the majority of ministers who identified themselves as being ordained (overall 77 percent of Latino/a ministers surveyed in the PARAL study indicated that they are ordained). Further, there is a strong correlation between formal religious education and ordination, job ranking and whether one is employed in full-time ministry, as Table 6 illustrates. Of the Latino/a ministers with seminary degrees, 90 percent are ordained, 79 percent are the highest-ranking person on their staff, and 74 percent work in full-time ministry. Comparatively, of those with no formal religious education, only 16 percent are ordained, just 13 percent occupy the highest-ranking position, and 44 percent are employed in full-time ministry.

Table 6. Relationship between Education levels and Ordination Status, Job Rank, and Full-time Ministry Status

	N = 883	Ordained	Highest Ranking	Full-Time Ministry
No formal religious education	55	16%	13%	44%
Certificate, bible college, or some seminary	119	36%	24%	64%
Seminary or postgraduate	684	90%	79%	74%

Source: PARAL NSLLPC data

As might be expected, Hispanic women encounter this education barrier more often than their male counterparts do, which can contribute to their being underrepresented in leadership positions within their churches and congregations. Nearly 19 percent (N = 163) of the PARAL

---

[11] This high number of Latino clergy with formal education reflects this sample's overrepresentation of Catholic and mainline Protestant ministers, since those denominations tend to both require and encourage formal education for their clergy. The percentage would be lower had independent and Pentecostal ministers been adequately represented in the sample.

study respondents were women, of which only 52 percent had received some type of seminary degree in contrast to the almost 86 percent of Latino ministers who had (see Figure 2). Fully two-thirds of Latino ministers in mainline churches hold a Master of Divinity or higher degree, while only slightly higher than one-third of Latinas do. A total of 17 percent of Latinas had no formal religious education, compared to only 4 percent of men; and 30 percent of Latinas reported having completed only a certificate or correspondence program, compared to just 10 percent of men.

The causes for this disparity are complicated by the fact that formal ordination[12] is not an option for women in certain churches (e.g., Roman Catholics, some Protestant groups). Since Master of Divinity degrees are often designed as a preparation for ordination, it is possible that women who belong to denominations that will not ordain them might not see the benefits of pursuing such education. Though, as we have mentioned, the PARAL study is not representative of the total Hispanic clergy in the U.S., the table below shows that the majority of female respondents who are ordained come from denominations that formally ordain women.

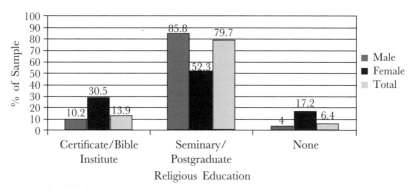

Source: PARAL NSLLPC data

Figure 2. Ministerial Religious Educational Attainment by Gender

---

[12] The PARAL survey asked participants to answer the basic question "Are you ordained?" without defining the term. Respondents thus were free to answer according to their own understanding of what it means to be ordained. This is evident in the fact that some Roman Catholic women answered in the affirmative, which suggests that they interpreted the question in terms of their role within the communities they serve, rather than according to whom the formal ecclesial structure defines as "ordained." See Table 9.

Table 7. Latina Ministers' Ordination Status by Denomination

N = 883	Number of Women	Women Ordained	% Women Ordained
American Baptist	88	11	3	27%
Christian Reformed	11	0	0	0%
Disciples of Christ	36	6	1	17%
Evangelical Lutheran Church in America	75	19	12	63%
Presbyterian Church, USA	32	3	3	100%
Roman Catholic	496	94	11	12%
Seventh-day Adventist	20	2	1	50%
United Church of Christ	6	4	2	50%
United Methodist Church	119	24	15	63%
Totals		163	48	30%

While the inability to be officially ordained might partly explain why in the PARAL study fewer Hispanic women have seminary degrees than Hispanic men, the survey found a similar gender gap in the overall educational levels of the respondents, which shows fewer Latinas receiving advanced degrees than their Latino colleagues. As the figure below illustrates, Latino men and Latina women follow each other closely in educational attainment until they reach college and associate degree levels of education. Latina ministers were more likely than their Latino counterparts to have some college or an associate degree, while Latino men were more likely than Latinas to have graduated from college or have earned a higher professional degree.

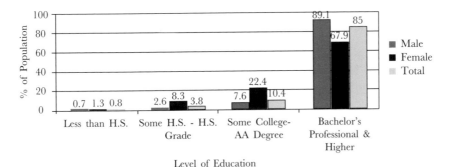

Source: PARAL NSLLPC data

Figure 3. Educational Atainment by Gender

Table 8. Disparity Between Latino and Latina Pastors

	N = 883	Highest Ranking	Full-Time Ministry
Female	163	25%	57%
Male	710	75%	72%

Source: PARAL NSLLPC data

This difference is significant because such the disparity in religious degrees is the overt reason some churches and congregations use for refusing women higher leadership positions, which in turn works to discourage women from pursuing their calls to ministry. Thus, as might be expected, Latino pastors occupy the highest-ranking position in their congregations more frequently than their Latina counterparts (see Table 8).

To be sure, increasing the educational opportunities for women in denominations that will not ordain them will not necessarily grant Latinas access to positions in their churches that are restricted to formally ordained clergy. This is evident in that only 36.1 percent of the Latinas shown in Table 8 as having certificates, some bible college, or seminary training, indicated that they are ordained.

Equally important to increasing access to seminary education for Latinas is making sure that educational curricula are relevant to the needs of the communities that Hispanic men and women will serve. Many focus group participants discussed how poorly their seminaries had prepared them for the actual work they are called to do. As one pastor put it: "Formation is not just a classroom, but it has to be based on real ministry." Pastor Enrique of Los Angeles summed up the problem in this way:

> In the modern seminary, it is mostly of the brain . . . [you] learn material, but you do not apply that material . . . When I graduated from my basic theological studies [and] . . . started to be a pastor of the church, I realized that what I learned in the seminary was not good for anything in the church.

Pastor Nestor of Raleigh, North Carolina, underscored the need for more practical course work, and noted how "in our seminaries, the emphasis on preaching, on mission, and on theology [has] been very good," but that attention to administrative skills and social action was lacking. Some pastors and lay leaders who came to ministry as a second career highlighted how their training in other fields provided what their seminary training lacked. Pastor Obed noted how his "social work career was very, very helpful. The . . . listening skills, comprehensive engagement, family systems theory, family therapy, case management process—that stuff was invaluable for me in ministry." A pastor from Chicago expressed his hope that pastoral education had improved since he had graduated twelve years ago, when he encountered a "lack of awareness of what was going on in the Hispanic ministry here in Chicago." He optimistically noted, "I think we have made relatively good progress on it now."

In some parts of the country progress is being made. For example, Pastor Naomi of Boston indicated, "Thank God many programs in leadership and management have surfaced, which is a very good thing." Pastors and leaders in Boston identified the Center for Urban Ministerial Education (CUME) of Gordon Conwell Seminary[13] in their city as one model of a seminary curriculum that is meeting the training needs of urban Hispanic ministers. Students in this Master of Arts in Urban Ministry program complete twenty courses, some of which are the standard courses of any Master's of Divinity program, but others which focus on urban theological studies, public ministry for church, inner-city ministry, and theology and ethics for urban ministry.

Conclusion: Empowering Latino Ministry for the 21st Century

As we mentioned at the outset, little social scientific study has focused exclusively on the Latino church or its leadership. The research data used here are an initial step toward filling the gaps in knowledge, and indicate important issues that we hope future research will further confirm and expand upon.

Though much remains to be learned about the complexity of Hispanic ministry in the United States, we are confident that the level of engagement we found among Latino/a ministers will only continue to increase. Both the focus group interviews and the PARAL study indicate that Latino/a ministers are far more than spiritual leaders in their churches, and are increasingly civically engaged in responding to the social needs of their faith communities. Whether

---

[13] The Center for Urban Ministerial Education (CUME) of Gordon Conwell Seminary is located at 363 South Huntington Avenue, Boston, MA 02130; tel. 617–983–9393; home page www.gordonconwell.edu/boston

working with youth to keep them from gangs or confronting housing, health, language, or immigration challenges, Latino churches and congregations throughout the U.S. provide an invaluable and often unrecognized service to their communities. Yet while these ministers are enormously resourceful individuals, the scope of needs they confront each day vastly exceeds any individual's capacity, however committed that person might be. Thus greater support and engagement from denominations is crucially needed to help ease the burden on individual ministers, and to connect their efforts to their larger church's lives.

As indicated by the responses from focus group participants, an analysis of seminary curricula is also needed. Latino/a pastors and lay leaders are saying that to be effective, they need to be better prepared for the demands they are likely to face. They also note that providing more practical education will help church leaders overcome their own communities' ambivalence toward higher education. As Pastor Gabriel of Chicago remarked:

> Any kind of education beyond the bachelor's level in our communities has historically been seen as a luxury, as something that is not needed to survive, as something that rich people do . . . I think that we can engage in reflection on how to present to people a theological education not as necessarily a socioeconomic defined enterprise but as a real useful tool needed in today's world to do effective ministry.

Both Hispanic women and men need improved educational opportunities, since a lack of educational credentials can restrict these ministers' chances of ordination, advancement to the highest ranks within their churches and denominational leadership, and access to positions that allow them to choose full-time ministry.

In light of the dearth of financial and other resources available to these communities, Hispanic ministers would also benefit from increased attempts to coalesce their efforts into a sustained political voice. As this study has indicated, existing networks and collaborative efforts can provide the ground upon which to begin transforming socioeconomically marginalized Latino communities into a political force capable of pressuring the broader society. The extensive interaction we have documented among Latino and non-Latino religious and community organizations has already helped make faith and civic communities aware of each others' needs and strengths, and has prompted people to join together across denominational and demographic lines to remedy particular problems.

Though we believe that the seeds have been planted for increased civic empowerment of the Latino community, the vital work being done by Hispanic ministers needs greater support and warrants further attention and research. A notable effort now underway is the Hispanic Capacity Project, Nueva Esperanza Inc.'s campaign to identify and supply the necessary training and resources to increase the serving capacity of Hispanic ministry in the U.S.[14] This increased attention will help broadcast the needs of these communities to a larger audience, and call attention to the insights that Latino/a religious leaders can offer the philanthropic community, local and national government leaders, and those seminaries and denominational bodies concerned with empowering the vital work of Hispanic ministers. The pastors and lay leaders who gave their time to this research have suggested ways in which their leadership and social ministries can be strengthened so that they might come closer to fulfilling their vision of good ministry. This chapter presents that data in the hope that it encourages the development of further strategies to facilitate the process.

References

Ammerman, Nancy Tatom. 1997. *Congregation and Community*. New Brunswick: Rutgers University Press.

Cnaan, Ram. 2002. *The Invisible Caring Hand: American Congregations and the Provision of Welfare*. New York: New York University Press.

Ebaugh, Helen Rose, and Janet Saltzman Chafetz. 2000. *Religion and the New Immigrants: Continuities and Adaptations in Immigrant Congregations*. New York: Altamira Press.

Kitchen, Jane. 2002. "The Hispanic Boom," Hispanicmagazine.com January–February.

Lummis, Adair T. 2003. "What Do Lay People Want in Pastors? Answers from Lay Search Committee Chairs and Regional Judicatory Leaders." *Pulpit & Pew: Research on Pastoral Leadership* (Winter). 3, 1–50.

Mata, Michael Mata. 1999. "Protestant Hispanics Serving the Community: Summary of Research Findings." Pew Charitable Trusts. July.

Nesbitt, Paula. 2001. *Religion and Social Policy*. New York: Altamira Press.

Segovia, Fernando F. 1996. "Aliens in the Promised Land: The Manifest Destiny of U.S. Hispanic American Theology." In Ada María Isasi-Díaz and Fernando F. Segovia, eds., *Hispanic/Latino Theology*, Minneapolis: Fortress Press.

Sherman, Amy L. 2003. "The Community Serving Activities of Hispanic Protestant Congregations." Unpublished report to the Center for the Study of Latino Religion, University of Notre Dame/AMEN.

Sikkink, David, and Edwin I. Hernández. 2003. "Religion Matters: Predicting Schooling Success among Latino Youth." Interim Report, 2003 Vol. 1 (January), Institute for Latino Studies, University of Notre Dame, 1–50.

---

[14] More information is available at www.esperanza.com.

Slessarav-Jamir, Helene. 2003. "Sustaining Hope, Creating Opportunities: The Challenge of Ministry among Hispanic Immigrants." Report for the Annie E. Casey Foundation.

Warner, Stephen R., and Judith G. Wittner, eds. 1998. *Gatherings in Diaspora: Religious Communities and the New Immigration.* Philadelphia: Temple University Press.

—— 2001. "North Carolina Growing Rapidly and Becoming More Diverse: Substate Statistics from the Census 2000 Redistricting Data." Raleigh: North Carolina Data Center, March 22.

—— 2002. "Educational Attainment of the Population 25 Years and Over by Sex, Hispanic Origin, and Race: March 2002." U.S. Census Bureau, Current Population Survey, March, Ethnic and Hispanic Statistics Branch, Population Division.

HISPANIC CATHOLIC LEADERSHIP: KEY TO THE FUTURE

Kenneth G. Davis, Andrew Hernández and Philip E. Lampe

Introduction

In this chapter, we continue to look at the issue of leadership with particular attention to Catholic Latino/as. The chapter's first task is to provide a general socio-demographic profile of Hispanic Catholics; second, it presents data on identification with and attitudes towards the Catholic Church (as well as the related matters of church attendance, membership and defections). Third, it looks at the degree of organizational participation and financial support among Hispanic Catholics; and finally, perceived and desired characteristics for leaders. Each of the chapter's four sections concludes with suggested implications for theology and ministry. The central conclusion is that because Hispanics are an increasingly important part of the Catholic Church in the United States (and society), Hispanic Catholic leadership development—especially among women, youth and young adults—requires an immediate and significant investment. Once formed, such leaders are very likely to contribute time, talent and treasure to the Church.

Although the research presented here does not draw upon focus groups or interviews like the previous chapter, much of the material is also the result of a collaborative effort. The National Community on Latino/a Leadership (NCLL)[1] conducted a survey of 2,662 Hispanic adults in the fall of 1999, commissioned by the National Catholic Council on Hispanic Ministry (NCCHM), an organization concerned with developing Hispanic leadership in a faith-based context.[2]

---

[1] Andrew Hernández was the lead investigator for NCLL; Adela Gallegos Flores represented NCCHM.

[2] The NCLL survey was a random-dial telephone interview of Hispanics 18 years of age and older in the states of California, Texas, New York, Florida and Illinois. Included was an oversample of Puerto Rican and Cuban American respondents, which was appropriately weighted to yield a minimum of 500 responses for each group.

Unless otherwise noted, data presented here are based on that NCLL survey.[3]

Socio-Demographic Profile of Hispanic Catholics

The Hispanic population is the fastest growing segment of the U.S. Catholic Church (and the society as a whole). An estimated 25 million Hispanic Catholics reside in the United States, a figure which constitutes about 33 percent of all U.S. Catholics. From 1970 to 2000, the number of Hispanic Catholics increased by over 18 million, or 264 percent. This increase accounted for 86 percent of all growth in the U.S. Catholic Church during that period.

Forty-one percent of Hispanic adults are under age 35; 30 percent are between 35 and 40 years old, and 29 percent are 50 years old and over.[4] Overall, Hispanics are younger than non-Hispanics, in part because of their higher birth rate and the large number of young immigrants. There is virtually no difference between the age structure of Hispanic Catholics and Hispanic non-Catholics.

A recent study by *Fe y Vida*, *La Red*, and the Southeast Pastoral Institute (SEPI) looks at similar data and concludes that 41 percent of Catholics under age 30 are Hispanic.[5] However, young Hispanics may be abandoning the Church. A recent study by the Hispanic Churches in American Public Life Project states that while 74 percent of immigrants are Catholic, only 66 percent of the second gen-

---

[3] With funding from the Lilly Endowment, NCCHM launched a six-year initiative in which it developed a training curriculum that integrates strategies for leadership development in education, civic participation, politics and community organization with the theological, spiritual and pastoral aspects of leadership. NCCHM piloted a model on a national scale in both English and Spanish. Later it produced a comprehensive program manual, *The Power to Serve: Latino/a Leadership for Church and Society*, to help institutions implement the successful model.

[4] In 1999 the Louisville Institute told the nation's bishops: "Given the fact that the Latino population in this country is overwhelmingly young (approximately 50 percent are under the age of twenty-six and over 33 percent under the age of eighteen), the Church ignores Hispanic youth at its own peril." This is an even stronger case than that presented here.

[5] This assumes that 70 percent of the Hispanic population in the U.S. is Catholic, and that 25 percent of the non-Hispanic White population is Catholic. Of course, if a greater percentage of the Church were Hispanic, an even larger percentage of young Catholics would be Hispanic.

eration, and 59 percent of third and later generations remain Catholic.

As with age, little difference exists between Hispanic Catholic and Hispanic non-Catholic marital status. Fifty-eight percent of both are married, 22 versus 23 percent are single, 10 versus 9 percent are either separated or divorced, 7 versus 8 percent are widowed, and 3 percent of both Catholics and non-Catholics are cohabiting.

Most Hispanics live in large cities. In nine of the ten largest cities in the United States ethnic minorities now constitute a majority of the population, with Hispanics being the largest minority in seven of these cities. Overall, Hispanics accounted for 62 percent of the population increase in the nation's 100 largest cities between 1990 and 2000 (U.S. Census Bureau 2001).

Hispanic households tend to be larger than those of non-Hispanic Whites. According to the Census Bureau, 78 percent of Hispanics have more than two people living in their households compared to 53 percent of non-Hispanic Whites. In addition, Hispanics have a higher birth rate than non-Hispanics, which means more children are present in the home. In 1996 the fertility rate for the general population was 2.03, while that of Hispanics was 3.0 (McFalls 1998: 3–48). According to the NCLL survey, 52 percent of Hispanic Catholics and 50 percent of Hispanic non-Catholics have children under the age of 18 living at home.

Households exist in neighborhoods. A neighborhood that is predominantly composed of one ethnic group constitutes what is termed an *enclave*, whereas one that is entirely composed of one ethnic group is usually termed a ghetto. Both of these are commonly referred to as a *barrio* if the residents are Hispanic. The type of neighborhood in which people live has important consequences. *Barrios*, for example, can be both functional and dysfunctional for their residents. Positively, they have a small-town, *gemeinschaft* quality that provides a more personal, friendly environment. This is particularly true for recently arrived immigrants who can make use of the *barrio* to reduce the culture shock inherent in international migration. According to one theory, *barrios* actually facilitate acculturation (Lal 1995). Negatively, *barrios* limit opportunities for residents by confining them to areas where access to better jobs, education, health care facilities, and personal security is less available (Santiago and Wilder 1991).

In an earlier study, the highest level of residential segregation between Hispanics and non-Hispanic Whites was in the northeastern region of the United States, while the least segregated was in the south (Massey and Denton 1987). Since 1990, many changes have occurred in the geographic distribution of the Hispanic population that may have affected regional segregation patterns. Previously it was common to think of Mexican Americans in the southwest, Cuban Americans in Florida, and Puerto Ricans in the northeast. Today, members of these and other Hispanic subgroups are located throughout the country. There are now twenty-one states where Hispanics are the largest minority (U.S. Census Bureau 2001).

Interestingly, Hispanic Catholics and non-Catholics tend to live in different kinds of neighborhoods. Forty-three percent of Catholics live in *barrios* compared to 35 percent of non-Catholics. Only 15 percent of Catholics live in predominantly non-Hispanic White neighborhoods compared to 17 percent of non-Catholics.[6] The remaining Hispanics live in ethnically mixed neighborhoods.

As noted in the previous chapter, Hispanics have less education overall than either non-Hispanic Whites or Blacks. Among Hispanics, Mexican Americans have the least amount of education of the three major subgroups. In 1998, 87 percent of non-Hispanics over the age of 24 had a high school degree compared to only 24 percent of Mexican Americans, 61 percent of Puerto Ricans and 66 percent of Cuban Americans. Although these relatively poor education levels are influenced by immigration, a recent study concluded that "Even after disaggregating the immigrant population from those statistics, however, Latino/a [school] dropout rates remain twice those of the non-Hispanic population" (Hernández and Davis, forthcoming). The picture for higher education is similar. According to the U.S. Census Bureau, while 27 percent of non-Hispanics had a college degree, only 8 percent of Mexican Americans, 11 percent of Puerto Ricans and 20 percent of Cuban Americans had received a degree.

According to the NCLL survey, Hispanic Catholics had less education than Hispanic non-Catholics. While 47 percent of Catholics had not completed high school, the corresponding figure for non-

---

[6] There is some evidence that interaction between Hispanics (specifically Mexican Americans) and non-Hispanics affects leadership. See Estrada Schaye, Carmen. 1995. "Religious Values and Leadership in Mexican Americans in Los Angeles." Ed. D. dissertation, Department of Education, Pepperdine University, Malibu, CA.

Catholics was only 39 percent. Meanwhile, 14 percent of Catholics had completed a college education compared to 17 percent of non-Catholics. The low educational attainment of Hispanics in general, and Catholics in particular, puts them at a distinct disadvantage in a credential-oriented society, as revealed in the following statistics on employment and income.

The greatest occupational difference between Hispanics and non-Hispanics is in the percentages of professionals/managers and farmers/laborers. There is also a large difference in these same occupations between the subgroups of Hispanics. In 1998, 33 percent of non-Hispanics held professional or managerial positions, compared to only 13 percent of Mexican Americans, 19 percent of Puerto Ricans and 25 percent of Cuban Americans (Weinberg 1999).

The unemployment rate for Hispanics has historically been much higher than for non-Hispanics, and continues to be so (U.S. Department of Labor 2002). Among Hispanics there is some difference between Catholics and non-Catholics, according to the NCLL survey. Non-Catholics too are slightly more likely to be employed, whether full or part-time, than Catholics (59 percent versus 54 percent). Most of those who are unemployed are either students, stay-at-home spouses, retired or unable to work. Of those who are employed, 40 percent of Catholics and 33 percent of non-Catholics have a direct supervisor who is also Hispanic. When asked how important it was that their supervisor understood Hispanic culture, 76 percent of Catholics and 71 percent of non-Catholics said it was very important.

The previous chapter looked at the income of Hispanic religious leaders, but actually the median income of all Hispanic families is below that of non-Hispanics. In 1998, Mexican American families earned 63 percent, Puerto Rican families 56 percent and Cuban American families 73 percent of the median income for non-Hispanic families. While overall the Hispanic income as a proportion of non-Hispanic income was 0.63, the proportion of Hispanic males to non-Hispanic males was 0.58. The proportion of Hispanic females to non-Hispanic females was 0.71 according to 1998 Census Bureau information. Thus, Hispanic females were experiencing less of a pay differential than males.

A comparison of the economic condition of the three main Hispanic subgroups to non-Hispanics in the United States for the year 1998 reveals that 9 percent of non-Hispanics were officially living in poverty compared to 28 percent of Mexican Americans, 33 percent of Puerto Ricans and 13 percent of Cuban Americans (Iceland 2003).

According to the NCLL survey, the overwhelming majority of both Catholic and non-Catholic Hispanics earned less than $40,000 a year. Based on annual family income, 79 percent of Catholics and 77 percent of non-Catholics are considered working class. These figures include 86 percent of foreign-born Hispanics. Only 16 percent of Catholics and 18 percent of non-Catholics are considered middle class, and approximately 5 percent of both are upper class. Remarkably, however, this is not how Hispanics view themselves. Only 45 percent actually perceive themselves as working class. Over half believe themselves middle class and 5 percent say they are upper class. Such perceptions are not uncommon. Immigrant Hispanics generally are more satisfied or optimistic about their economic situation than U.S.-born Hispanics, perhaps because the former compare themselves to the previous situation in their homeland, whereas the latter compare themselves to fellow U.S. citizens.

NCLL survey respondents were queried about the probable future of the Hispanic community and their own ability to achieve the American Dream. In response, Catholics exhibited greater confidence in the future of the average Hispanic than did mainline Protestants (62 percent versus 57 percent) or Pentecostals (42 percent). Only nondenominational Hispanics showed greater confidence—67 percent. Catholics were the most optimistic (77 percent) when asked if the American Dream was attainable for the majority of Hispanics. In response to the same question, 74 percent of nonaffiliated and 70 percent of mainline Protestants answered affirmatively.

When asked what the most important part of the American Dream was, the most common answer for Catholics (37 percent) was a better life for their children. Only 8 percent indicated financial success and security. Mainline Protestants more frequently indicated (29 percent) that the dream meant living up to their potential, compared to only 6 percent who said financial success and security. More Pentecostals (26 percent) cited a better life for their children and 10 percent indicated financial success and security. Thus, financial success and security are the least important part of the American Dream for most Hispanics.

The Census Bureau's 2000 population report found that 12.8 million Hispanics were foreign-born, comprising 39 percent of all

Hispanics. However, the NCLL survey, which was limited to Hispanic adults, found that 53 percent were foreign-born. Infants and the very young are less likely to immigrate, especially without proper documents, resulting in an overrepresentation of adults. Because the vast majority (86 percent) of foreign-born Hispanics are Catholic, over half (56 percent) of all Catholic adults are foreign-born. The opposite is true of Hispanic non-Catholics, most of whom (55 percent) are U.S.-born.

As may be expected, a similar pattern is found with citizenship. Whereas 74 percent of Hispanic non-Catholics are U.S. citizens, only 63 percent of Hispanic Catholics are citizens. Almost six million Hispanic Catholic adults are not yet U.S. citizens. This deprives both the Hispanic community and the Catholic Church of a more effective voice in government.

NCLL survey participants were given the choice to participate in English or Spanish. Sixty-three percent of Catholics and 52 percent of non-Catholics selected Spanish. Forty-six percent of Catholics and 39 percent of non-Catholics indicated they speak only Spanish. Another 43 percent of Catholics said they are bilingual, speaking both English and Spanish. In the home, 63 percent of Catholics and 54 percent of non-Catholics indicated that Spanish is spoken most often. Only 21 percent of Catholics and 29 percent of non-Catholics said that English is spoken most often at home. Over 80 percent of those who the spoke Spanish indicated they could also read it. Among U.S.-born Hispanics, 33 percent of mainline Protestants speak English exclusively compared to 21 percent of Evangelicals or nondenominationals, and 24 percent of Catholics. However, 60 percent of Catholics are bilingual compared to 59 percent of Evangelicals and nondenominationals, and 50 percent of mainline Protestants.

This demographic profile notes a pattern of class, language, nativity and citizenship differences between Hispanic Catholics and non-Catholics. Protestants tend to have slightly higher levels of education and income, and are less likely to live in predominantly Hispanic neighborhoods, work under Hispanic supervisors or speak only Spanish. While a majority of Protestants are U.S.-born, a majority of Catholics are foreign-born. This can explain the fact that 74 percent of Protestants, but only 63 percent of Catholics, are U.S. citizens. It can also help explain differences in language, education, income, and place of residence. These findings are consistent with those of the last chapter, where further implications for them are explored.

For Hispanics, the Catholic Church in the United States is again largely an immigrant church. This means that the Church and its leaders may be called upon for assistance in social, financial and spiritual matters. It also means that Hispanic Catholics are different in this respect from other Catholics who are predominantly U.S.-born. Thirty years ago, only 15 percent of U.S. Catholics were first-generation immigrants, 25 percent were second-generation, 40 percent were third-generation, and 20 percent were fourth-generation (Greeley 1977: 38). Today, the situation is dramatically different. For example, the Washington Post/Henry J. Kaiser Family Foundation/Harvard University 1999 National Survey on Latinos in America concluded that today's Hispanic Catholics are majority immigrants.

Previous studies[7] as well as the NCLL survey indicate that Hispanic mainline Protestants generally have higher social class status (measured by indicators such as income and education) than members of Pentecostal or Evangelical churches. These latter Hispanics are more similar to Catholics in social class.

The differences based on place of birth are even greater. Among U.S.-born Hispanics, 63 percent of mainline Protestants, 67 percent of Jehovah's Witnesses or Mormons, and 75 percent of Evangelicals or nondenominationals have household incomes of less than $40,000 annually compared to 70 percent of Catholics. For foreign-born Hispanics the percentages are 77 percent of Jehovah's Witnesses or Mormons, 84 percent mainline Protestants, and 87 percent Evangelicals or nondenominationals, compared to 86 percent of Catholics. Interestingly, foreign-born Jehovah's Witnesses and Mormons fare better than even mainline Protestants, perhaps because these communities tend to offer greater mutual support to their members than the other faith communities. Such differences have previously been noted and seem consistent with those presented in the final chapter of this book.

What are the theological and pastoral implications of this socio-demographic profile? The most intriguing implication may be the faith and optimism of Hispanics (especially Catholics) despite their

---

[7] See, for instance, Hernández, Edwin, "Moving from the Cathedral to Storefront Churches: Understanding Religious Growth and Decline Among Latino Protestants" in *Protestantes/Protestants*, edited by David Maldonado. Nashville: Abingdon Press, 1999.

relatively poor socioeconomic situation. This data may support the assertion of Eduardo C. Fernández, S.J.: "What is the factor that accounts for the resiliency of U.S. Latinos? Again, their theologians are now beginning to explore an inherent world of meaning—a spirituality, one might say—that provides an unmistakable source of strength" (Fernández 2000:28). Of course, Fernández does not suggest that poverty creates optimism or that neglect promotes faith. Nonetheless, further theological investigation appears merited.

Pastors, of course, must attend to the rising numbers of Catholic Hispanics, their increasing immigration, concentration in *barrios*, and the challenges stemming from their poor income and educational levels. Religious publishers and educators must consider the large numbers who prefer Spanish. However, the most important pastoral implication may be the urgent need to provide ministry (especially through leadership development) to Hispanic Catholic youth.

IDENTIFICATION WITH AND ATTITUDE TOWARDS THE CHURCH

Even the chapters of this book reflect the fact that there is disagreement over the exact number of Catholics in the United States, as well as the number of Hispanic Catholics.[8] This latter question has two facets: what proportion of U.S. Catholics is Hispanic, and what proportion of U.S. Hispanics is Catholic. The Catholic population has usually been estimated at between 25 and 28 percent of the nation (Roof and McKinney 1987: 230). In an August 2000 Gallup Poll on religious preference, 27 percent of the respondents indicated they were Catholic. This means there are approximately 76 million Catholics in the United States. When the estimate is based on parish registration figures, however, it appears that there are approximately 63 million Catholics, who constitute 23 percent of the population. Yet this number obviously under-represents the reality since many people, including families, are unregistered at any given time, even though they are regular churchgoers.

To determine the number of Hispanic Catholics we must rely on survey data, since official church membership rolls do not identify

---

[8] There are methodological reasons for these differences.

members by race or ethnicity. Some surveys are interested in determining the ethnicity of Catholics, while others are interested in determining the religion of Hispanics. This makes comparisons and conclusions elusive, especially since sampling frames and methodologies also differ among the various studies. Moreover, the results of some of the most ambitious studies are still not final. Therefore, the following data is meant to be informative but not conclusive.

A national study of adult Catholics conducted by the Catholic Pluralism Project in 1995 found that 16 percent of the respondents identified themselves as Hispanic.[9] The same results were obtained in a more recent study by the Center for Applied Research in the Apostolate (CARA) Catholic Poll 2000. Based on these percentages, the number of Hispanic Catholics would range between 9,982,600, or 16 percent of the membership base Catholic population, and 12,157,600 of the 2000 general survey Catholic population estimates. These findings suggest that in 2000, Hispanic Catholics numbered between 10 and 12 million out of a total Hispanic population of over 35 million. This would mean that only one-third of all U.S. Hispanics are Catholic. However, a conclusion that only 33 percent of Hispanics are Catholic is contradicted by a number of larger, national surveys that report the percentage to be between 56 and 69 percent, as illustrated in the following table:

Survey (Year)	Percentage of Hispanics Reported as Catholic
Citizen Participation Study (1989)	66%
General Social Survey, Roper Center (1990–1996)	67%
Voter News Exit Poll (1996)	66%
CARA Catholic Poll (2000)	56%
Social Capital Community Benchmark Survey-Seguaro Seminar, Harvard University (2000)	69%

---

[9] Data found at http://www.thearda.com/arda.asp.

Most of these surveys were conducted in English, which means their findings probably under-represent the true number since 46 percent of Catholic Hispanics and 39 percent of non-Catholics speak only Spanish. The largest national surveys, which are those with the smallest margins of error, find the percentage of Hispanics who are Catholic to be even greater, between 72 and 80 percent. The 1990 Latino/a National Political Survey (NLPS) of 2,817 Hispanics found that 73 percent of the respondents identified themselves as Catholics. Later, the 1994 Hispanic PAC USA National Survey of 1,420 respondents reported the same results. More recently, the 1999 Kaiser/Harvard University National Latino/a Poll (HKF) of 2,417 respondents found the percentage of Hispanics saying they are Catholic to be 72 percent. Finally, the 2000 National Community for Latino/a Leadership Survey (NCLL) discovered that 80 percent of the respondents reported they are Catholic. Based on these larger, national surveys, the percent of Hispanics who are Catholic appears to be between 72 and 80 percent. Therefore, the number of Hispanic Catholics can be estimated to be 25 million, or one-third of all Catholics in the United States. This data also suggests the likelihood that as the U.S. population becomes more Hispanic, it will also become more Catholic.

According to these same national surveys, between 12 and 16 percent of Hispanics identify themselves as Protestant, and between 7 and 19 percent indicate they are unaffiliated or have no religious preference. The findings of the NLPS, HKF and NCLL surveys show that although a majority of all Hispanics are Catholic, there is a difference between the three major Hispanic subgroups in the percentage of Catholics. The number of Mexican Americans who identify themselves as Catholics ranges between 77 and 87 percent, Cuban Americans between 66 and 80 percent and Puerto Ricans between 65 and 70 percent. While Mexican Americans are the most Catholic, Puerto Ricans are the most Protestant, at 21 to 22 percent, and also the most likely to be unaffiliated, at 9 to 13 percent.

As previously mentioned, however, recent large-scale national surveys have found that between 72 and 80 percent of Hispanics identify themselves as Catholics. Even Survey America 2001 found that 70 percent of Latinos identify themselves as Catholic. All this would seem to confirm Hunt's analysis of the General Social Survey of Latino/a data sets that found little or no increases in the percentage of Hispanics who identify themselves as Protestant during the 1990s. However, it does seem that the percentage of U.S. Hispanics who are Catholic did decline over most of the past century. Sociologist Meredith McGuire wrote that "... many Latinos do not find the Catholic church in the United States to be a strong source of belonging; indeed many have become Protestant, but many more simply do not identify with a Catholicism so foreign to their own cultural experience" (McGuire 1997: 191). A number of studies appear to support this assessment. One recent survey conducted in Los Angeles County found that 79 percent of Hispanic immigrants are Catholic, compared to 63 percent of those born in the United States. In addition, although 89 percent of the immigrants said they were raised Catholic, only 79 percent still consider themselves Catholic. Among U.S.-born Hispanics, the percentages are 79 percent raised Catholic and 63 percent still Catholic. As both groups aged, they were less likely to consider themselves Catholic. While some converted to different religions, others just ceased to embrace any religion (*America* 2001). Greeley presents a similar picture (1997: 12–3), reporting that 85 percent of Hispanics were raised Catholic, but only 67 percent continue to be Catholic.

Some reasons for Hispanics' religious switching may have less to do with doctrinal issues and more to do with structural differences between Catholic and Protestant churches. In general the latter are smaller, members are more likely to know each other, there is greater opportunity for lay participation, and the congregational rather than episcopal structure allows greater lay leadership (Verba, Schlozman, and Brady 1995: 245). It has also been suggested that some Hispanics see conversion as an aspect of assimilation or a means of possible upward mobility.[10]

While it appears certain there has been a decline in Catholicism among Hispanics in the United States, the magnitude of this decline is in question. Greeley reports that in the early 1970s, 78 percent of Hispanic Americans were Catholic but by the mid-1990s this figure had fallen to 67 percent—representing a loss of approximately .5 percent per year. The previously mentioned *Fe y Vida* survey reported that 74 percent of first-generation Hispanics, 66 percent of

---

[10] Both hypotheses are found in Hunt, L. L. 2001. "Religion, Gender, and the Hispanic Experience in the United States: Catholic/Protestant Differences in Religious Involvement, Social Status, and Gender-Role Attitudes." *Review of Religious Research* 43(2): 139–60.

the second generation, and 59 percent of the third generation were Catholic. Meanwhile, a study reported by Hunt found that 83 percent of first-generation Hispanics identified themselves as Catholics compared to 64 percent of third-generation Hispanics. Differences between these studies are significant, although all three indicate a generational decline in identity with the Church. The questions, therefore, are not whether a decline occurred, but how large and why.

Whatever their denomination, 95 percent of Hispanics in three separate surveys, the NCLL, HKF and CBS, indicated that religion is an important part of their lives, compared to 88 percent of the general population who participated in the Gallup 2000 survey. The NCLL survey also found that among Hispanics, 96 percent of Catholics compared to 89 percent of non-Catholics said it was important. Hispanics in general not only consider religion important, but they also have a favorable opinion of the Catholic Church.[11] The HKF survey found that 75 percent of Hispanics have a favorable opinion, including 54 percent who indicated very favorable. This is compared to 64 percent of the general public who expressed a favorable opinion, and 18 percent very favorable in the Gallup Poll. In the former survey, 19 percent of Hispanics indicated an unfavorable opinion and 8 percent very unfavorable of the Church, while in the latter poll 27 percent of the general public expressed an unfavorable opinion, and 8 percent very unfavorable.

This favorable attitude towards the Catholic Church includes its priests. Recent studies have shown that Hispanic Catholics prefer to consult priests about their problems rather than lay professionals. They seek clerical help not only for moral problems, but also depression, suicidal feelings, drug and alcohol abuse, job loss, and marital difficulties, whether or not the priest has special training in those areas. Non-Hispanic Catholics, however, prefer to consult someone who has special training, whether priest or lay professional. Overall, 72 percent of Hispanics would rather talk to a trained or untrained priest than a trained lay professional, compared to 57 percent of Non-Hispanics (Kane and Williams 2000). This continued confidence

---

[11] According to at least one published opinion, this does not seem to have been affected even by recent scandals. See Rodriguez, Raymond. 2002. "Latino Catholics Retain Trust in Parish Priest." *Hispanic Link* 20(13): 3. See also the commentary by Gregory Rodriguez, *Los Angeles Times*, April 7, 2002.

in clergy means that the study of their role within the Hispanic context—the subject of the next chapter—is essential.

However important religion or religious leaders are to them, and despite their generally favorable opinion of the Church, Hispanics are not the most likely to attend church services. African Americans have the highest rate of church attendance, although Hispanics have a higher rate than non-Hispanic Whites. The 1989 Citizens Participation Study found that 53 percent of Hispanics attended church regularly compared to 48 percent of non-Hispanic Whites. The 2000 Social Community Benchmark study found that 47 percent of Hispanics attended church weekly compared to 40 percent of non-Hispanic Whites. In a recent survey of Hispanics conducted by the Tomás Rivera Policy Institute, 45 percent of the respondents indicated they attended church services at least once a week. Forty-three percent of all respondents attended services in Spanish, 27 percent attended services in English and 30 percent attended services in Spanish and/or English.

Finally, the NCLL survey reported that 41 percent of Hispanics attended church services at least once a week, compared to 35 percent of the general public who answered the Gallup Poll.[12] It is likely, however, that a difference in attendance exists between the various nationality groups of Hispanics.[13]

For Latinos, church attendance does not necessarily mean registering at a church. An analysis of an over-sample of the 1999 Gallup Poll data found 54 percent of Hispanic Catholics were registered members of a local parish, compared to 70 percent of non-Hispanic Whites (D'Antonio 1999). More recently, the Social Capital Community Benchmark Survey 2000 found that 46 percent of Hispanics were

---

[12] Earlier studies of church attendance among U.S. Catholics by nationality indicated that Germans were the most active, while Italians and Hispanics were among the least. See Greeley, Andrew, "Ethnic Variations in Religious Commitment," in *The Religious Dimension: New Dimensions in Quantitative Research*, edited by Robert Wuthnow. New York: Academy Press, 1979. Also Abramson, Harold, *Ethnic Diversity in Catholic America*. New York: John Wiley, 1973.

[13] For instance, 41 percent of Mexican Americans attend Mass at least once a month while 47 percent report they never go. Among those born in Mexico, the corresponding percentages are 51 percent versus 41 percent. See De la Garza, Rodolfo O., et al. *Latino Voices: Mexican, Puerto Rican and Cuban Perspectives*. Boulder, CO: Westview Press, 1992. See tables 3.21 and 2.26.

registered members compared to 67 percent of non-Hispanic Whites and 71 percent of African Americans.[14]

Although Hispanics place a greater importance on religion, have a more favorable attitude towards the Church, and attend services more frequently than non-Hispanic Whites, they are less often registered members of a parish. There are several reasons that may explain this behavior. First, approximately 46 percent of Hispanic Catholics speak only Spanish. Many of these probably hesitate to become registered members of any parish without Spanish-speaking ministers. Second, a large number of Hispanics are undocumented immigrants, and, as such, they might be reluctant to register their names and addresses.[15] Third, in some of the immigrants' homelands, parish registration is not common, especially in small towns or *ranchos*. Finally, immigrants tend to be more mobile and do not stay or plan to stay in one place for an extended length of time. Many also plan to return home and therefore do not feel the need to register since they believe that they will only be in the United States temporarily.

The data reflects the great importance that religion holds for Catholic Hispanics, their generally positive opinion of the Church, and yet their relative lack of formal church registration and involvement. This paradox may be explained by the way many Hispanics practice their faith, that is, through a domestic or neighborhood expression of their own popular Catholicism. While popular Catholicism does not cause less church registration, it may be constitutive of how many Hispanics are Catholic, and that particular manifestation of Catholicism may not always include formal registration.[16] It would

---

[14] One-third of all Catholics in the United States are not registered in their local parishes. See page 205 of Froehle, Bryan and Mary L. Gautier. *The Catholic Church Today*. Maryknoll, N.Y.: Orbis Books, 2000.

[15] This situation may be even more pressing given popular opinion toward immigrants after the events of September 11, 2001.

[16] For studies on parish life and popular Catholicism among Hispanics see the following two dissertations: Kelliher Jr., Thomas D., *Hispanic Catholics and the Archdiocese of Chicago, 1923–1970* (Ph.D. dissertation, Department of Theology, University of Notre Dame, Notre Dame, IN, 1996). Kelliher concludes, "Since Hispanic Catholicism was to a large extant a household religion and was not centered on parish life . . . by the end of the 1960s most Hispanics still displayed little interest in Chicago parish life." Treviño, Roberto R. *La Fe: Catholicism and Mexican Americans in Houston, 1911–1972* (Ph.D. dissertation, Department of Theology, Stanford University, Stanford, CA, 1993). Treviño concludes, "They selectively participated in the institutional Church and clung to home and community-based religious practices."

appear that theologians are quite correct to explore the importance of this peculiarly Hispanic way of being Catholic (Espín 1997: 2–5).

Is the exodus of Hispanics from the Church slowing or accelerating? If so, why? In recent years, there has been a growth (albeit still inadequate) in the Church's ministry to Hispanics. Has this been successful in slowing the exodus? If so, such efforts certainly deserve the attention of pastors, because identifying successful pastoral strategies bodes well for their replication.

DEGREE OF ORGANIZATIONAL PARTICIPATION AND FINANCIAL SUPPORT

An often-cited study by González and La Velle reports that the vast majority of Hispanics (88 percent) are not actively involved in parish activities, and most (60 percent) feel they are not encouraged to become involved (1985: 127). However, two other studies published ten years apart found that one-fourth of Hispanics participate in church activities other than attending services. Although the Barna Research Group study in 1999 had no corresponding data regarding non-Hispanics, an earlier CPS study in 1989 found that African Americans showed the greatest participation with 35 percent, followed by 27 percent of non-Hispanic Whites. Hispanics are the least involved in non-liturgical church activities. There is some evidence that Hispanics who become Protestants are more religiously involved than those who remain Catholic. This is particularly true for women (Hunt 2001). Yet such an increase in religious participation and zeal is not uncommon for converts to any faith and is a recognized part of the conversion experience. Hispanics who were raised Protestant were not found to show this same religious fervor.

The CPS and Barna studies also found parallels when looking at financial support for churches by ethnic group. While between 72 and 80 percent of African Americans financially support their church, and between 63 and 71 percent of non-Hispanic Whites do; only 57 to 61 percent of Hispanics support their churches. These studies, however, failed to distinguish between Catholics and non-Catholics.

The NCLL survey did distinguish between Catholics and non-Catholics and found that 23 percent of Catholics (compared to 31 percent of non-Catholics) indicated they had donated either time or money to some club, organization or group within the last year. Of those who indicated organizational affiliation over the last year, 40 percent of Catholics and 44 percent of non-Catholics were actively involved in some aspect of the organizational life of a local church. Among Hispanics, not only are Catholics somewhat less likely than non-Catholics to be involved in church-related organizations, but also when they are involved they are less likely to volunteer, attend meetings or hold office. Fifty-nine percent of Catholics volunteer, 56 percent attend meetings and 17 percent hold office compared to 70 percent of non-Catholics who volunteer, 72 percent attend meetings and 21 percent hold office. Nevertheless, organizationally involved Catholics are just as likely as non-Catholics (89 versus 90 percent) to contribute financially to their churches.

Approximately three-fourths of adult Hispanics say a close personal relationship with God is a top priority; 85 percent say their faith is very important in their daily lives; 77 percent say that Mary as the Mother of God is very important to them, and 63 percent say they believe the Bible is totally accurate in its teaching. In addition, in an average week 81 percent pray, 33 percent read the Bible, and 15 percent participate in small groups for spiritual purposes.[17]

Twenty-five percent describe themselves as "born again Christians." No distinction was made between Catholics and non-Catholics, but it is probably safe to say that Catholics were underrepresented in this last category since this particular expression is decidedly more Protestant than Catholic.

Taken together, this data presents interesting theological and pastoral questions. For instance, the data shows that Catholic Hispanics are now more likely to be immigrant with all the socioeconomic (education, income, politics) and cultural effects (differences in language, history, self-identity) that immigration entails. Should not the great numbers of Hispanic Catholics who are immigrants (further complicated by the events of September 11, 2001) both inform pastoral practice and influence theological reflection?

Another important issue is one that Allan Figueroa Deck identified in 1989, namely, the importance of small Christian communities among Hispanics (Figueroa Deck 1989).[18] Such very local church

---

[17] A very important way that Catholic Hispanics participate in church is through the various small Christian communities. See page 54 of Lee, Bernard J., *The Catholic Experience of Small Christian Communities*. Mahwah, N.J.: Paulist Press, 2000.

[18] RENEW still appears to offer the most successful methodology in this respect.

involvement is not only of pastoral import, but deserves the attention of ecclesiology. Moreover, since the present data seems to show that when Hispanics do participate in the local church they also donate, this would seem to influence both the practice and theology of stewardship. Ecclesiology and stewardship must both attend to the development of leaders. Leadership and a sense of ownership or belonging are also pastoral issues of great import.[19] For that reason, we now turn to the issue of leadership in the U.S. Hispanic Catholic Church.

PERCEIVED AND DESIRED CHARACTERISTICS OF LEADERS

Altogether, Hispanics comprise 5.4 percent of the Catholic clergy in the United States. In 2000 there were 366 U.S. Catholic Bishops, 24 (that is, 7 percent) of whom were Hispanic.[20] Most of these are auxiliary bishops serving dioceses with large Hispanic populations. There were also 1,818 Hispanic priests, or 4 percent of all U.S. priests. This translates into approximately 13,700 Hispanic Catholics for every Hispanic priest. In addition, there are 1,340 Hispanic permanent deacons which accounts for 11 percent of all such deacons. Vowed religious in the U.S. are even less than 5 percent Hispanic. While these numbers represent a general improvement over the past, they also indicate a great underrepresentation of the community that constitutes one-third of the entire U.S. Catholic Church.[21]

---

[19] See Chapter One of Davis, Kenneth G. and Yolanda Tarango, eds. *Building Bridges: The Pastoral Care of U.S. Hispanics*. Scranton, PA: University of Scranton Press, 2000.

[20] In January 2002 there were 25 active Hispanic bishops with 4 retired (plus two deceased and one in Puerto Rico). (Telephone interview with Rosalva Castañeda of the United States Catholic Conference of Bishops Secretariat for Hispanic Affairs, January 18, 2002).

[21] Comparing Catholic parishes that are at least 40 percent Hispanic with those that are Black, Asian, Native American or non-Hispanic White, it appears that the former, together with their Asian counterparts, have on average a greater number of priests, deacons and lay staff per parish, more Masses per week, as well as higher average numbers of parishioners participating in the sacraments. These differences are likely to be a function of the larger size of such parishes (Froehle and Gautier, *The Catholic Church Today*, 135, 144, 155).

According to a 1999 report of the Bishops' Committee on Hispanic Affairs, there were 6,545 Hispanics in lay ministry formation, constituting 21 percent of those in formation. There were also 1,040 Hispanic parish lay ecclesial ministers, or 4 percent of the total (Froehle and Gautier 2000: 33–5). Historically, most Hispanic leaders in the Church have been lay (Dolan and Figueroa Deck 1994).[22] A study by F. J. Woods of Hispanic leaders conducted in San Antonio in the 1940s described them as educated, bilingual, middle class *mestizos* who had lived in the United States longer than most and who were active in the church as well as social ethnic organizations (Woods 1976: 63–89).[23] The NCLL survey discovered some similarities as well as some important differences with these characteristics of Hispanic leaders.

Currently, leaders are still more likely to be older, educated, and married with children living at home than the average Hispanic Catholic. However, there are two important differences between the findings of these studies. Today most church leaders are immigrants and working class. Foreign-born Hispanics comprise 56 percent of all Hispanic Catholics, but account for nearly 70 percent of local church office holders. And 54 percent of those local church leaders come from households with annual incomes of less than $40,000.

The NCLL survey also found that while female Hispanics constitute 56 percent of the Hispanic Church membership, they are only 43 percent of church leaders. This percentage appears quite low in light of the large and significant role women play in the popular religious life of the Hispanic community (Stevens-Arroyo and Diaz-Stevens 1994). It is particularly so when the results of the survey reveal that more females agree (26 percent) with the statement that "women make better leaders than men" than agree (24 percent) that

---

[22] The chapters by Moisés Sandoval (131–65) and Marina Herrera (166–205) are particularly pertinent. Note also that any account of U.S. Hispanic Catholic leadership must mention César Chávez. While we await a biography that adequately deals with his faith, see Day, Mark. *Forty Acres: César Chávez and the Farm Workers.* New York: Praeger, 1971.

[23] Her definition of a leader is still helpful, namely, a person who "offers some solution to the problems of the ethnic group. He has not only an acceptable plan of action designed to meet these problems, but also an appreciable following" (5). For an excellent explanation of Hispanic Catholic leadership see Azevedo, Marcello. "Hispanic Leaders: Faith and Culture in the New Millennium." *Chicago Studies* 36:3 (December 1997) 230–4.

"men make better leaders than women." On the other hand, 30 percent of males believe that men were better leaders compared to 15 percent of females. Nevertheless, a majority of both sexes agree that there is no gender difference in leadership abilities.[24] Catholics were somewhat more egalitarian than non-Catholics.

Some priests are even asking questions about female leadership in the Church, such as one at the "Hispanic Ministry in the 21st Century" summit who commented that ". . . leadership within the Church is a hierarchical reality . . . Deaconate, Priesthood and Episcopacy are . . . strictly reserved exclusively for men and too often the contributions of Hispanic religious and laywomen have been overlooked. This reality can bring about the temptation to talk about Hispanic ministerial leadership only in terms of the leadership of men."

Most females and males believe that women are as good as or better leaders than men. Overall, two-thirds of Hispanics indicate there is little difference between the leadership abilities of men and women. Hispanic Catholics are less likely than non-Catholics to believe that men are better leaders than women (26 percent vs. 32 percent) and more likely to agree that women are better leaders than men (22 percent vs. 19 percent). This more positive attitude towards female leadership on the part of Catholics might be traced to women's role in popular religion and Hispanics' high esteem for the Virgin Mary.

Woods also identified the following functions of Hispanic leaders:

1) to help their group realize that injustices need not be accepted and that change is possible;
2) promote group integration within the system;
3) represent the group to itself and others;
4) build consensus;
5) negotiate and build coalitions between groups;
6) coordinate group efforts towards common goals;
7) identify and encourage new leaders.

---

[24] At the same time, leadership may be exercised differently between men and women. At April 13, 2002 conference at Notre Dame called "Recovering the U.S. Hispanic Catholic Heritage," those who presented on "Latina Faith, Evangelization, and Leadership" (Antonia Castañeda, Aria María Díaz Stevens, Anita de Luna, and Anna María Padilla) noted that for women, leadership includes: (1) sacrifice as service to family and community; (2) formation of youth; (3) creation of social space to claim opportunities.

Another recent study of Hispanic leaders indicated similar functions:

1) to integrate foreign-born and U.S.-born Hispanics;
2) provide a bridge between Hispanic and non-Hispanic communities;
3) serve as role models;
4) reduce tension due to cultural differences.[25]

Obviously, the role of a leader is multi-dimensional. At the center of the leader's role is the need to serve and represent his or her people, as Gloria, a Catholic lay leader in San Antonio, Texas, articulated in the previous chapter: "For me the words that come to mind are enabler, catalyst."

Representing one's people may be problematic at times for Hispanic Catholic leaders, especially the clergy, if there is or appears to be a conflict of interests between Hispanics and non-Hispanics. Leaders may feel a conflict inherent in their dual role of serving and representing the Church while serving and representing *la raza*. One study of Hispanic priests revealed that a majority (58 percent) were not satisfied with the Church's response to social problems in their communities. An even larger majority (84 percent) felt their fellow Hispanics lack an adequate voice in the decision-making of the Church, and also believed (82 percent) that Hispanics experience discrimination in the Church (Cadena 1989). Chapter Three updates these findings with a newer study of Hispanic, Catholic clergy.

What do Hispanics see as the most desirable qualities for leaders? Both Catholic and non-Catholic respondents to the NCLL survey overwhelmingly indicated that the three most important traits were honesty, trustworthiness and integrity. Overall, 60 percent of respondents indicated that qualities associated with personal character were most vital to them. Another 10 percent identified qualities associated with competence, such as intelligence, good communication skills and efficiency. Next, 8 percent selected qualities related to compassion and caring, and 6 percent to community service and respect for the community. There was virtually no difference between the preferences of Catholics and non-Catholics except concerning education,

---

[25] See Harada, Masaaki, "Study Urges Strong Latino Leaders." *The Albert Lea Tribune*, January 8, 2002. See also Thomas W. Florek's D.Min. thesis, *Constructing A Theological Methodology for a Lay Leadership Formation Situated in the Midwest Pastoral de Conjunto*. Catholic Theological Union, Chicago, IL.

intelligence and experience. Catholics (8 percent) placed a greater value on these than did non-Catholics (4 percent).

Catholics and non-Catholics diverge significantly over the importance given to the ethnicity of a leader. A majority of Catholics (55 percent) believe that Hispanic leaders represent their values better than non-Hispanic leaders, compared to 40 percent of mainline Protestants, 47 percent of Pentecostals, and 35 percent of nonaffiliated. Sixty-two percent of Catholics versus 64 percent of Pentecostals, 56 percent of nonaffiliated, and 53 percent of mainline Protestants believe that Hispanic leaders better reflect their views on important issues. Similarly, 57 percent of Catholics compared to 56 percent of Pentecostals, 53 percent of mainline Protestants and 39 percent of nonaffiliated believe that Hispanic elected officials care more about them than non-Hispanic officials.

Given the importance that Catholic Hispanics place on the ethnicity of their leaders, it is worthwhile to note the leadership provided by Hispanic permanent deacons. A 1999 survey of the deaconate in the Hispanic community, based on information from 137 of 180 dioceses, found 1,400 incardinated Spanish-speaking deacons, most of whom came from Mexico or Puerto Rico. There were also 135 Hispanic candidates in deacon formation programs. Approximately 87 percent of both Hispanic deacons and deacon candidates were bilingual, while 8 percent spoke only Spanish. This language proficiency was reflected in the difference in the number of continuing formation programs which were conducted in English (63 percent) and in Spanish (11 percent). Fourteen percent of the dioceses reported having distinct formation programs for Hispanic deacon candidates. Responding to a question about how well-received Hispanic deacons were by priests, 50 percent said such deacons were well-received by Hispanic priests and 60 percent by non-Hispanic White priests. The question, "Does the local church perceive Hispanic/Latino deacons as ordained for the whole Church" elicited a 60 percent affirmative response.[26] The following chapter explores these important issues in greater depth.

---

[26] United States Conference of Catholic Bishops' Secretariat for the Diaconate, November 2, 1999, provided to the authors by Enrique Alonso of the Asociación de Diáconos Hispanos.

All of the above data suggests helpful insights for theologians and pastors. One of the topics that U.S. Hispanic theologians wrestle with is *lo cotidiano*, or the everyday, real-life issues facing their community. These theologians apparently have generally been quite accurate in their assessment of *lo cotidiano*. In particular, one might point to the continuing lack of female Church leadership despite Hispanic acceptance of it.[27]

Although the issue was not raised, it does appear from the preceding information that the ethnicity of the clergy and lay church leaders may be of even greater importance than gender to the laity, especially among Catholics. Undoubtedly, some non-Hispanics have made significant contributions as leaders; nonetheless, the work of Ana Maria Diaz-Stevens and Anthony Stevens-Arroyo notes the desire of Hispanics to have leaders who are themselves Hispanic (1998).[28] If this is so, it means that for the Church to meet the leadership demands of the Hispanic community, it needs decidedly more Hispanic priests and lay leaders. Although this is a daunting challenge, other research has provided some insight (Hernández and Davis, forthcoming). It may be that a leadership program directed towards females is needed, much like the diaconate program for males.

CONCLUSION

As time has shown, a prediction made a decade and a half ago has proven very accurate—that is, Hispanics

> ... have strong cultural and religious bonds, which will no doubt continue to shape the religious communities. Catholicism especially will be influenced by these newer immigrant streams and will continue to have distinct ethnic *enclaves* within it. The Spanish-speaking constituency will expand more rapidly than any other sector within American

---

[27] Among the most important leadership organizations for Hispanic women is Las Hermanas. See Lara Medina, Manuel, *Las Hermanas: Chicana/Latina Religious-Political Activism, 1971–1997*. Ph.D. dissertation, Department of American History, Claremont Graduate University, Claremont, CA, 1998.

[28] See also Díaz-Stevens, *Oxcart Catholicism on Fifth Avenue*. Notre Dame, IN: University of Notre Dame Press, 1998. Another classic but little known example of the influence of a non-Hispanic leader is contained in Sr. Valdez, Mary Paul. *The History of the Missionary Catechists of Divine Providence*. San Antonio: The Missionary Catechists of Divine Providence, 1978.

Catholicism. Thus it is reasonable to expect a gradual but significant shift in Catholic constituency and religious and spiritual life as these influences are assimilated in the years ahead (Roof and McKinney 1987: 15).

U.S. Hispanic theology has also largely been accurate in its assessment of the context of its own community. It has rightly emphasized the experience of *diaspora* (through conquest or immigration), popular religion (particularly devotion to Mary and the concept of *fiesta*), small Christian communities, and the need to negotiate the peculiar experience of U.S. Hispanics who live on cultural (including differences in race and levels of acculturation) borders. The data indicates that this theology that claims to be contextual has actually been true to its context (Davis and Castillo-Coronado 2001). Evaluating the Church's pastoral response to this context is more difficult, but certainly necessary. One can look at the response of the U.S. Church's hierarchy in its *National Pastoral Plan for Hispanic Ministry*.[29] The above data suggests that evaluation is needed particularly in the areas of youth ministry, leadership, immigration, and stewardship.[30]

While Hispanics, who comprise approximately one-third of all U.S. Catholics, are important to the future of the Church, young Hispanics are even more so. This is because they encompass 41 percent of all Catholics under age 30, and 44 percent of all Catholics under age 10. In the nation's two most populous states, California and Texas, over 70 percent of Catholics under age 30 are Hispanic. Census Bureau statistics indicate that between 1990 and 2000, the Hispanic population between ages of 15 and 29 grew 54 percent, while the non-Hispanic White population decreased by 11 percent. Meanwhile, the Hispanic population under age 10 increased by 62 percent compared to a 10 percent decrease in the non-Hispanic White population. According to the Census Bureau, this trend will continue.

---

[29] National Conference of Catholic Bishops Secretariat for Hispanic Affairs (Washington, D.C.: United States Catholic Conference, 1987). Charles McCarthy privately compiled a helpful index. The more recent Encuentro 2000 document updates the National Pastoral Plan, although it doesn't replace it.

[30] Small Christian communities referred to as *comunidades eclesiales de base* or "small ecclesial communities" receive attention (paragraphs 19, 27–29, 33, 37–38, 40–45, 47, 49–50, 61–63, 65, 70, 77–79, 84). Popular religion is only mentioned directly in paragraph 11 and spirituality is recognized (16, 68, 84, 86, 94–96), but probably underdeveloped. Evaluation (paragraphs 6, 43, 84–92) of pastoral practices is mentioned throughout; however, there is no authoritative plan for accountability.

To meet the needs of this growing portion of the Church's population, some parishes in certain dioceses have established peer youth programs, usually organized and directed by the members themselves, which may or may not include an adult advisor. Such advisors are either paid or volunteers. Unfortunately, few such programs exist, and only 35 dioceses have trained personnel to develop and coordinate them. In ten of these dioceses the coordinators are only part-time. Youth and young adult ministry does seem to receive some priority in the *National Pastoral Plan* (paragraphs 12, 34, 51, 53, 55–56, 64–66, 72, and 79). Nonetheless, there is an obvious and growing need to attend to Hispanic youth and young adults. For instance, the following chapter notes how few Latinos consider the priesthood as well as how few have had personal contact with priests: could these issues be related?

The importance of leaders/leadership is evident in (paragraphs 17, 24, 32–33, 58, 60, 68–69, 77–78, 84) as well as under some categories such as laity, women, diocesan personnel, priests, etc. Commentaries on leadership in this document stress the goal of communion:

> Throughout the whole Pastoral Plan, the words "leader," and "pastoral ministers" and, at times, "pastoral agents" are easily interchanged. There is a slight emphasis on the use of the word "leader" when it refers to an organizational, administrative and advocacy service, and the use of the words "pastoral ministers" or "ministries" when it speaks of more ecclesial services. However, according to the model of a communitarian Church, both of them must be interpreted as true services to the community of brothers and sisters because the Lord did not come to be served but to serve (Vizcaíno 1992).

Relative inattention to immigration (paragraphs 4, and 10–11 as well as mention of some countries of origin) probably reflects the difference between the percentage of U.S.-born versus immigrant U.S. Hispanics between the 1980s and today. More attention probably needs to be focused here. The real challenge evident in the *National Pastoral Plan*, however, appears to be attention to stewardship. Not only is there virtually no mention of the issue, moreover, the repeated phrase "In accordance with budget procedures of the respective entities involved" often meant that no special budget or fundraising efforts were directed toward implementing this otherwise fine document. Perhaps the best assessment to date concludes that it ". . . represents a huge advance toward a pastoral praxis . . . falls short of the best that we might hope for from the Church's ministry" (Connors 1997: 333).

This necessary yet still lacking shift of investment and the identification of new sources of funds has probably been one reason for the relatively tiny number of Hispanic professional and clergy leaders, especially among women, youth and young adults. Some shift of those resources commensurate with the percent of Hispanics in the Catholic Church toward that leadership development could eventually generate new sources of funding, since Hispanics apparently do contribute financially to churches in which they feel ownership and exercise leadership.[31] This may partly explain why Protestant Hispanics, with much greater leadership of the same ethnicity, also contribute much more to their churches (Wagner and Figueroa Deck 1999).

The title of this chapter argues that Hispanic Catholic leadership is the key to the Church's future. The National Catholic Council for Hispanic Ministry (NCCHM) commissioned this study because of its mission to "[empower] . . . Hispanics in both church and society by identifying, convoking and developing leadership among its member organizations and their constituencies." Accordingly, the most important argument we make is that Hispanic Catholic leadership development (especially among women, youth and young adults) requires an immediate and significant investment, but once formed, such leaders are very likely in turn to contribute time, talent and treasure to the Church.

This chapter has examined leadership from a specifically Catholic perspective, but with attention to the generally perceived and desired characteristics of leaders. We found that among Hispanics, desired characteristics of leaders were more personal (e.g., integrity) than professional (e.g., specific skills), and that leaders were expected to offer practical as well as spiritual aid. Although the word "networking" was not used, leaders were expected to build coalitions and bridges, as well as promote integration. Such networks were perceived as important resources. Barriers (or limitations) to leadership

---

[31] Note that this implies giving more than money. For instance, most seminarians in the U.S. are now required to study the Spanish language and Hispanic cultures. Is it not time that permanent deacons or at least professional lay ministers more often do the same?

included financial and educational ones—as noted in the previous chapter—although here it appears that such barriers may be even greater for Catholics than for Protestant Hispanics, and for women. Once again common limitations and shared resources are common threads running through the chapters of this book. Chapter Three will explore in more detail the various specific types of Catholic Hispanic leadership, including both ordained and lay leaders.

References

America. 2001. "Latinos Becoming Less Catholic." 185(6): 5.

Cadena, Gilbert. 1989. "Chicano Clergy and the Emergence of Liberation Theology." *Hispanic Journal of Behavioral Science* 11: 117–20.

Connors, Michael E. 1997. "The National Pastoral Plan for Hispanic Ministry as a Strategy for Inculturation Among Mexican Americans." Ph.D. dissertation, Department of Theology, University of Toronto, Toronto, Canada. Pp. 333.

D'Antonio, William. 1999. "Latino Catholics: How Different?" *National Catholic Reporter* October 29.

Davis, Kenneth G. and Jesús Castillo-Coronado. 2001. "U.S. Hispanic Theologians: A Sketch of What They Are Doing." *Louvain Studies* 26: 3–26.

Diaz-Stevens, Ana Maria and Anthony Stevens-Arroyo. 1998. *Recognizing the Latino Resurgence in U.S. Religion: The Emmaus Paradigm*. Boulder, CO: Westview Press.

Dolan, Jay P. and Allan Figueroa Deck, eds. 1994. *Hispanic Catholic Culture in the U.S.: Issues and Concerns*. South Bend, IN: University of Notre Dame Press.

Espín, Orlando O. 1997. *The Faith of the People: Theological Reflections on Popular Catholicism*. Maryknoll, NY: Orbis Books.

Estrada Schaye, Carmen. 1995. "Religious Values and Leadership in Mexican Americans in Los Angeles." Ed. D. dissertation, Department of Education. Pepperdine University, Malibu, CA.

Fernández, Eduardo, S.J. 2000. *La Cosecha: Harvesting Contemporary United States Hispanic Theology (1972–1998)*. Collegeville, MN: The Liturgical Press.

Figueroa Deck, Allan. 1989. *The Second Wave: Hispanic Ministry and the Evangelization of Cultures*. Mahwah, NJ: Paulist Press.

Froehle, Bryan and Gautier, Mary L. 2000. *The Catholic Church Today*. Maryknoll, NY: Orbis Books.

Gonzalez, Roberto O. and Michael J. LaVelle. 1985. *The Hispanic Catholic in the United States: A Socio-Cultural and Religious Profile*. New York City, NY: Northeast Catholic Pastoral Center for Hispanics.

Greeley, Andrew. 1977. *The American Catholic: A Social Portrait*. New York City, NY: Basic Books.

———. 1997. "Defection Among Hispanics." *America* 177(8): 12–13.

Harada, Masaaki. 2002. "Study Urges Strong Latino Leaders." *The Albert Lea Tribune*. January 8.

Hernández, Edwin and Kenneth C. Davis. 2003. *Reconstructing the Sacred Tower*. Scranton, PA: The University of Scranton Press.

Hunt, Larry L. 2001. "Religion, Gender, and the Hispanic Experience in the United States: Catholic/Protestant Differences in Religious Involvement, Social Status and Gender-Role Attitudes." *Review of Religious Research* 43(2): 139–60.

Iceland, John. 2003. *Dynamics of Economic Well-Being, Poverty 1996–1999*. Current Population Reports, P70–91. U.S. Census Bureau, Washington, DC.

Kane, Michael N. and M. Williams. 2000. "Perceptions of South Florida Hispanic Anglo Catholics: From Whom Would They Seek Help?" *Journal of Religion and Health* 39(2): 107–21.

Lal, Barbara Ballis. 1995. "Symbolic Interaction Theories." *American Behavioral Scientist* 38: 421–41.

Massey, Douglas and Nancy Denton. 1987. "Trends in the Residential Segregation of Blacks, Hispanics and Asians: 1970–1980." *American Sociological Review* 52: 802–25.

McFalls Jr., Joseph. 1998. "Population: A Lively Introduction." *Population Bulletin* 53(3): 3–48.

McGuire, Meredith. 1997. *Religion: The Social Context.* 4th ed. Belmont, CA: Wadsworth.

Roof, Wade Clark and William McKinney. 1987. *American Mainline Religion.* New Brunswick, NJ: Rutgers University Press.

Santiago, Anne and Margaret Wilder. 1991. "Residential Segregation and Links to Minority Poverty: The Case of Latinos in the United States." *Social Problems* 38: 492–515.

Schmidley, A. Dianne. 2000. U.S. Census Bureau, *Current Population Reports, Series P23–206, Profile of the Foreign-Born Population in the United States 2000.* Washington, D.C.: U.S. Government Printing Office.

Stevens-Arroyo, Anthony and Ana Maria Diaz-Stevens, eds. 1994. *An Enduring Flame: Studies on Latino Popular Religiosity.* New York City, NY: Bildner Center for Western Hemisphere Studies; 116, 175

Weinberg, Daniel H., PhD. 1999. U.S. Census Bureau. "Income and Poverty 1998—Press Briefing." Retrieved from http://www.census.gov/hhes/income/income98/prs99asc.html on May 13, 2005.

U.S. Census Bureau. 2001.*Projections of the Resident Population by Age, Sex, Race and Hispanic Origin 1999–2100.* Washington, D.C.: U.S. Government Printing Office.

Verba, Sidney, Kay Lehman Schlozman and Henry E. Brady. 1995. *Voice and Equality: Civic Voluntarism in American Politics.* Cambridge, MA: Harvard University Press.

Vizcaíno, Mario, Sch.P. 1992. Christian Leadership as Service. Pp. 347–8 in *Prophetic Vision: Pastoral Reflections on the National Pastoral Plan for Hispanic Ministry.* Edited by Soledad Galerón, Rosa María Icaza, and Rosendo Urrabazo. Kansas City, MO: Sheed and Ward: 347–348.

Wagner, Lilya and Allan Figueroa Deck, eds. 1999. *New Directions for Philanthropic Fundraising* 24 (Summer 1999): 59–74.

Woods, Frances Jerome. 1976. *Mexican Ethnic Leadership in San Antonio, Texas.* New York City, NY: Arno Press.

LATINO/A CATHOLIC LEADERS IN THE UNITED STATES

Mark M. Gray and Mary L. Gautier

Introduction

The focus on Catholics continues in this chapter, but with a somewhat different methodology. The more than 40 years of experience in social science research on the Catholic Church by the Center for Applied Research in the Apostolate (CARA) makes it possible to analyze a variety of previously gathered data regarding Latino/a Catholics.

For this chapter, results are presented from a series of CARA Catholic Polls (CCP), a national random sample telephone survey of the adult Catholic population, data from its two priest polls (2001 and 2002), its deacon poll (2001), and its lay ecclesial minister poll (2002) with respect to Latino/as in leadership positions in the Church.[1]

We also incorporated data from CARA's *Catholic Ministry Formation Directory* to describe characteristics of Latino/as in formation for leadership in the Catholic Church.

To develop an understanding of the challenges facing Hispanic leadership in the Catholic Church, we identified characteristics of Latino Catholic parish life today, as reported in CARA's national database of parish life, the National Parish Inventory (NPI).

This chapter presents the results of this data as a portrait of the current state of Latino leadership and leadership formation in the Catholic Church. It begins with a look at the general Hispanic Catholic population, and then details the current estimated proportions of lay ministers, deacons and priests who self-identify as Latino/a.

---

[1] In spring 2003, the Center for the Study of Latino Religion at the Institute for Latino Studies of the University of Notre Dame commissioned the Center for Applied Research in the Apostolate (CARA) to conduct a study of Hispanic leadership, leadership formation, and ministry challenges in the Catholic Church in the United States as baseline research for the Latino/a Religious Leadership Inventory.

However, since one indication of how these figures may change in the near future is to calculate the percentage of Latino/as among those men and women who are currently in formation programs, the chapter next looks at lay ministry, deaconate, and priesthood training programs. We end with the broader context for all of this data, namely, a look at Latino parish life.

The Latino/a Catholic Population

CARA's recent national survey of the Catholic population, the CARA Catholic Poll (CCP) 2003, estimates that 28 percent of the adult Catholic population self identifies as Hispanic, Latino/a or Spanish (margin of error ±3.5 percentage points).[2] Of these respondents, 85 percent say they speak at least some Spanish at home, and half of them (51 percent) preferred to be interviewed in Spanish.

As is widely recognized, the Latino segment of the U.S. Catholic population has grown in the last decade. A Gallup national telephone poll of Catholics conducted in 1992 estimated that 19 percent of Catholics self-identified as Hispanic.[3] However, some of the increases in the estimated number of Catholics who are Latino over the years could also reflect greater efforts by survey researchers to reach the Hispanic population. A combination of factors including interview language preferences, mobility, and general unwillingness to participate in surveys among Hispanics may have systematically led to lower estimates by survey researchers in the past. CARA has placed strong emphasis in its telephone polls on reaching respondents who self-identify as Latino and those who prefer to be interviewed in Spanish. CARA's survey weights are also designed to provide the most accurate population estimates possible.

CARA survey questions provide multiple terms for racial and ethnic identification, thereby supplying a variety of ways in which a respondent may identify himself or herself. For this study the ques-

---

[2] The American Religious Identification Survey (ARIS) 2001 conducted by the Graduate Center of the City University of New York estimates that 29 percent of adult Catholics are Latino/a or Hispanic. However, this study was conducted with English interviews only.

[3] Other national surveys specific to the Catholic population conducted since 1992 have estimated a somewhat smaller Latino segment.

tion, "are you of Spanish, Hispanic, or Latino descent?" is most important. For simplicity, from this point forward in the chapter we will use the term "Latino/a" to refer to any respondent who said they were of Spanish, Hispanic, or Latino/a descent. The 28 percent Latino/a share of the adult Catholic population will also be used throughout this to measure the degree to which Latino/as are underrepresented in leadership positions relative to their presence in the Catholic population. The CARA Catholic Poll (CCP) 2001 (margin of error ±2.3 percentage points) asked respondents if they had ever considered becoming a lay ecclesial minister, priest, or religious sister or brother.

There are no significant differences between Latino/as and non-Latino/as who say they have considered becoming a lay ecclesial minister or between Latina and non-Latina women who say they have considered becoming a sister or nun. However, male Latino Catholics are much less likely than male non-Latino Catholics to say they have considered becoming a priest or brother (13 percent compared to 24 percent).

These results indicate that any under-representation of Hispanics among lay ministers or religious sisters cannot be attributed to differences in interest. However, disproportionately low numbers of Latinos serving as Catholic priests or religious brothers may be in part due to a lower likelihood among male Latino Catholics to have considered these vocations to the same degree that male non-Latino Catholics have.

The comparatively lower levels of interest in becoming a priest or brother among Latino Catholic men are not limited to one observation. Since CARA started asking the question, "Have you ever considered becoming a priest or a brother?" in the CCP, male Latino respondents have always been less likely to say that they have ever considered becoming a priest or a brother.

However, one apparent trend is that the percentage of male Latino Catholics who say they have considered becoming a priest or brother has declined. In 2000, some 21 percent responded that they had considered becoming a priest or brother, but by 2003 only 7 percent agreed with this statement. The question is open-ended in regard to time frame in that it asks the respondent whether they have "ever considered," so dramatic changes in this relatively short span of time would be unusual. Thus, what these data more likely indicate is a growing reluctance among Latino men to say they have considered

Tables 1 and 2

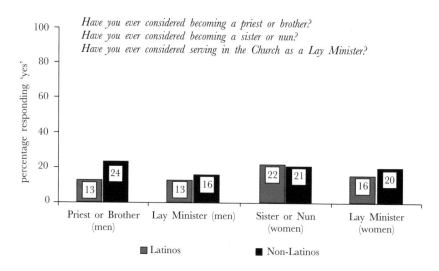

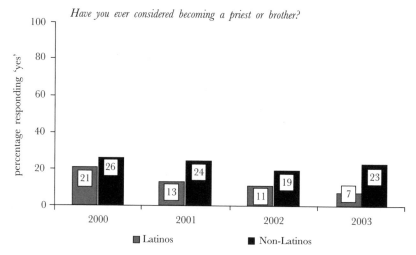

becoming a priest or brother that may not reflect the actual levels of consideration.[4] Regardless, male Latino Catholics are less likely than male non-Latino Catholics to *say* they have ever considered

---

[4] The variance in samples also contributes to the differences. Each survey has its own margin of error and each is based on a different group of respondents.

becoming a priest or brother, and in the past four years they seem to have become even less likely to do so.

At the same time, this reluctance appears not to be based on some growing negative assessment of priestly vocations. Instead it seems to be more grounded in their personal view that they themselves would not consider being a priest. Evidence of this can be found in their willingness to encourage other men to become priests.

In CCP 2003, male Latino Catholics were just as likely as male non-Latino Catholics to agree that they have "ever encouraged someone to pursue a vocation as a priest" (15 percent). Moreover, those Latino/as that have encouraged others are slightly more likely than non-Latino/as to say they would do so again now (63 percent compared to 55 percent). Doing so "now" is significant in that it measures their willingness to encourage priestly vocations after cases of Catholic priests sexually abusing children and adolescents became widely reported in the media in 2002. This question, following the "have you ever" inquiry, was designed to gauge the impact on encouragement of any diminishing evaluations of priesthood in light of the scandals.

Other factors may also be important in explaining why male Latino Catholics are less likely to say they have ever considered becoming a priest or brother. Male Latino Catholics are less likely than male non-Latino Catholics to agree that they have "ever known a Catholic priest on a personal basis, that is, outside formal interactions at church or school" (47 percent compared to 61 percent). To the degree that they have had less personal exposure to priest role models, they may be less aware of the vocation as a personal option.

Another factor may be differing cultural responses to the requirement of celibacy. There is no significant difference between male Latino Catholics and male non-Latino Catholics in their level of agreement with the statement, "Have you ever considered serving in the Church as a lay minister?" In this case, celibacy is not a requirement for lay persons (who are not vowed religious). However, this does not imply that male Latino Catholics would more seriously consider priestly vocations if celibacy were not a requirement. In fact, male Latino Catholics are much *less* likely than male non-Latino Catholics to agree that "married men should be ordained as priests" (47 percent compared to 73 percent).

Latino/a Lay Ecclesial Ministers

In the wake of the Second Vatican Council's call for the laity to become more active in Church life, lay persons[5] and vowed religious—including many Latino/as—responded by becoming lectors, Eucharistic ministers, pastoral council members, religious educators, music ministers, youth ministers, pastoral associates, and in some cases parish directors.

The evolving nature of these opportunities and contributions has at times made it complex to distinguish those who are formally appointed to a leadership position within the structure of the institutional church and those working as lay ministers without specific pastoral responsibilities in a formal ecclesial context. The United States Conference of Catholic Bishops recognizes that "the boundaries that distinguish ecclesial ministers from other lay ministers and from all the laity are flexible and permeable" (National Conference of Catholic Bishops). However, some generally discussed parameters can help define boundaries.

First, the word *lay* underscores the fact that persons in this group remain first, foremost, and always members of the laity. The word *ecclesial* denotes not only that the ministry of these lay persons has a place within the communion of the Church, but also that it is to be submitted to the judgment and supervision of the hierarchy. It is not simply an activity undertaken on personal initiative.[6]

Social science demands even greater precision. In CARA's 2002 telephone poll of 795 parish-based lay ecclesial ministers (margin of error ±3.5 percent) those surveyed included any parish staff member besides a priest, deacon, or seminarian working or volunteering for a parish at least 20 hours in a typical week, excluding secretaries and other clerical workers,[7] maintenance workers, and school employ-

---

[5] The term "lay persons" is used here to refer to lay persons who are not vowed religious brothers or sisters. Although vowed religious are technically lay persons under canon law, we exclude them from the term for the purposes of this report.

[6] Ibid.

[7] Business managers are included although their roles are not exclusively pastoral; they are mentioned in some Church documents about lay ministry. In the course of CARA's survey of lay ecclesial ministers, it became evident how difficult it is to distinguish business managers from other financial and clerical workers. Also some workers whose primary roles are secretarial also do some pastoral ministry for their parishes. Thus parish workers with titles such as "bookkeeper," "secre-

ees. This is very nearly the same definition used by Murnion and DeLambo (1999) in their 1997 survey of lay ministers. One difference is that Murnion and DeLambo limited their study to ministers who are paid for their work. Volunteers (so long as they are considered "staff members" by the parish) were included in CARA's definition to account for the possibility that some poorer parishes probably have unpaid staff members.

Six percent of lay ecclesial ministers surveyed (49 respondents) in CARA's Lay Ecclesial Ministers Poll self-identified as Latino/a—well below what would be expected if the number of Latinos in lay ecclesial ministry mirrored the number of Latinos in the Catholic population. The resulting small number of Latinos among respondents makes comparisons to non-Latinos complicated. It is only possible to make very general inferences about differences between Latino/as and non-Latino/as with these data. The findings presented may suggest real differences in the population, but care should be taken not to overstate the significance of these differences.

Respondents were asked about their primary area of ministry. Nine in ten Latino/a lay ecclesial ministers said their primary work was

Table 3. Primary Area of Ministry for Latino and Non-Latino
Lay Ecclesial Ministers

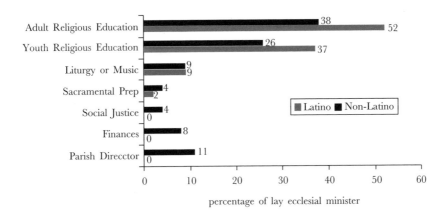

percentage of lay ecclesial minister

tary," and "administrative assistant" were not interviewed as lay ecclesial ministers unless some of their responsibilities are also pastoral. Those with managerial titles such as "business manager," "office manager," and "administrator" were generally included even if they had no pastoral responsibilities.

in adult or youth religious education. None of the Latino/a lay ecclesial ministers surveyed said they were parish administrators without
a resident priest pastor (canon 517.2), or that their primary work
was in ministries related to finances or social justice.

There are a number of other notable differences between Latino/a
and non-Latino/a lay ecclesial ministers. Although both are similarly
likely to be vowed religious, female, and to have earned at least a
bachelor's degree, in addition to being younger, Latino/a ministers
are proportionately less likely than non-Latino/as to have earned a
graduate degree, to be married, to have attended Catholic schools,
or to have been enrolled in ministry formation programs that lead
to graduate ministry degrees or to certification by a diocese.

Latino/a lay ecclesial ministers who have been enrolled in a ministry formation program are equally likely as non-Latino/as to have
received financial assistance from a parish, but less likely to have
received financial assistance from a diocese.

Table 4. Profiles of Latino and Non-Latino Lay Ecclesial Ministers

	Latino	Non-Latino
Vowed religious	14%	16%
Married (lay persons only)	57	69
Female	82	81
Age		
18 to 29	9	6
30 to 49	51	33
50 or older	40	61
Highest Level of Schooling		
High school degree or less	6	7
Some college	12	15
Bachelor's degree	41	24
Graduate or professional school	41	54
Catholic Schooling		
Elementary/middle school	57	70
High school	37	53
College or university	60	67
Study in Ministry Formation Program		
Attended ministry formation program	76	85
– Received financial assistance		
from a parish to attend	62	59

Table 4 (*cont.*)

	Latino	Non-Latino
– Received financial assistance from a diocese to attend	11	20
Attended before becoming a minister	41	50
Attended after becoming a minister	31	42
Has a graduate degree in ministry	29	36
Certified by a diocese for ministry	31	44

Canon 231.1 requires that "lay people who are pledged to special service of the Church, whether permanently or for a time, have a duty to acquire the appropriate formation which their role demands."

A 2002 report of the United States Conference of Catholic Bishops' Subcommittee on Lay Ministry of the Committee on the Laity identified a growing trend among dioceses to create standards and a certification process for lay ecclesial ministry positions that reflect the principle of canon 231.1 (National Conference of Catholic Bishops 1999).

To the extent that these processes would require graduate education or enrollment in ministry formation programs that require a college degree, Latinos who wish to serve as lay ecclesial ministers may face higher entry hurdles than non-Latinos. The figures presented above detail the profile of Latino/as *already* serving as lay ecclesial ministers. They do not represent the profile of all Hispanic Catholics who could potentially be interested in a lay ecclesial ministry career.[8]

Nineteen percent of Latino/as in the adult Catholic population that were surveyed in CCP 2003 had attained at least a bachelor's degree and 5 percent had attended a graduate or professional school. By comparison, 40 percent of non-Latino/a Catholics had attained at least a bachelor's degree and 16 percent had attended a graduate or professional school.

Most Latino Catholics do not have educational backgrounds that would meet the requirements for many graduate ministry formation

---

[8] Ideally, one would try to isolate those in the Catholic population who say they have considered a vocation and then further segment the analysis among men and women and Latino/as and non-Latino/as in this group. However, the share of Latino/as who have considered a vocation creates a total number of respondents that is too small for statistical inference.

programs whereas at least four in ten non-Latino/a Catholics likely do. Hispanic Catholics may also be less able to assume the financial costs of attending graduate ministry programs that might be required to obtain or advance in a lay ecclesial ministry position. More than six in ten (63 percent) Latino Catholics live in households with a combined annual income of less than $40,000, compared to three in ten (30 percent) non-Latino Catholics.

Scholars and Church representatives readily admit that Latinos, and ethnic and racial minorities in general, are underrepresented among lay ecclesial ministers.[9] The U.S. Conference of Catholic Bishops' Subcommittee on Lay Ministry of the Committee on the Laity reasons that, "some members of these communities are recent arrivals in this country, and many, though not all, are poor" (United States Conference of Catholic Bishops). They also note "within the so-called minority communities, ministry is clearly seen as a service to the community, but rarely is it recognized as a profession or career. The bulk of the work is done by volunteers." (United States Conference of Catholic Bishops 1999). This appears to mirror some of the findings of the previous chapter.

CARA's Lay Ecclesial Ministers Poll shows that Latino/a ministers are disproportionately more likely than non-Latino/a ministers to be working for their parish as a volunteer (25 percent compared to 12 percent) and those Latino/as that are receiving a wage or salary for their ministry work are not compensated as well as non-Latino/as. Nearly eight in ten (78 percent) Latino/a lay ecclesial ministers who receive some form of payment for ministry earn less than $30,000 per year for that work. By comparison, fewer than six in ten (59 percent) non-Latino/as earn less than $30,000 per year for their ministry work.

---

[9] This has been consistently recognized for more than a decade. Zeni Fox, in *New Ecclesial Ministry* (2002), writes, "The overwhelming majority of the new ministers are white. . . . In general, traditional church leaders from minority communities are not being successfully recruited" (p. 17). Bryan Froehle and Mary Gautier, in *Catholicism USA* (2000) write, "Hispanics/Latino/as are under-represented among lay ecclesial ministers relative to their proportion in the Catholic population overall" (p. 157). Philip Murnion et al., in *New Parish Ministers* (1992) writes, "There is a drastic problem of the very few Hispanic and African American ministers" (p. 18).

Canon 231.2 ensures that lay persons serving in a ministry position for the Church have a right to "worthy remuneration befitting their condition, whereby, with due regard also to the provisions of the civil law, they can becomingly provide for their own needs and the needs of their families." To the degree that lay ecclesial ministry does not provide Hispanic families with a living wage, it may be a job some cannot afford to seek. As further proof, nearly eight in ten (78 percent) non-Latino/a lay ecclesial ministers earning an income as a minister report that their ministry income is smaller than other income sources in their household. Yet only 57 percent of Latino/a lay ecclesial ministers report that their ministry income is smaller than other income sources in their household. Hence although paid Latino/a lay ministers earn less for their ministry than non-Latino/as, they rely on that income more to meet the needs of their households.

Latinos in the Catholic population do not show disproportionately low interest in becoming lay ecclesial ministers. However, they are more likely to have disproportionately lower levels of socio-economic resources from which to draw to meet the professional and educational standards being developed for lay ministry leadership positions. Even Latinos who currently serve as lay ecclesial ministers—primarily as religious educators—are more likely than non-Latinos to lack ministry degrees as well as certification, and they are more likely to earn less for their work or provide it as a volunteer. In sum, the Latino/a disproportionality in lay ecclesial ministry may not be a function of interest but of resources in the context of evolving institutional requirements for service as a lay ecclesial minister in the Catholic Church.

Latino Permanent Deacons

Pope Paul IV restored the permanent deaconate in 1967, creating an ordained leadership position within the Catholic Church that was open to married men. Permanent deacons are distinguished from transitional deacons in that they are not planning to become ordained priests. Permanent deacons can be married—and most are. More than nine in ten permanent deacons (95 percent) are married or are widowers. In 1975, there were just 898 permanent deacons in the United States. In 2002, 13,277 permanent deacons were serving the

Church in a variety of ministries including 117 administering parishes in the absence of a resident priest pastor (canon 517.2).

CARA's Deacon Poll 2001 included 804 deacons (margin of error of ±3.5 percent) randomly selected from a national list of all permanent deacons, active and retired, obtained from *The Official Catholic Directory*. Ten percent of those surveyed (79 respondents) self-identified as Latino.[10] This is half of what would be expected if the number of Latino deacons mirrored the number of Latinos among males 35 years of age or older in the Catholic population (approximately 20 percent).[11]

More than nine in ten deacons—Latino and non-Latino alike— say they first "seriously considered" the vocation after they turned 30 years of age and nearly half say this occurred after the age of 45. More than nine in ten agree that if they had a chance to "do it all over again" that they would still become a deacon and that they are happy in their ministry. Latino deacons are more likely than non-Latino deacons to become candidates for the priesthood and then be ordained within one year (8 percent compared to 1 percent). Latino deacons—much like Latinos in the general Catholic population—are much less likely than non-Latinos to say they had ever considered becoming a priest or religious brother. Half of all non-Latino deacons (51 percent) say they had considered a priestly or vowed religious vocation whereas only 35 percent of Latino deacons say they had ever thought of becoming a priest or religious brother.

Many deacons continue to work in other professions in addition to their part-time (bi-vocational) ministry. A third of Latino deacons work full-time in ministry. Latino deacons are more likely than non-Latino deacons to say they are able to spend as much time in their ministry as they would like (70 percent compared to 57 percent). Latino deacons are also more likely than non-Latino deacons to serve more than one parish (30 percent compared to 16 percent).

---

[10] This estimate is similar to the 11.5 percent of deacons who are Latino reported in *The National Study on the Permanent Deaconate of the Catholic Church in the United States*, 1995.

[11] Canon 1031.2 allows single men to become a candidate for the permanent diaconate at the age of 25. A married man cannot become a candidate until he is 35, "with the consent of his wife."

There are no significant differences between Latino and non-Latino deacons in the types of ministry they engage in. The most common, in which more than nine in ten deacons are involved, include presiding at funerals, assisting in Masses, celebrating baptisms, and presiding at Communion services. About eight in ten say they preach homilies, witness marriages, provide ministry to the sick, and provide religious education.

However, there are differences in the types of groups served by Latino deacons and non-Latino deacons. Latino deacons are more likely than non-Latino deacons to serve the poor and non-Latino deacons are more likely to serve the elderly.

Table 5. Groups Served by Latino and Non-Latino Deacons

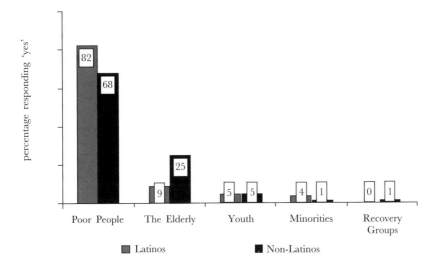

More than nine in ten Latino and non-Latino deacons agree that their formation and training prepared them for their ministry, although seven in ten say continuing education or ongoing formation would be "very useful." Nearly nine in ten Latino deacons (88 percent) say they would be willing to serve as a parish administrator in a parish without a resident priest pastor. By comparison, about three in four non-Latino deacons (76 percent) say they would be willing to serve as a parish administrator in the same situation.

Table 6. Profiles of Latino and Non-Latino Permanent Deacons

	Latino	Non-Latino
Marital Status		
Married	87%	91%
Widowed	8	4
Never married	5	4
Separated or annulled	0	1
Age		
35 to 44	1	2
45 to 59	32	32
60 or older	67	66
Highest Level of Schooling		
High school degree or less	24	11
Some college	44	29
Bachelor's degree	18	31
Graduate or professional school	14	29
Weekly Hours of Ministry Work		
Less than 24 hours a week	65	62
25 to 49	19	26
50 to 74	12	11
75 or more	4	1
Income		
Paid for ministry	24	27
Has a secular job	34	38
Weekly Hours of Secular Work		
(of those with a secular job)		
Less than 24 hours a week	7	11
25 to 49	59	57
50 to 74	30	31
75 or more	4	1

Latino deacons are also more likely to agree with the statement, "priests understand and accept the role of deacons." Nine in ten Latino deacons (90 percent) say priests understand and accept their role, whereas only one in four non-Latino deacons (77 percent) agree with that statement.

Latino and non-Latino deacons are similar in age, marital status, receiving payment for their ministry, in their likelihood of having a secular job, and the hours they work at it. However, Latino deacons are much less likely than non-Latino deacons to have a college degree or to have attended a graduate or professional school.

The United States is home to 135 diaconate formation programs. Admissions requirements generally include recommendations from a pastor, support from the candidate's wife (if married), and letters of reference. Although a small number of dioceses do require an undergraduate or graduate degree, most do not require academic prerequisites, and therefore the greater likelihood among Latinos not to have earned a college degree is not necessarily an impediment to serving.

LATINO PRIESTS

The CARA Priest Polls conducted in 2001 and 2002 included a national random sample of Catholic priests (1,234 and 902 respondents, respectively, for margins of error of ±2.5 percent and ±3.3 percent). The 2002 survey included an additional random over-sample of priests ordained after 1991 (301 respondents for a margin of error of ±5.8 percent).

Undoubtedly, the Latino population is more underrepresented in the priesthood than in either lay ministry or the deaconate, but there are indications that this is beginning to change. The CARA Priest Poll in 2001 estimated that 3 percent of Catholic priests were Latino; a year later, the 2002 survey estimated 2 percent.[12] Among priests ordained since 1991, however, 8 percent self-identify as Latino. The current relatively low numbers of Latino priests may be a reflection of the earlier reported finding that Latino males are less likely than non-Latinos to consider priestly vocations (CCP 2001–2003). The small proportion of Catholic priests that self-identify as Latino creates challenges in analyzing survey data, due to the small number of Latino priests interviewed. However, some basic patterns and differences can be identified that may suggest real differences in the population of all priests. Care should be taken, however, in interpreting these differences.

---

[12] According to CCP 2003, 28 percent of male adult Catholics self-identify as Latino.

Tentatively there is some indication that Latino priests ordained since 1991 may be more likely than Latino and non-Latino priests overall to at least "somewhat agree" with the statement "I have seriously thought about leaving the priesthood in the last five years" (21 percent compared to 11 percent of non-Latino priests ordained since 1991 and non-Latino priests overall, and 5 percent of Latino priests overall). About seven in ten Latino priests—both newly ordained and overall—are diocesan priests rather than religious priests, such as Jesuits or Franciscans, compared to six in ten non-Latino priests overall and almost eight in ten non-Latino priests who have been ordained since 1991.

Latino priests are less likely to report that they spend a lot of time doing administrative or supervisory work in their parishes. Only about one in ten Latino priests—both newly ordained and overall—say they work more than ten hours a week in parish administrative work or supervisory duties, compared to about four in ten non-Latino priests overall and about one quarter of non-Latino priests who have been ordained since 1991. Latino priests are also slightly less likely than non-Latino priests to agree with the statement, "I would prefer to spend less time on administrative and supervisory work."

Latino priests also report significant involvement as leaders in the communities where they minister. About six in ten Latino priests—both newly ordained and overall—say they are at least "somewhat involved" in civic or community affairs, compared to six in ten non-Latino priests overall and about four in ten non-Latino priests ordained since 1991. This is a fact worth keeping in mind when reading the following chapters, which look at the community-serving activities of Hispanic religious leaders.

In part because of the limited number of Latino priests surveyed, there is no indication that Latino priests are more likely than non-Latino priests to serve larger or smaller parishes, on average, in terms of registered households. About three in four Latino and non-Latino priests report serving in just one parish. Both Latino and non-Latino priests are most likely to say they celebrate five Masses in an average week.

Latino and non-Latino priests differ somewhat in terms of the location of parishes where they serve. Half of Latino priests overall serve a parish in a large city compared to one in four non-Latino priests, who are more likely to serve a parish in a small town or rural area (51 percent). Among priests ordained since 1991, Latinos are somewhat more likely than non-Latinos to serve in a large city (35 percent compared to 19 percent).

In the overall population of priests, Latinos are younger and more recently ordained than non-Latino priests. More than half of Latino priests are younger than 45, compared to 15 percent of non-Latinos. Because Latino priests are disproportionately younger, they are also more likely than non-Latino priests to be ordained after 1990 (53 percent compared to 14 percent).

There are not significant differences in the percentage of Latino and non-Latino priests who have attended Catholic schools. More Latino than non-Latino priests report they were involved in a parish youth group (56 percent compared to 37 percent). Latino priests are more likely than non-Latino priests to say they have attended a seminary both overall (95 percent compared to 76 percent) and among those ordained since 1991. Latino priests are less likely to report that they attended college before entering seminary or novitiate.

Table 7. Profiles of Latino and Non-Latino Priests

	Latino	Non-Latino
Age		
18 to 34	16%	2%
35 to 44	37	13
45 to 64	31	44
65 or older	16	41
Time of Ordination		
Before 1950	5	6
1950 to 1969	10	44
1970 to 1989	32	36
1990 or later	53	14
Schooling and Formation		
Attended Catholic elementary	68	79
Participated in a parish youth group or CYO	56	37
Attended Catholic high school	74	74
Attended college before entering seminary or novitiate	26	41
Attended college seminary	95	76

While Latino men in the Catholic population are less likely to have considered becoming a priest, Latino priests are no less likely than non-Latino priests to say they would, or have encouraged other men to become a priest. All Latino priests surveyed said they would encourage (compared to 95 percent of non-Latinos) and that they have encouraged others in the past (all non-Latino priests also say they have encouraged others in the past). More than eight in ten Latino and non-Latino priests say they are satisfied with their lives as priests and about nine in ten strongly agree that if they had the chance to do it all over they would become a priest again.

The incongruity between the Latino percentage of the Catholic population and the Latino percentage of Catholic priests cannot be directly attributed to any institutional or educational factors using the data analyzed here. Other than their age and year of ordination, Latino priests have comparable levels of preparation and satisfaction with their ministries. Other than slight differences in the time spent doing administrative as well as supervisory work, and the urban versus rural location of their parishes, there are not major differences in the profiles of Latino and non-Latino priests as measured by this survey data.

Thus, understanding the roots of the disparity between the size of the Latino population and the number of Latino priests appears to be more a question of the differences in the consideration of the vocation as has been noted in the analysis of CARA's polls of the Catholic population (CCP). This is an important trend to understand, as the data presented here suggest that the already low likelihood of consideration of priestly vocations by Latinos could be declining even further.

LATINO/AS IN MINISTRY FORMATION PROGRAMS

The previous sections of this chapter detailed the current estimated proportions of lay ministers, deacons, and priests who self-identify as Latino/a. Next we calculate the percentage of Latino/as among those men and women who are currently in formation programs for leadership roles. Data collected for CARA's *Catholic Ministry Formation Directory* is used in this section to detail current levels of Latino/a enrollment in the more than 600 priesthood, deaconate, and lay ecclesial ministry formation programs sponsored by the Church in the United States.

LAY ECCLESIAL MINISTRY PROGRAMS

Lay ecclesial ministry formation programs currently exist in 147 of 194 (76 percent) Catholic dioceses and eparchies (a total of 312 programs). According to the 275 lay ecclesial ministry formation programs that have enrollments and provided CARA with information about the racial and ethnic composition of their participants, there are 3,558 Latino/as currently attending lay ecclesial ministry formation programs in the United States. This represents about 12 percent of all participants enrolled in these programs in 2003. That percentage is lower than what would be expected if participant enrollments mirrored the proportion of Latino/as among all adult Catholics, yet it is significantly higher than the 6 percent of lay ecclesial ministers who self-identify as Latino/a. The dioceses with the programs that, on average, have majority Latino/a enrollments are Lubbock, Texas (92 percent), Miami, Florida (67 percent), Galveston-Houston, Texas (66 percent), San Bernardino, California (60 percent) and Austin, Texas (52 percent). A total of 57 lay ecclesial ministry formation programs (18 percent) report that they are able to provide instruction in Spanish.

DIACONATE PROGRAMS

Diaconate formation programs currently exist in 128 of 194 (66 percent) Catholic dioceses and eparchies (a total of 135 programs). According to the 112 diaconate formation programs that have enrollments and provided CARA with information about the racial and ethnic composition of their participants, there are 465 Latinos currently attending a diaconate formation program in the United States. This represents about 18 percent of all deacon candidates enrolled in these programs in 2003. This percentage is very near what would be expected if Latino diaconate enrollments mirrored the proportion of Latinos, among Catholic males, 35 years of age or older (20 percent), and it is significantly higher than the 10 percent of deacons currently serving the Church who self-identify as Latino. The dioceses with the programs that, on average, have majority Latino enrollments are Lubbock, Texas (79 percent), Las Cruces, New Mexico (67 percent), Galveston-Houston, Texas (62 percent), San Antonio, Texas (60 percent), Yakima, Washington (57 percent), and Chicago,

Illinois (52 percent). Thirty-six deaconate programs (27 percent) report that they are able to provide instruction in Spanish.

PRIESTLY FORMATION PROGRAMS

Priestly formation programs at the high school, college, and post-graduate level currently exist in 69 of 194 (36 percent) Catholic dioceses and eparchies (a total of 196 programs and houses of formation). According to the 176 priestly formation programs that have enrollments and provided CARA with information about the racial and ethnic composition of their seminarians, there are 919 Latinos currently attending priestly formation programs in the United States.[13] This represents about 17 percent of all students enrolled in these programs in 2003. This percentage is below what would be expected if Latino priestly formation enrollments mirrored the proportion of Latinos, among adult Catholic males (28 percent), yet it is significantly higher than the 2 to 3 percent of priests currently serving the Church who self-identify as Latino. The dioceses with the programs that, on average, have majority Latino enrollments are Brownsville, Texas (100 percent), El Paso, Texas (100 percent), Miami, Florida (77 percent), San Bernardino, California (63 percent), and Los Angeles, California (59 percent).

These formation program statistics reveal that the proportion of Latinos preparing to serve the Church is much higher than the proportion of Latinos among those currently in ministry. As CARA's survey data show, Hispanics serving the Church as lay ministers and priests are proportionately younger than non-Hispanics in those ministry positions.[14] It is evident that there is an emerging younger Latino segment of those preparing for or already serving in ministry in the Catholic Church.

The formation program data also provide a wider context in which to evaluate the finding that adult Latino men in the Catholic pop-

---

[13] There are an additional 31 U.S. Latino seminarians attending priestly formation programs in Mexico, Belgium, Rome and the U.S. Virgin Islands that are sponsored by, or especially for, U.S. seminarians.

[14] There is no significant age difference between Latinos and non-Latinos who serve as deacons. This may be in part due to the minimum age restrictions associated with this vocation.

ulation are less likely than adult non-Latino Catholic men to say they have considered becoming a priest. The CCP results reflect the percentage of men in the Catholic population who considered becoming a priest, but did not follow through with that idea. The formation program data show Latinos are not under-represented to the same degree among those who consider becoming a priest and then actually enter a formation program.[15]

LATINO/A PARISH LIFE

To understand the development of Latino leadership in the Catholic Church, one must evaluate parish life among Latinos. Parishes are the reservoirs from which future leaders of the Church emerge. Anything that can be identified about parish life more specific to the experience of the Latino population helps explain how Hispanic leadership in the Church could possibly be developed beyond its current levels, and indicate the needs of predominantly Hispanic parishes.

CARA has collected information from Catholic parishes in the United States in its National Parish Inventory (NPI) database since 1998. CARA uses a simple, one-page, mailed questionnaire or Internet-based survey that is given to each parish in the United States periodically. Those parishes that complete the questionnaire have their information recorded. For those parishes that do not return a survey, CARA relies on information supplied by dioceses, *The Official Catholic Directory,* and any existing information from previous NPI data collections where possible.

CARA's NPI questionnaire includes questions regarding the percentage of registered parishioners who are African American/Black, Hispanic/Latino/a, Asian, Anglo/White, or Native American. Currently, CARA has received race and ethnicity data from about four in ten parishes. Those parishes that have not provided race and ethnicity data are, on average, smaller than those that have provided

---

[15] It is possible that some of the men surveyed in the CCP actually did at one time enter a priestly formation program but did not go on to become priests. Yet this share is likely to be extremely small. In some surveys CARA has asked a follow up question probing how seriously the respondent considered becoming a priest. In CCP 2001 about 2 percent of adult Catholic men say they had considered becoming a priest "very seriously."

information in terms of the number of registered households, registered parishioners, seating capacity, and the number of Masses. Thus, information on race and ethnicity collected from the NPI should be considered in light of the under-representation of smaller parishes.

Table 8. Parishes by Percentage of Registered Parishioners who are Latino, National Parish Inventory

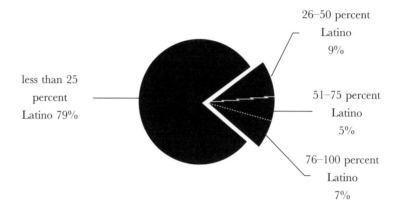

Among those parishes that have provided CARA with race and ethnicity data, about eight in ten report that 25 percent or less of their registered parishioners are Latino/a. More than one in ten parishes report that a majority of their registered parishioners are Hispanic.

The CCP-based estimate of 28 percent of the adult Catholic population self identifying as Latino/a is used to sort parishes into two categories.[16] The first includes all parishes that have provided CARA with race and ethnicity data that also report at least 28 percent of their parishioners are Latino/a. The second includes all parishes that have provided CARA with race and ethnicity data that report fewer than 28 percent of their parishioners are Latino/a.

---

[16] Registered parishioners also include children, and when this is taken into account, the number of Latinos in the total Catholic population, of any age, is larger than 28 percent. However, the exact percentage of Latinos among the total Catholic population, of any age, is more difficult to estimate using survey research studies. To use the estimate of greatest accuracy and to remain consistent with the figure used throughout this report, 28 percent is used here as a cut-point between the two categories.

Table 9. Profiles of Parishes by Percentage of Parishioners
Identified as Latino, National Parish Inventory

	Parishes that are 28% or more Latino	Parishes that are less than 28% Latino
Masses		
Average number of weekend Masses	5	5
Average number of weekday Masses	6	6
Has at least one weekend Spanish language Mass	70%	13%
Size of Parish		
Average seating capacity	519	528
Average number of registered households	1,155	1,083
Average number of registered parishioners	2,959	2,809
Average attendance at *all* Masses on a typical October weekend	1,407	1,188
Average number of infant baptisms per year	129	32
Average number of funerals or memorial services per year	32	30
Parish Staff		
Average number of diocesan priests	1.6	1.5
Average number of religious priests	1.7	1.5
Average number of deacons	1.7	1.5
Average number of religious brothers	1.3	1.1
Average number of religious sisters	1.8	1.5
Average number of lay ecclesial ministers	4.8	4.9

Of the parishes in these two groups, those with more Latino/as have a slightly larger average number of registered households, registered parishioners, and Mass attendance. Parishes with more Latino/as are also more likely to offer Mass in Spanish, which requires a priest who is at least somewhat fluent in that language. Seven in ten parishes with 28 percent or more Latino/as offer at least one Spanish Mass per week, compared to 13 percent of parishes that have fewer than 28 percent Latino/a parishioners. There is no difference between the two groups of parishes in terms of the average number of Masses offered on a weekly basis and average seating capacities; parish staffing patterns are very similar.

One distinct difference between parishes where at least 28 percent of parishioners are Latino/a and those parishes with fewer Latino/as, is the average number of baptisms performed (129 per year compared to 32 per year). This, in relation to the average number of funerals, indicates that parishes with larger numbers of Latino/as are growing at a faster rate than parishes with fewer Latino/as.

CONCLUSION

This review of CARA survey data reveals that the percentage of Latino/a priests, deacons, and lay ecclesial ministers serving the Catholic Church do not currently mirror the size of the Catholic population that self-identifies as Latino/a. However, there is also evidence in these surveys and in CARA's ministry formation data to indicate that there are more representative numbers of Latino/as among those who recently entered ministry or who are preparing for leadership positions in the Church in formation programs.

One useful representative example is a comparison of Latino priests and seminarians. CARA estimates that there are approximately 900 Latino priests currently serving the Church in the United States, and CARA ministry formation data indicate that 919 Latino men are currently enrolled in priestly formation programs in the United States. Thus, there are indications that there are at least as many Latino men currently preparing to be priests as there are Latino men currently serving the Church as priests.

It is difficult to isolate with the data utilized here the historical reasons for Latino/a under-representation in Catholic ministry. However, there are indications that issues related to how Latino men evaluate the vocation of priesthood may have been an important factor in explaining the disproportionality between the Latino population and Latino priests. There are also some issues related to eligibility and affordability of formation programs that are often required for ministry positions. Too often, Latinos in the Catholic population may lack the educational and financial resources to pursue these formation programs, a situation not unlike other denominations as will be seen in the following chapters.

What emerges from the findings in this chapter is a Catholic Church in transition. The Hispanic Catholic population is growing, as is the number of Latino/as preparing for Catholic ministry positions. Whether the proportion of leaders in the Church who are Latino/a grows as fast as the proportion of Catholics who are appears to be partly dependent on issues related to formation requirements, cultural issues regarding the considerations of vocations, and the availability of Latino/a leadership role models.

The next chapters shift the focus to Hispanic Protestant congregations and leadership. Although differing methodologies, definitions, and sampling make comparisons difficult, they present some parallels that the reader may identify and researchers might later explore.

Among all the mainline denominations, sufficient Hispanic religious leadership poses a challenge. In general this does not appear to be for lack of desire by Hispanics to lead congregations, but rather obstacles such as the cost of education and the lack of resources to meet that cost. One also sees Latino/a ministers whose families are dependent upon their salary (and who sometimes augment that salary with extra-ecclesial work), and ministers quite likely to be engaged in the civic affairs of their communities. As the book's introduction suggests, Hispanic religious leaders may have more in common across denominations than previously thought.

REFERENCES

Zeni Fox. 1997. *New Ecclesial Ministry: Lay Professionals Serving the Church*. Theological Book Service.

Froehle, Bryan and Mary L. Gautier. 2000. *Catholism USA: A Portrait of the Catholic Church in the United States*. Maryknoll, NY: Orbis Books.

Murnion, Msgr. Phillip J. 1992. *New Parish Ministers*. New York: National Pastoral Life Center.

Murnion, Msgr. Phillip J. and David DeLambo. 1999. *Parishes and Parish Ministers*. New York: National Pastoral Life Center.

National Conference of Catholic Bishops Subcommittee on Lay Ministry. "Lay Ecclesial Ministry: The State of the Question." Report presented at a U.S. Bishops' general meeting, November 1999, Washington, DC.

HISPANIC MINISTRY IN FOURTEEN PROTESTANT DENOMINATIONS

Adair Lummis

Introduction

While the last two chapters looked at Catholicism, this chapter summarizes major issues in Hispanic ministry but compares them across fourteen Protestant denominations. Like the earlier essays, it too will look at general denominational statistics, data specific to (Protestant) clergy, and current strategies. Readers can begin to see both similarities and contrasts between Catholic and Protestant Hispanic ministry and leadership, including common limitations and resources among Hispanic ministers across denominations.

Sources for this chapter include: 1) material downloaded from denominational websites; 2) interviews conducted with national denominational leaders working in the area of Hispanic ministry, using question areas proposed by Edwin I. Hernández; 3) several additional interviews with or e-mail responses from those who keep statistics for their denominations; 4) material mailed by those interviewed.

Measuring the Hispanic Presence

Among the larger Protestant denominations in the United States, how many Hispanic congregations are there, and how large is their membership? How many Hispanic clergy hold leadership positions? Accurate counting is not an easy task. While denominations keep the most accurate current records on numbers of congregations, for some it is only within the last few years that they have kept records of how many of their total congregations are Hispanic. Further, denominations may differ in how they define a "Hispanic congregation." For example, the research office of the Evangelical Lutheran Church in America (ELCA) categorizes a congregation as Hispanic if it has 30 percent or more Hispanic members. This precision in definition is likely not true of most denominations. Usually, denominations do not have a reporting form for the ethnic/racial composition of their congregations with definitions widely accepted by their own regional judicatories or congregations.

Another source of difficulty in making cross-denominational comparisons relates to what the national denominational office or its individual regional judicatories count as a congregation. For instance, Southern Baptist Convention (SBC), Reformed Church in America (RCA), and Christian Reformed Church (CRC) and United Methodist Church (UMC) make a distinction in reporting statistics between established churches and church-type mission when reporting numbers of Hispanic congregations. However, this is not as true in other denominations, mainly because their middle judicatories use different categories and reporting forms, resulting in some tallying total numbers of Hispanic congregations by counting established churches and new church starts together.

Denominations, particularly the mid-sized and larger ones, generally have no way of knowing the ethnicity of members because annual congregational reports do not categorize people by ethnic or racial identity. No national records are kept for individual members at all in most denominations. Therefore, the number of Hispanic members a denomination has is typically estimated in one of two ways—either by the number of adult members in congregations classified as Hispanic or the number who subscribe to the national Hispanic office mailings (usually in Spanish).

Both criteria present problems that lead to underreporting of a denomination's Hispanic/Latino members. For example, many Latino/as do attend new churches specifically intended to attract Spanish-speaking persons in an area. However, because in some denominations these "works in formation," missions, and home churches are not recognized as "real" congregations when counting members (such as in UMC), those Latino/as who attend are missed in both denominational membership totals and ethnic counts.

A greater source of underreporting across denominations, mentioned by several interviewees, is that neither way of estimating total Hispanic membership is likely to catch second- and third-generation Hispanics whose first language is not Spanish. Rather, it is more likely that those born in the United States whose first language is English, if churched at all, are attending mixed ethnic churches where the services are in English, attending congregations which are not classified as "Hispanic," or failing to request denominational mailing in Spanish.

DENOMINATIONAL STATISTICS

Table 1 summarizes the numbers for Hispanic congregations, members and clergy for fourteen denominations and where possible, compares figures for "recently" and "five years ago."[1] The table, compiled in 2003, shows substantial differences among denominations in total numbers of Hispanic congregations, members, and clergy. The size of each denomination is one likely contributing factor to its Hispanic totals; hence the table lists denominations in terms of their overall, present number (regardless of ethnicity). For each denomination, the recent total of Hispanic congregations is followed with the percentage that Hispanic congregations represent of all their congregations. Question marks in the table indicate where information was unobtainable.

Table 1. Hispanic Congregations, Membership and Clergy in
14 Protestant Denominations, 2003

DENOMINATION	CONGREGATIONS		MEMBERS		CLERGY	
	Recently	5 years ago	Recently	5 years ago	Recently	5 years ago
A. *VERY LARGE DENOMINATIONS* Over 35,000 congregations						
1. Southern Baptist[2] 41,000 total congregations	2,650 6.46%	?	200,000	?	2,500	2,000
2. United Methodist 36,000 total congregations	300 > 1%	323	50,000	47,757	531	441
B. *LARGE DENOMINATIONS* 10,000 to 12,000 congregations						
3. Assem. of God 11,800 total congregations	1,918 16%	1,706	600,000	500,000	3,600	2,500

[1] In Table 1, the dates corresponding to the most recent data available vary from December 1999 to March 2003. In gathering this information we found that the larger denominations are more likely to be a year or two late in reporting statistics on congregations and members, usually because the national statistical or research office must wait until all the congregations have filed their reports.

[2] Updated information provided by Bob Sena of the North American Mission Board via electronic mail, received August 26, 2003. By way of comparison, Roman Catholics have 4,000 majority Hispanic parishes or 20.6% of their total with 25.25 million Hispanic members and 2,900 Hispanic clergy. See the United States Catholic Conference of Bishops website, http://www.nccbuscc.org/hispanicaffairs/demo.htm.

Table 1. (*cont.*)

DENOMINATION	CONGREGATIONS		MEMBERS		CLERGY	
	Recently	5 years ago	Recently	5 years ago	Recently	5 years ago
4. Presby. Ch USA 11,300 total congregations	285 2%	220	35,000	22,261	366	300
5. Evangel. Lutheran 10,900 total congregations	108 1%	85	38,706	29,424	166	126
C. *MID-SIZED DENOMINATIONS*	6,000 to 8,000 congregations					
6. Episcopal Church 7,145 total congregations	200 3%	?	50,000	?	110	?
7. Ch of God, Cleve. 6,177 total congregations	569 9%	495	44,872	34,759	588	438
8. Luth Ch Mo. Synod 6,150 total congregations	150 2%	65	12,000	8,000	150	100
9. Unit. Ch of Christ 6,145 total congregations	34 > 1%	22	11,687	?	50	40
D. *SMALLER DENOMINATIONS*	Under 6,000 congregations					
10. American Baptist 5,802 total congregations	362 6%	329	35,457	33,206	?	?
11. Seventh-day Adv. 4,297 total congregations	853 20%	590	121,000	88,000	500	380
12. Disciples 4,036 total congregations	123 6 %	75	6,000	?	160	110
13. Reform. Ch, Am. 910 total congregations	39 3%	35	5,000	3,600	46	38
14. Christn Refm. Ch. 832 total congregations	23 3%	18	1,537	1,000	23	17

INCREASING HISPANIC MEMBERSHIP AND LEADERSHIP

Although this varied Hispanic presence has its roots in the differences in polity, theology, church history, cultural ethos, and geographical distribution of the denominations studied here, another factor is also pivotal: the amount and kind of attention denominations are giving to Hispanic ministry.

Scholars, the media and church publications describe Hispanic immigrants and their children as the fastest growing ethnic group in America. Denominational position papers further report that Latinos are the fastest growing ethnic minority in their membership, although most of the Protestant denominations deplore the fact that they are successful in getting less than 1 percent of these first- and second-generation Latinos into their congregations.

Exceptions to the above generalization are the evangelical and Pentecostal denominations, which have been more effective in drawing a substantial number of Hispanic immigrants into their U.S. congregations without special efforts to target Latinos. The success of these denominations is attributed (particularly by analysts from the less successful, traditionally Anglo denominations) partly to their emotional, lively worship services which are more in keeping with the Hispanic culture than the kinds of services that are typical of the traditional, mainly Anglo denominations. This may be one reason why the Assemblies of God (AOG) has experienced continued increase in Hispanic membership over recent decades. Also, the Assemblies of God grew in part from its Hispanic roots in the United States as well as a substantial evangelism ministry in Spanish-speaking countries. The Church of God in Christ, although much smaller than AOG, is similarly finding it fairly easy to attract and keep Hispanic members.

The traditional, mainly Anglo, denominations are to different degrees trying to design and implement policies and programs that would help them attract more Latino members. To do that effectively, they need to know more about Hispanic cultures. Reports and position papers on denominational websites make some of the following similar points:

• A probable large majority of first-generation Latino/as are living below the poverty line, constrained from bettering their financial situation by 1) having Spanish as a first language combined with

minimal facility in English; 2) little formal education—proportionately
few have more than a high school degree.

- Many first-generation Latino/as are from Pentecostal backgrounds.
  This predisposes immigrants and their children to be mainly drawn
  to U.S. congregations with a more energetic and joyful worship
  conducted in Spanish.
- Among first-generation Latinos, however, there is often diversity
  in educational attainment, occupation, location, family situation,
  and other demographics. Differences also exist among immigrant
  groups in the culture and the way they speak Spanish, attributed
  mainly to corresponding differences in their countries of origin.
- The greatest difference among Hispanic/Latino persons is between
  generations in the United States. Approximately 30 percent of the
  Hispanic/Latino residents in the mainland United States are young
  adults. Most of these young adults were born, raised, and educated in the U.S. They have English as a first language, and may
  not be fluent in Spanish. While the second and third generation
  young adults may identify with and appreciate some elements of
  the Hispanic culture (music, festivals, food, customs), they are
  thought to predominate in the majority of Latino/as who are
  presently unchurched.
- Denominations in this study have paid most attention to Spanish-
  speaking, first-generation Latinos and their young children in policy and programming. They are just recently realizing the need
  to use quite different approaches to reach teens and young adults
  among the offspring of Hispanic immigrants.

The major thrust of the Protestant denominations studied here has
been to develop Spanish-speaking congregations and to find or edu-
cate bilingual, preferably Hispanic, clergy to lead them. In most current denominational work, these two activities occur together although
one may be prior to the other.

In one model, Latino people in a neighborhood gather as a small
group without a designated pastor, typically as a house church, and
sometimes as a "daughter chapel" or outreach ministry of a larger,
mixed ethnicity or Anglo congregation. If the regional denominational office is aware of this group, and if the group appears stable
and growing, these officials will likely give them hymnals, prayer
books, and Christian education resources written in Spanish. Lay
leaders who emerge from this worshipping community are encour-

aged to undertake special education from the denomination in areas such as preaching, denominational doctrines, and evangelism techniques. The lay leader(s) may then become denominationally certified or ordained as pastors of this mission, which with further expansion may become an established congregation. These lay or "local pastors" who show particular promise may be denominationally encouraged to undergo further ministerial training, particularly in new church starts, toward becoming further educated and possibly ordained.

In the second model of denomination outreach, Latino/a pastors are expected to start their own congregations and are given substantial training in how to do this. These pastors can be present among the immigrants or actually recruited from other countries. However, as alluded to in the first model, probably most have moved from being active lay leaders to pastoral candidates for further certification or ordination. These Latino/a candidates are given access to theological education and ministerial training that is mainly conducted outside of seminaries in their region—sometimes through Bible colleges but primarily through special judicatory educational programs within the region or (as in one CRC) through on-line courses. In some denominations this training is augmented by several weeks a year at the denominational seminary.

Those that complete the advanced program with distinction or who are particularly outstanding in expanding their congregation and its ministries are likely to be ordained to a restricted order, which acknowledges them as denominationally-recognized church planters, evangelists, and pastors. Completion of such programs, however, typically does not give Latinos full clergy status in those mainly Anglo denominations, because most clergy have Master of Divinity (M.Div.) degrees. However, the more promising graduates of these alternate theological programs are likely encouraged and given financial support to obtain further theological education that will qualify them for full clergy status.

Hispanic Clergy: Numbers and Training

Clergy play a fundamental role in bolstering Hispanic churches, but most national denominational offices have a hard time obtaining accurate information on the number of active clergy. Clergy who serve in ministries outside the parish (such as denominational executives and senior staff, institutional chaplains, pastoral counselors) may not be counted in official totals, for example. Ordained persons who are secularly employed but donate pastoral time are typically missed in clergy counts altogether.

National offices in the denominations with loose connections to their relatively autonomous regional judicatories—such as American Baptist Churches (ABC) and to some extent Disciples of Christ (DOC) and United Church of Christ (UCC)—do not even try to keep accurate statistics on clergy, leaving it up to their regional judicatories to track and report. In these denominations, as well as several others, the issue is further confused because clergy from a different denomination pastor an unknown number of their smaller congregations.

Moreover, clergy can be fully ordained, ordained to a lesser order which is restricted in location or type of ministry, or not ordained at all but rather certified as preachers, evangelists, or lay pastors. This is another reason why several denominations that make extensive use of clergy of these different types and levels (AOG, UMC) do not try to keep accurate national tallies of how many clergy they have.

Although the fourteen denominations studied here are currently making an effort to track the number of their Hispanic congregations, this is not as likely for their Latino/a clergy. Sometimes this is because there are no national records kept of clergy by race or ethnicity. For instance, ABC national statistics do not "maintain information on the ethnicity of individual leadership at this point in time."

The varying levels of clergy status and definitions of who should be counted as "clergy" within denominations are also a source of major confusion in comparing numbers of Latino/a clergy across denominations. Latino/a clergy serving mixed ethnic or predominantly Anglo churches are especially likely to be missed in the Hispanic count. This situation frequently occurs where there is an oversupply of Hispanic clergy for Hispanic congregations, such as in the AOG and Seventh-day Adventists. In other denominations, Latino/a clergy with master's degrees may find that they can get a much better paying pastorate in a mixed ethnicity or Anglo rather than Hispanic church.

Table 1 gives numbers for the Latino/a clergy in twelve of the fourteen denominations listed. Yet candidly, many of these numbers represent, to quote Bobby Sena of SBC, "a guestimation!"

Across denominations most Latino clergy are men. To be sure, CRC and LCMS do not certify or ordain any women as pastors regardless of ethnicity, and SBC does not encourage their congregations to call or ordain any women as pastors. However, even in those denominations in which women are one-third or more of the active clergy, women are still less than 5 percent of all Hispanic clergy. There are two exceptions to this rule: the Presbyterian Church of the United States of America (PCUSA), where women represent about 10 percent of the Hispanic clergy, and UCC, where women represent 20 percent of Hispanic clergy.

According to the individuals interviewed for this study, there appear to be divergences in formal education requirements among the denominations and hence corresponding differences in attainment among Latino/a pastors. By way of illustration, at least a two-thirds majority of Latino/a pastors have no college degree in the Assemblies of God, Church of God-Cleveland, the Disciples and the Baptist denominations (ABC, SBC), as these denominations have no formal minimum educational requirements for ordination.

Other denominations typically do require high school graduation for certification or ordination as pastor. The Episcopal Church, the United Church of Christ, and the United Methodist Church report very mixed educational attainments for their Latino/a clergy, but best estimates are that between one-third and one-half of the clergy in these denominations have four-year college degrees.

Denominations with the highest proportion of college-educated Latino/a pastors are the Christian Reformed Church, the Presbyterian Church USA, and the Reformed Church in America, in which over half of the Latino/a clergy have four-year college degrees. The different levels of clergy status within the denomination can affect this distribution. For example, Latino/a pastors who want some level of ordained status rather than certification alone must also have a four-year college degree in the Evangelical Lutheran Church, Lutheran Church Missouri Synod, and Seventh-day Adventists.

Denominations in this study with the highest proportion of Latino/a clergy with master's degrees are the Presbyterians (90 percent), Seventh-day Adventists (50 percent), and the United Church of Christ (40 percent). The great majority of Latino/a clergy in the other eleven denominations do not have master's degrees.

Though denominations might prefer that all their ordained Latino/a clergy have M.Div. degrees, few actually do. Entering a seminary master's degree program requires a four-year college degree. This is an obstacle for many Hispanic pastors, even when they have financial support to eventually attend seminary. Qualified Latino college grad-uates who want to get the M.Div. typically can get some scholar-ship funds for seminary. However, denominations rarely have funds or access to foundations that will provide financial support for the required college education of Latino/a students who specifically express interest in ministry.

What these denominations do make available and in most cases require for the certification and ordination of the Latino/a pastors is theological grounding in the core beliefs and polity of their denom-ination. This is especially important in the traditional Anglo denom-inations, because the incoming Hispanic members and pastors are likely to have been reared in a very different religious tradition.

Promoting excellence in ministry for Latino/a clergy in most of these denominations should ideally include funds for college or seminary. Yet most support this leadership either solely or mainly through continuing education and fellowship opportunities (region-ally and/or nationally) for certified or ordained pastors of their respective denomination.

Hispanic pastors are recognized as the best recruiters of new Hispanic clergy, but the extent to which pastors of Hispanic con-gregations feel appreciated and connected with their denominations affects their efforts to interest young persons to consider the min-istry. One source of affirmation for current pastors is the biannual, annual or biennial gatherings of Hispanic pastors (and often their families). These gatherings typically include further ministerial train-ing, particularly in evangelism and church planting, as well as oppor-tunities for these pastors to share, pray, strategize, and support one another. Restrictions on available funding for travel make it difficult to hold national denominational conferences just for Hispanic/Latino clergy and religious leaders. However, five denominations have recently executed or are planning such national meetings.

Given this data on clergy, traditional, historically Anglo denomi-nations which hope to attract Hispanic/Latino members have to decide whether to:

1) Insist on a policy that pastors have college and preferably M.Div. degrees knowing that this will net them very, very few Latino/as interested in pastoring Hispanic congregations in the foreseeable future; or

2) Recruit and train lay leaders to be pastors of their present Hispanic

congregations or to pursue another "alternate" leadership path requiring less formal education—a policy which will net them far more Hispanic pastors, congregations, and members in a shorter time.

In times of declining mainline Protestant national and regional resources for special ministries, the latter is more cost- and time-effective. Denominations are increasingly using this second approach not only for finding pastors for Hispanic congregations, but to fill pulpits of all their small, poorer congregations that cannot afford M.Div. graduates or even college-educated pastors.

A dilemma in the more traditional, mainly Anglo, denominations where an M.Div is virtually required for full clergy status is that heavy use of this second approach results in most of the Hispanic clergy attaining lesser status in the denominational hierarchy than most of the Anglo clergy. This lower status can leave Hispanic clergy without the same voting privileges as Anglo clergy and without equal opportunities for career advancement within the denomination. This situation has already prompted several Hispanic national and regional leaders to raise concerns about the education and/or ordination status of Latino/a pastors in their denominations.

Planning and Strategy

How do denominations increase their Hispanic membership? National and judicatory denominational staff persons distribute materials, arrange continuing education events, and directly consult with those trying to start or strengthen Hispanic congregations. In addition, some denominations have national funds to immediately assist their regional judicatories to stimulate new church development (albeit often less now than in former years). Although national funds for new church development typically cover other than Hispanic congregations, in some denominations (SBC and ELCA) national funds are expended in innovative resource design and staff allocation to assist the growth of Hispanic membership.

The Southern Baptists have developed a new church planting kit specifically for Hispanic congregations, as well as radio and TV spots for broadcasting on Spanish language channels. The Evangelical Lutheran Church has three executive staff located in regional offices that are paid to give half of their time to establish new Hispanic churches and work with those Hispanic churches still in need of assistance. In the American Baptist Church, there is some national money to augment the salaries of pastors of new or struggling Hispanic churches. Several denominations have given special priority to funding new Hispanic church starts. In the Christian Reformed Church, half of the whole denomination's mission budget goes for starting new non-Anglo congregations, and of that amount probably one-third of the grants are for Hispanic congregations. In the United Methodist Church, any conference can get $50,000 from a national denominational fund for starting new Hispanic ministries if the conference matches this with $50,000 from its coffers; 25 conferences have done so.

Regional judicatories usually have a closer link to Hispanic constituencies within their borders than do national offices, and therefore much of the Hispanic mission strategy and implementation is left to the regional judicatories. Yet, without a national denominational effort as well, some of the traditional, mainly Anglo regional judicatories might well remain unacquainted with people of Hispanic ethnicity in their area.

These fourteen denominations differ as to whether they have an active strategy for Hispanic ministry on the national level. For some, such a national plan is a formal document being implemented. For others, there is no national plan as yet—only national planning. Denominations with formal, national strategies for Hispanic ministry now being implemented include the American Baptist, Episcopal, Lutheran Church Missouri Synod, Presbyterian, Southern Baptist, United Church of Christ, and United Methodist.

Interviews, website postings, and material from these national strategy reports as well as other publications, highlight several issues of concern that most of the fourteen denominations struggle with:

• Getting current numbers (or best estimates) of Hispanic congregations, members and clergy (of all levels) to the national Hispanic office appears problematic in many of these denominations. These numbers might well help national offices in their design of strategies for strengthening Hispanic ministry. Are there ways denominations can improve the collecting and reporting of statistics on Hispanic congregations, members, and clergy?

• Diversity may exist among Hispanics immigrants, depending in part on their country of origin, cultural mores, ways of speaking

Spanish, preferred worship styles, and educational as well as economic backgrounds. What is the best approach to evangelism and church planting for Hispanic first-generation families from different backgrounds?

- Divergences most often exist between Hispanic immigrants and their second- and third-generation offspring raised in the United States. Second- and third-generation Latinos are likely to differ from their first-generation parents and grandparents in their fluency in English or Spanish, as well as in their lifestyles, occupations, values, and religious affiliations (if any). What are the best ways to reach the second and third generation?
- New Hispanic church members often come from different faith backgrounds and worship traditions than what is core to the mainline, mainly Anglo denominations. How can a denomination teach these new members what is fundamental to denominational identity, as well as find ways to include their cultural preferences in worship?
- Relatively few members of Hispanic congregations have an education beyond high school. How best can denominations work with Hispanic congregations to encourage their young people to get further education in any field, but particularly in ministry?
- In the traditional, mainly Anglo, denominations where most of the fully-ordained clergy have M.Div. degrees, a majority of the Latino/a pastors do not have graduate seminary education and are likely to be ordained to restricted orders or certified as lay pastors. If this situation continues, what are the implications for continued recruitment of Latino/a clergy, and the expansion of Hispanic ministries in these denominations in the next five to twenty years?
- National denomination leaders usually are aware that the Hispanic population in the United States is increasing faster than any other ethnic group. Most would desire to have a larger proportion of this population within their congregational membership than is currently the case. Some denominations have increased their national church attention to Hispanic ministry. In others, particularly those that are in the midst of "restructuring" or "downsizing" on the national level, the "ethnic desks" or offices for Hispanic ministry are threatened with loss of funds, staff, and even separate existence. How does support of a national Hispanic office presently influence Hispanic ministry? In the future, what would the effect be if the present national support were reduced? What could be done if this national support for Hispanic ministries is increased?

Although undeniable differences exist between Hispanic Protestant and Catholic ministry and ministerial leadership, these common concerns reveal that there are many parallels as well. Both Catholics and Protestants have some difficulty obtaining accurate statistics and communicating that information from the local level to the denominational leadership. Both are limited by the difficulty in attracting and retaining sufficient numbers of highly educated Hispanic clergy. Both seem to intuit that doing so would require involving Hispanics in recruitment (that is, encouraging networking among Hispanics) as well as significant financial support for education. Indeed, the preceding list of concerns could describe almost any denomination, as well as the ministerial leadership of virtually all Hispanics.

Cross-denominational similarities become further evident in the next chapter, which explores Hispanic Protestant congregations that provide social services in their communities. For all their important doctrinal differences, Hispanic Christian congregations and clergy are rising creatively to common challenges in diverse settings around the country.

THE COMMUNITY-SERVING ACTIVITIES OF HISPANIC PROTESTANT CONGREGATIONS

Amy L. Sherman

INTRODUCTION

Specifically Protestant, Hispanic congregations are the focus of this chapter, which is based on a survey of pastors and leaders from 468 such communities and case studies of eight Hispanic, church-based compassion ministries, described in Table 1. After a discussion of methodology below, we proceed with an overview of our findings, a review of the literature, a more detailed discussion of the findings, and finally research questions and conclusions that we call "Lessons Learned."

In May 2002, AMEN (*Alianza de Ministerios Evangélicos Nacionales* or National Alliance of Evangelical Ministries, a multidenominational group of Latino evangelical leaders) and the Hudson Institute fashioned a research project with two components:

(1) a national survey of Hispanic pastors to identify the kinds of church-based, community-serving ministries that are currently operational;

(2) case studies of 8 to 10 Hispanic congregations (of small to medium size) actively involved in community social services of various types.

From September 2002 through May 2003, the Hudson Institute's Faith in Communities Initiative and their subcontractor, the Urban Leadership Institute, together completed a survey of 468 Hispanic (predominantly Evangelical) Protestant pastors in the United States. The survey focused on the community-serving activities of these congregations.

Hudson staff also conducted in-depth site visits and interviews at eight Hispanic congregations operating various community outreach initiatives. The nature of those programs is listed in Table 1.

Table 1. Listing of Case Studies

Church Name	Location	Denomination	Size	Ministry Type
El Encino	Downey, CA	Evangelical Covenant	<100	community center
Path of Life	Riverside, CA	Pentecostal	150	men's residential rehab
Centro Cristiano Misionero Internacional	Orlando, FL	non-denominational	125	job training
El Tabernáculo	Houston, TX	Assemblies of God	500	at-risk teens
Iglesia Metodista Hispanic de Bethesda	Bethesda, MD	Methodist	66	ESL
My Friend's House	Whittier, CA	Assemblies of God	300	housing
Leon de Judah Congregational Church	Boston, MA	Congregational	800	college prep
Iglesia Cristiana Emmanuel	Atlanta, GA	Christian & Miss. Alliance	135	health clinic

OVERVIEW

In the course of this work, we gathered important information regarding the community-serving activities of Hispanic Protestant congregations in the United States. Through our survey, pastors and leaders at 468 Hispanic churches indicated whether and how their congregations serve their neighbors.

The study shed light on the range of services offered, the most common forms of community involvement, and the reasons why some congregations are not active in outreach ministry.

The findings also reveal how collaboratively these congregations work when implementing community programs and how even modest-sized Hispanic congregations are capable of conducting impressive social service programs. Like most other churches, Hispanic Protestant congregations tend to be more active in short-term, relief-oriented programs (food and clothing assistance) than in longer-term, more "development-oriented" ministries. Nonetheless, a significant number are engaged in delivering the latter kinds of services. The Hispanic churches represented in our sample sponsor a variety of family support and human service initiatives such as parenting classes, GED and ESL training, family counseling, teen mentoring, after-school tutoring and recreational programs, outreach to prisoners, and substance abuse recovery programs. Fewer were involved in community development or economic development activities.

We have also identified a number of networks of Hispanic pastors that, to varying degrees, are attempting to advance the vision of church-based community outreach ministry, provide "how to" training and guidance, and/or facilitate collaborative efforts to address community needs.

Finally, like authors in previous chapters, we have seen that existing networks and theological training programs geared to Hispanic ministry candidates are insufficient. Although many formal and informal networks exist, most concentrate on fellowship, prayer, and cooperative evangelism efforts. Relatively few focus on encouraging and facilitating church-based, community ministry. There are theological training programs and bible institutes specifically serving the Hispanic community, but relatively few offer training programs directly relevant to the work of church-based social service provision or community development. This lack of training is especially distressing given the number one lesson learned from the on-site, in-depth examination of eight church-based Hispanic community ministries; namely, that committed, competent, visionary leaders are *the* key resource necessary for viable outreach programs. In most of the eight case studies, one or two key leaders were absolutely essential. Without their skills, dedication, and creativity it is difficult to imagine these programs continuing.

LITERATURE ON HISPANIC CHURCH-BASED COMMUNITY SERVICES

We know much more about the community-serving activities of African American congregations than we do about the work of predominantly Hispanic/Latino congregations. Numerous books have been published on the former topic, some looking at African American congregations nationally and others describing the community development activities of one or a few particular African American churches (see, for example, Andrew Billingsley, *Mighty Like A River*, 1999; C. Eric Lincoln and Lawrence Mamiya, *The Black Church in the African American Experience*, 1990; Samuel Freedman, *Upon This Rock*, 1993; Nile Harper, *Urban Churches, Vital Signs*, 1999). No seminal books exist on the community impact of Hispanic congregations to compare to Billingsley's on the Black church. Of course, this fact makes the data in this volume all the more important.

Various national studies on congregational outreach give us a picture of how congregations serve communities, but in most of these surveys, Hispanic churches make up only a very small part of the sample. Almost always, data specific to the Hispanic congregations is not disaggregated and analyzed.

For example, the 1998 National Congregations Survey (Mark Chaves, principal investigator) examined 1,236 congregations nationwide, gathering a wealth of data. One question in the survey asked the respondent to indicate whether or not the church had "participated in or sponsored a social service in the last twelve months." Overall, 56.3 percent of respondents answered "yes" while 43.3 percent said "no." Only 29 congregations out of the 1,236, though, could be considered "Hispanic" churches to any degree. (That is, 29 were churches where at least 45 percent or more of the regular adult attendees consider themselves Hispanic or Latino.) Among these 29 churches, engagement in social service was low. Respondents from 21 (72 percent) indicated that their congregations had not participated in or sponsored any social service in the past year.

The wording of the question, however, is problematic. Not all pastors may interpret the phrase "social service" to mean the kinds of informal community ministries conducted by many congregations. Ram Cnaan, in his in-depth examination of hundreds of congregations in Philadelphia, discovered that often, church leaders would initially say that their church offered no social services. However, as he probed further, he would hear about youth programs that engaged neighborhood students or a men's ministry that distributed food in the community. The leaders would not necessarily label these efforts among the needy as "social programs." They thought only large, formal initiatives, often undertaken in conjunction with the government, constituted "social services" (Tennant 2003). Thus, it is possible that more than 8 of the 29 Hispanic congregations noted above were engaged in some form of community ministry. Nonetheless, this is far too small a sample size to draw any robust conclusions.

The 2001 Faith Communities Today study, conducted by the Hartford Seminary's Institute for Religion Research, is the largest survey of congregations ever conducted (n = 14,301). Overall, it found that almost 9 out of 10 churches provide assistance to individuals and families in need. This generally agrees with the data gathered by Cnaan and summarized in his book, *The Newer Deal*. The Hartford study found that, overall, 88 percent of congregations offered emergency financial assistance, 85 percent offered food assistance, 60 percent helped with clothing, 45 percent with medical attention, 46 percent with crisis counseling, and 38 percent with shelter. Congregations were also involved in providing longer-term or ongoing help beyond these short-term relief programs. Thirty-eight percent were involved in prison ministry, 33 percent in drug rehabilitation, 32 percent offered tutoring programs, 14 percent were active in assisting immigrants, and 45 percent served senior citizens.[1]

The Faith Communities Today study, however, offers little information about the activities of majority-Hispanic congregations. These churches appear underrepresented in the Hartford sample. That sample was composed primarily of denominational groups. Within the sub-sample of American Baptist Churches, for example, only 3 percent were congregations led by a Hispanic/Latino pastor. The non-denominational sub-sample divided the race of church participants only into "Black," "White," and "other," making it difficult to estimate the number of congregations with dominant Latino/a membership. Within the sub-sample of Southern Baptist congregations, only 2.7 percent were majority-Hispanic. Not surprisingly, the Assemblies of God sub-sample included the highest number of Hispanic-led congregations: 6.7 percent of the total 691 congregations in this sample reported having a Latino/Hispanic pastor. Assuming that those congregations are majority Hispanic (though the presence of a Hispanic pastor is no guarantee), only about 41 of the 691 churches could be considered Hispanic. But no separate analysis was conducted on the community-serving activities of those congregations.

David Maldonado Jr.'s edited volume, *Protestantes/Protestants: Hispanic Christianity Within Mainline Traditions* (Nashville, TN: Abingdon Press, 1999) analyzes a survey of approximately 300 Hispanic pastors within mainline Protestant denominations (United Methodist, Disciples of Christ, Presbyterian Church USA, and the Lutheran Evangelical Church of America). Eighty-three percent reported that their congregations were involved in community ministries, but information on the specific types of social service their churches offered was not gathered.

---

[1] Carl S. Dudley, "Reaching Out: FACTs on Community Ministries." Available at http://fact.hartsem.edu/topfindings/topicalfindings_article8.htm.

Michael Mata of the Urban Leadership Institute at the Claremont School of Theology has written two important papers with information on the community-serving role of Hispanic congregations.[2] The first, "Protestant Hispanics Serving the Community: Summary of Research Findings" (Pew Charitable Trusts, July 1999), is the most directly relevant. This paper evaluates the community and leadership development roles of 134 Hispanic Protestant churches in southern California; 32 were studied in depth. Mata found that these congregations were significantly engaged in community-serving ministries. Some 131 different service programs were identified, ranging from mental health/counseling services to housing, job training, substance abuse recovery, and emergency assistance to childcare, ESL, and tutoring for elementary school-age children.

Other important examinations of Hispanic church-based community ministry underway include those being conducted through the Hispanic Churches in American Public Life (HCAPL) project. HCAPL commissioned the Tomás Rivera Institute to conduct in-depth ethnographic studies in several selected communities, which include interviewing congregational leaders about their community outreach activities. The conclusions, some of which are outlined in the penultimate chapter of this book, reveal important new insights.

At the University of Pennsylvania, Ram Cnaan has analyzed survey interviews conducted with leaders of Hispanic congregations in Philadelphia, the results of which will be published in a forthcom-

---

[2] Mata's other paper is a comprehensive literature review of studies on the role of faith in Hispanic families ("The Hispanic Family and Faith," Annie. E. Casey Foundation, May 1999). His review cast a wide net, however, and the paper discusses several studies of faith as an aspect of the Latino family health care system, including physiological, emotional, and mental health. In this section, he discusses Davis et al., "The Urban Church and Cancer Control: a Source of Influence in Minority Communities" *Public Health Reports* (QJA), 1994 Jul-Aug; 109 (4): 500–6). This study examined a congregational-based cervical cancer control program in Los Angeles County that served over 1,000 Hispanic women. Hispanic congregations have also sponsored many substance abuse recovery programs. Probably the most notable is that of Victory Outreach International, an organization operating over 400 rehabilitation homes serving predominantly Hispanic urban communities. Mata's review also cites two city-focused dissertations on the community serving impact of Hispanic congregations (Aponte, Edwin, "Latino Protestant Identity and Empowerment: Hispanic Religion, Community, Rhetoric and Action in a Philadelphia Case Study, Temple University 1998 and Carabello Ireland, Elba R., "The Role of the Pentecostal Church as a Service Provider in the Puerto Rican Community of Boston, Massachusetts: A Case Study," Brandeis University, 1991).

ing book. In addition, Catherine Wilson completed a Ph.D. dissertation based on ethnographic studies of a few key, well-known Hispanic ministries (Nueva Esperanza in Philadelphia, The Latino Pastoral Action Center in New York City, and The Resurrection Project in Chicago). These studies will prove to be vital contributions to the literature.

At the University of Notre Dame, the Center for the Study of Latino Religion has also launched several important studies of community-serving activities of Latino congregations throughout the country. The findings of the Center's Latino Church Social Service Capacity Study, for example, will shed light on the extent and capacity of well-established Latino faith-based organizations across 17 metro areas, which together account for one-third of the Latino population in the United States.

All of these efforts are encouraging, but until very recently there has been a significant dearth of knowledge about the community impact of Hispanic congregations—and much more research is needed.

FINDINGS FROM THE SURVEY OF HISPANIC PROTESTANT CONGREGATIONS

Against this backdrop, the AMEN survey, though not based on a scientifically-designed, random sample, is a significant exploratory study. Leaders from 468 predominantly Hispanic congregations—all Protestant and primarily Evangelical—completed self-reporting survey questionnaires to provide the data for the study.

The survey used two similar questionnaires. First, approximately 35 percent of the pastors completed a shorter pilot survey. A second, longer survey included all the questions listed on the pilot questionnaire, and was completed by 65 percent of the pastors.[3] At an

---

[3] 161 respondents completed a shorter, seven-question version of the survey. This pilot questionnaire was then expanded to include a few additional questions (the original seven questions were also repeated). 307 respondents, or 65 percent, completed the slightly longer questionnaire. The longer version included four additional questions to gather background, descriptive information about the churches (number of members in the church, number of regular adult attendees, language the worship service is conducted in, and year the church was founded). It also included a question about whether the church cooperated with other local institutions in its community service activities, and if so, asking the respondent to list those partnering organizations.

"n" of 468, this data set was over three times larger than any of the largest known previous inquiries of Hispanic pastors about their community ministries (i.e., Mata's research in southern California).

The AMEN survey used a convenience sampling technique. One component of the sample frame was drawn from the attendees at the 2002 *Cumbre* conference co-sponsored by AMEN in Pasadena, CA. This event gathered some 500 Hispanic church leaders. At the conference, survey questionnaires were distributed for completion during a plenary session. Approximately 260 surveys were gathered. Later analysis, however, revealed that in a significant number of instances, more than one respondent filled out a questionnaire about the same congregation. Also, some of the surveys were incomplete; others were about para-church ministries rather than congregations, and a few represented churches in Mexico or Central America. The usable number of surveys garnered from the *Cumbre* event was 161.

To enlarge the sample frame, various lists of Hispanic congregations were compiled using information gathered from the Internet and from key gatekeepers who were knowledgeable about the Hispanic evangelical community. These included lists of:

- Hispanic churches (by state) extracted from a large national database of congregations developed by the group Churches Around the World (*Iglesias Cristianas Alrededor del Mundo*);
- Majority-Hispanic Seventh-day Adventist churches nationwide (from denominational information);
- Hispanic congregations from Virginia, Maryland, and Washington, DC compiled by the nonprofit agency Ethnic Harvest;
- Hispanic congregations in the Seattle-Tacoma area compiled by the nonprofit agency Ethnic Harvest;
- Nazarene Hispanic congregations nationwide (from denominational information);
- Hispanic Baptist pastors (from articles in *The Baptist Standard*);
- United Brethren Hispanic congregations nationwide (from denominational information);
- Hispanic Mennonite churches nationwide (from denominational information);
- Hispanic pastors in Georgia (from a directory compiled by the nonprofit *Arca de Noé*);
- Hispanic American Baptist churches nationwide (from denominational information);

- Hispanic Evangelical Covenant churches nationwide (from denominational information);
- Hispanic churches in Florida from the website (now expired) www.rwf2000.som/CH/Florida.htm.

Using these lists and the names of Hispanic pastors suggested by approximately 30 "gatekeepers," we were able to submit a database containing approximately 600 pastors' names, telephone numbers, and church names to staff at the Urban Leadership Institute (ULI) at the Claremont School of Theology. From this database, ULI completed telephone interviews with 144 pastors.[4] Hudson Institute staff also completed telephone interviews with over 50 respondents; a printed version of the questionnaire was distributed to Hispanic pastors gathered at the 2003 Promise Keepers convention; a printed version of the questionnaire was also distributed to Hispanic pastors enrolled in classes at Vanguard University; a printed version was distributed to a gathering of Hispanic pastors affiliated with Kingdom Coalition (Southern California) as well; and an e-mail version of the questionnaire was sent to those Hispanic pastors with email addresses that had attended the *Cumbre* event but from whom we had not received a completed survey. From all the sources, the eventual total of 468 completed interviews was reached.

The "bottom line" question of the survey was whether or not the church offered community-serving programs. The question was worded in such a way as to flesh out the meaning of the phrase "social services" and to make clear that both formal and informal programs were of interest. Approximately 73 percent of those surveyed indicated that their congregations did offer community-serving activities (see Table 2).

Respondents were drawn from 35 states, although California and Texas were disproportionately represented. Other states with significant numbers of respondents included Florida, Georgia, and North Carolina.

For approximately two-thirds of the sample, we have data available on church size. The average size of these surveyed congregations,

---

[4] A substantial number of the telephone numbers proved inoperable. In addition, some pastors were virtually impossible to reach even when interviewers placed ten or more calls to them. The actual refusal rate, when a pastor was reached, was very low. These interviews, plus the completed surveys from the *Cumbre* event, make up the bulk of the 468 total respondents in the AMEN survey.

measured by number of regular adult attendees, was 233. This number is skewed, however, by some mega-churches in the sample. One pastor interviewed, for example, served a congregation of 5,000 attendees, and several others served congregations of over 1,000 attendees. The median size of the congregations in the AMEN study (for which we collected this information) was 135 regular attendees.

Nearly 70 percent of the pastors interviewed provided information on the year their church was founded. The founding years ranged from 1850 to 2003. Half of the churches on which age data was captured were founded in 1987 or before. The median age of the churches in the sample providing this information was 16 years.[5]

Table 2. Extent of Community Outreach by Hispanic Congregations

"Does your church offer community ministries; that is, 'social services' such as assistance with food, tutoring, job training, etc., to help people in the community? (These ministries may be formal, with established offices and volunteers or paid staff, or may be informal. We are interested in both types.)"

YES	72.8 percent
NO	27.2 percent
n = 468	

Hispanic churches provide an impressive array of services.[6] The Hispanic church leaders reported forty-nine different types of community ministries. These ranged from short-term, relief-oriented efforts such as emergency financial help, toy distribution campaigns at Christmas, and food or clothing assistance to more long-term, relational ministries such as mentoring of youth, job training and placement, life skills classes, and literacy and GED programs. They also included community development initiatives such as housing programs, health care ministries, charter schools, and daycare centers. The top twelve most common services provided are listed below.

---

[5] Out of the 236 churches that reported having social services and reported the year in which the church was founded, 51 (22 percent) were established in or after 1998. Thus, 78 percent of the churches with community serving ministries, on which we have age data, have been in existence for at least five years.

[6] Due to the exploratory nature of the study and the sampling used, it is not possible to distinguish between those programs that are professionally certified and those that are not.

Table 3. Twelve Most Common Types of Social Service Programs Offered

Service Type	Number of Churches	Percent of Churches
1. Pastoral counseling	260	55.6 percent
2. Food assistance	247	52.8 percent
3. Family counseling	210	44.9 percent
4. Clothing assistance	192	41 percent
5. Referrals to other helping agencies	162	34.6 percent
6. Emergency financial assistance	128	27.4 percent
7. Aid to immigrants	93	19.9 percent
8. ESL classes	87	18.6 percent
9. Aid to prisoners and their families	77	16.5 percent
10. Tutoring programs	72	15.4 percent
11. Substance abuse rehab/counseling	56	12 percent
12. Parental training	50	10.7 percent
n = 468		

The Hispanic churches we examined are apparently less able to provide material resources such as cash assistance and clothing to families in need, than are the (mainly White) churches represented in
the Hartford FACT study (see Table 4). However, the Hispanic
churches offer much personal assistance in the form of pastoral and
family counseling, youth tutoring, parenting and life skills classes,
ESL classes, and (not surprisingly) aid to immigrants.

Table 4. Comparison of Hispanic Church-Based Community Services
        and FACT Data on Congregation-Based Social Services

Service Type	Hispanic Churches (percent active)	FACT Churches (percent active)
Food assistance	53 percent	85 percent
Clothing assistance	41 percent	60 percent
Emergency financial assistance	27 percent	88 percent
Aid to immigrants	20 percent	14 percent
Substance abuse rehab/ counseling	12 percent	32 percent
	n = 468	n = 14,301

In the AMEN survey, 338 of the 341 respondents who indicated
that their church conducted community ministries specified what
those ministry programs were. In total, an impressive 2,039 programs
were listed. The vast majority of the churches represented in the

study offered more than one social service program. Over 80 percent listed more than three programs from our list of 23 possibilities (they could also check "other" and describe a service they were operating that was not included in our list).[7] Very few indicated operating only one program. On average, each congregation provided 6.03 services.

Four samples from Andrew Billingsley's survey data examining the community-serving activities of African American congregations provide some comparisons to the findings from the AMEN survey.[8] Billingsley surveyed 315 Black congregations in the northeastern portion of the United States, 320 Black congregations in the north-central region, 320 in the Midwest, and 80 congregations from Denver in a convenience sample. The table below shows how active these Black churches were in providing some kind of outreach ministry. Based on this comparative data, Hispanic congregations are as active in providing community services as are African American congregations.

Table 5. Percentage of congregations indicating that they have one or more community-serving programs

Hispanic	Black/NE	Black/NC	Black/Midwest	Black/Denver
72.8 percent	69 percent	66 percent	66 percent	75 percent
n = 468	n = 315	n = 320	n = 320	n = 80

We were also interested in whether or not Hispanic congregations that were active in providing community services were also working in cooperation with others. Hence, in the longer version of the survey, utilized in 65 percent of the interviews, we included a question about whether the churches collaborated with other local institutions such as schools, the police, or other churches. In total, 232 respondents answered this question. Of these, 56 percent said that they

---

[7] The 23 services listed were: food assistance, clothing assistance, emergency financial assistance, referrals to other helping agencies, homeless services, tutoring, teen mentoring, Head Start, daycare/childcare, GED, ESL, substance abuse counseling/rehab, pastoral counseling, aid to immigrants, job training, health programs, citizenship classes, legal assistance, life skills, parenting classes, teen pregnancy prevention programs, family counseling, and aid to prisoners.

[8] Some caution, of course, is needed in making this comparison, since the wording of Billingsley's questionnaire regarding provision of community services differed from the wording employed in the survey of Hispanic congregations.

partnered with other organizations, agencies, or congregations while 44 percent indicated they did not have such partnerships. The most common partners identified were other churches, nonprofit social service organizations, and the police department. Table 6 provides further detail.

Table 6. With Whom Do Hispanic Churches Partner
in Outreach Programs?

Partner	Number of churches
Other churches	28
Police Department	24
Social service nonprofits	21
Schools	15
Courts/probation/parole	13
Local government	7
Hospitals	5
Food bank	5
Fire Department	3
After-school centers	1
Lawyers	1
Counseling centers	1
Emergency Personnel	1

It is difficult to match this data precisely against that of studies completed by other researchers, since questions were worded differently. As noted, in the AMEN survey, we simply asked whether or not the church partnered with other local institutions; then we asked them to name the groups with whom they worked.

Ram Cnaan's survey of 887 Philadelphia churches raised two inquires probing this topic. The first asked respondents whether the church worked with other faith-based organizations (FBOs) in developing and delivering their social services. Approximately one-third said they did. The second asked respondents whether they collaborated with secular organizations; 38 percent indicated they did. With these findings in mind, it appears that we can offer a tentative hypothesis that Hispanic congregations are at least as likely, and perhaps slightly more likely, than churches in general to cooperate with others in implementing community programs.

Indeed, collaboration seems the norm for each of the eight churches whose community ministries we examined by case study. These congregations were working with local public schools, local government agencies, other churches, the business community, and the police or court system (see Table 7):

Table 7. Types of Collaboration Exemplified by the Case Study Ministries

Church	Ministry Focus	Partners
Iglesia Cristiana Emmanuel	health center	state government, business
My Friend's House	housing/daycare	HUD, business, local govt. agencies
Centro Cristiana	job training/mentoring	business, other churches
León de Judah	college prep	Nellie Mae, Inter-Varsity, other churches, high schools, HEIC
El Tabernáculo	teens at risk	schools, police
El Encino	community center	schools, secular nonprofits
Path of Life	men's rehabilitation	courts, police, local govt., business
Iglesia Bethesda Metodista	ESL	schools, public library, other churches

However, 127 respondents (roughly 27 percent of those surveyed) indicated that their churches were not involved in providing community social services. We asked these church leaders to tell us more about the reasons why they were not currently engaged in such programs. They could select as many of the possible reasons listed below as they felt accurately represented their situation. If none of these reasons fit their experience, they could select "other" and respond in their own words. Some responses were:

> "We are a very small church and have no resources for outreach ministry."
> "We believe it is more important to engage in evangelism than in outreach ministry or social services."
> "We have the desire to help the community, but we are not sure how to start effective programs."
> "We have future plans to do more outreach in the community, but right now we are focused on other priorities."
> "There are individual church members who minister in the community in various ways, but the church as a whole does not operate formal outreach programs."

The most common reason given by church leaders for not being more active in community ministry was the third choice, namely, lack of "know-how." These pastors indicated that they had the desire to better serve the community, but were uncertain about the steps needed to launch an effective ministry. Almost 55 percent of those in congregations not reporting outreach ministries gave this response.

The second most common reason for not offering social services, selected by 46 percent of the non-active group, was that the church was small and had no resources for doing outreach programs. Only 8 percent said that the reason their church was not involved in community service was because they believed it was more important to engage in evangelism than it was to conduct outreach ministry or social services.

For those eager to see Hispanic congregations vibrantly active in serving their communities, the survey results are encouraging. Not only is the number of already active churches high (73 percent), but the findings from those churches that are not active leave much room for hope. For example, 38 percent of the churches without social services indicated that although their congregations have no current programs, they had future plans to engage in social services. And roughly one-third indicated that individual congregants were already performing community service even though the church as a whole lacked formal outreach programs. Finally, survey respondents indicated that the number one reason for being unengaged was not theological skepticism about the legitimacy of community outreach, but rather a simple lack of knowledge about how best to go about starting service programs.

A few observations, though, should temper this good news. First, as noted earlier, the AMEN survey was not a scientifically random one. Many of the respondents were drawn from among church leaders that attended major conferences (*Cumbre* and Promise Keepers). It may that leaders pre-disposed to be active in such events are more likely than their counterparts to also be active in community service.

Second, a small portion of the survey respondents included students in a class taught by Dr. Jesse Miranda at Vanguard University. Again, it is may be that these more educated pastors tend to be more active in community-serving ministries than those who are less educated.

Third, although nearly all the respondents indicated that their social services programs benefited persons within the church family and neighborhood/city residents, we have no way of knowing from the data collected whether a majority of those served are from outside the serving church.

Fourth, some may question whether "pastoral counseling" is a community-serving activity (and pastoral counseling was the single most common form of social services reported).

Finally, as reported above, only a small percentage of the survey respondents representing churches without outreach programs admitted that the reason for their inactivity was theological. But many of the gatekeepers (network leaders and/or heads of well-known Hispanic faith-based organizations) we interviewed said that the problem of theological skepticism about the legitimacy of social ministry remains a significant issue in the Hispanic Evangelical community.

Hudson researchers invested substantial energies in attempting to identify key gatekeepers and networks of Hispanic churches. While there seems to be a fair number of both formal and informal networks of Hispanic churches around the country, we found that few exist for the specific purpose of encouraging or providing community service programs. Most exist for prayer and fellowship. When the churches in a given network do collaborate, the focus is often on evangelistic endeavors. When we asked gatekeepers and leaders of networks why this was so, most explained that it is easier to sponsor worship activities, such as praise services or prayer meetings, than it is to wrestle with the entrenched, long-standing social problems that exist in the surrounding community.

To increase Hispanic church-based community ministries, collaborative networks like those described above are helpful. Enhanced training in community outreach for future Hispanic pastors should also contribute to expanding churches' capacity to serve surrounding areas.

Initially, we had hoped to conduct an ambitious, nationwide scan of theological training programs geared to Hispanics to identify how many of these programs offer specific training in topics related to church-based community ministry (e.g., courses in community or economic development, how-to seminars on conducting community needs/assets assessments, internships at Hispanic faith-based organizations, etc.) However, the work required to compile lists of Hispanic pastors to contact for the survey was so time-consuming and labor-intensive that we were unable to fully accomplish this component.

In the end, we were able only to look briefly at 25 institutes and seminaries with programs geared specifically to Hispanic students. We found that less than half (10 of the 25) offered significant courses or programs relevant to training in holistic ministry (Table 8).

Table 8. Hispanic Training Programs

Training Program	Community Ministry Focus?	Comments
San Antonio Bible Education	Limited	leadership dev; creative VBS
Hispanic Bible School	Yes	"Hisp. Urban Issues & the Church"
Rio Grande Bible Institute	Limited	1 holistic ministry course at certificate program level
Hispanic Institute of Theology (Concordia Seminary)	Limited	"contextual leadership dev" church planting
Hispanic Baptist Theological School	Limited	"contextual evangelism," counseling
Seminario Bíblico del Sur de California	Limited	
Hispanic Ministries Program (McCormick Theological Seminary)	Unknown	
Instituto Teológico del Oeste	Unknown	significant emphasis
Ctr. for Urban Studies & Ethnic Leadership, Vanguard University	Yes	
Hispanic Ministries Program, Hartford Seminary	Yes	"Urban Ministry in Hisp Context" required hands-on experience in community
Centro Hispano de Estudios Teológicos	Yes	handful of courses
Atlantic International Bible Institute	No	
Instituto Ministerial Hispano	No	
Loyola Marymount	Limited	"Pastoral Care," substance abuse, counseling
Word Bible School	No	
Goshen College	Yes	Supervised community ministry
Asbury Theological Seminary	Yes	handful of courses
Instituto Hispano at Loyola University	Limited	1 course
El Seminario Bíblico Fundamental de Sur de California	No	
Haggard Graduate School (Azusa Pacific University)	Yes	Concentration in Urban Ministry
Perkins School of Theology	Yes	"Christianity and Social Justice," "Community organizing"
Oblate School of Theology	Limited	1 course in "Contemporary Issues in Hispanic Ministry"
Catholic University	Limited	"Church and Social Issues"
Houston College of Biblical Studies	Yes	significant emphasis
Interdenominational Training Institute	Yes	significant emphasis

LESSONS LEARNED

The first group of lessons relates to research methods. The most cost-effective method of garnering surveys was distributing them at major events. We did not even consider doing a surface mail version of the survey since we expected an abysmal rate of return.

We were unsure about the value of survey distribution via email. We learned it was an ineffective method. Those surveyed by email were aware of AMEN, and the survey was accompanied (twice) by a cover note from John Mendez of AMEN. Nonetheless, only three people in roughly 100 responded.

We also attempted to use gatekeepers as distribution agents for the survey. This, too, failed. Despite securing commitments from several gatekeepers to distribute the surveys at their network meetings, only one actually did. We did find that the gatekeepers were helpful in directing us to individual churches or pastors operating community programs. It was largely based on their input that we were able to put together a list of 35 potential case study sites from which we eventually picked eight. We also tried to use denominational leaders as survey distribution agents. These individuals were without exception unhelpful and unresponsive.

With regard to the telephone survey, subcontracting with ULI was an effective strategy. Their interviewers—native Spanish speakers and ministry candidates—were able to develop a rapport with the pastors that facilitated the pastors' willingness to participate in the survey.

The other group of lessons we learned cluster around the issue of leadership. From the case studies in particular, and from analysis of significant Hispanic church-based community ministries that we did not visit on-site, we clearly saw the importance of visionary, committed leadership. This must not be underemphasized in any strategy to expand or enhance the scope of Hispanic church-based outreach efforts. In every case study and every robust church-based community ministry we found, in huge measure the program resulted from the work of one or two key leaders.

These leaders appear to be motivated primarily by their own personal histories. One was an immigrant from Cuba and knew personally the challenge of integrating into life in the United States. She has now invested over twenty years operating a highly organized ESL program. Two others had been drug abusers and lived at various rehabilitation centers until they were healed. Now the two have launched a men's residential recovery home designed in large measure by a kind of positive plagiarism—that is, imitating the best models they have personally experienced and avoiding practices they saw were ineffective. Another leader grew up impoverished in Colombia; today he is passionate about seeing that poor Hispanics have access to decent health care.

Some of the leaders were mentored, although rarely by fellow Hispanics. A few had formal training or education that was relevant to the skills and knowledge they needed to launch their specific outreach ministries. Most, though, just "figured out how to do things" on their own. They had an entrepreneurial, can-do spirit and incredible perseverance. They did express a desire to know about others from whom they could learn, as well as about resources (websites, organizations, training conferences, or materials) from which they could benefit.

The vast majority instinctively realized that they needed to connect to public institutions—the police, the court system, the schools, and local or state government—to realize their visions. None expressed fear of potential "church-state" conflicts. All believed that their efforts would enjoy greater credibility if they wooed public officials or civic leaders "to their cause." All also revealed an ability to "know what they didn't know," and to quickly identify other churches, FBOs (usually non-Hispanic), or even secular nonprofits that were operating the kinds of programs they dreamed of implementing.

Finally, almost without exception, these leaders felt isolated. Other pastors they knew were either lukewarm about or hostile to their efforts. A few made comments about being perceived as "odd men out" among their peers. Some admitted that initially, their own congregations had been either skeptical or indifferent to the outreach programs they wanted to implement. These leaders said that they had "gotten ahead of their flock" and had had to go back and cast vision and "pull people along." In most cases, their ministries had received little publicity or praise. Typically, they were not aware of other Hispanic Christian leaders who were active in operating outreach ministries like their own. They expressed interest in networking with other Hispanic peers passionate about community ministry.

CONCLUSION

Hispanics are now America's "majority minority." By various indices, Hispanics may be considered the poorest minority as well. In distressed urban centers, Hispanic youth are at significant risk for dropping out of school, joining gangs, or getting pregnant as teens. Hispanics rank high among the medically uninsured and many are underemployed. These problems are well known and well documented. What is not as well known and well documented is the effort that Hispanics of faith are investing in meeting these challenges. The AMEN survey reveals that far from being unaware of or unengaged in the life of their communities, Hispanic congregations do reach out to try to make a difference.

At the same time, the Hispanic faith community does not yet have the strong infrastructure of faith-based social services that the African American community enjoys. African American capacity-building intermediaries exist. Training conferences and how-to materials relevant to the Black community are available. A young Black pastor can, without much effort, connect with an African American mentor or leader who has experience in community ministry—and probably right within his or her own city.

The situation is vastly different for the Hispanic community, though recent growth and efforts by the two largest and most reputable Hispanic FBOs (Nueva Esperanza and LPAC) are bringing training, capacity building, and resources to local Hispanic congregations and FBOs. More of these kinds of efforts are critical. Many Hispanic pastors are willing to become more involved in community outreach, but they need help to get started. And, as our survey revealed, many pastors have already led their congregations in serving their communities. Their efforts provide a foundation on which to build, so that the talents, energies, and assets of the Hispanic Christian community can be unleashed for community transformation.

Repeatedly, this book has suggested that without ignoring the doctrinal differences among Christian denominations to which Hispanics belong, there are important commonalities. The study summarized here shows, for example, that ministers across denominations share the common limitation of a lack of practical training to begin social service programs. The few visionary leaders who have successfully implemented such programs all feel isolated and wish to network with others. This suggests a key question: is it possible to "agree to disagree" on doctrine while at the same time working together as Christians for the common good of Hispanic neighborhoods? The next chapters explores this and related issues among Latino congregations in several cities, including Chicago.

REFERENCES

Dudley, Carl S. "Reaching Out: FACTs on Community Ministries." Available at http://fact.hartsem.edu/topfindings/topicalfindings_article8.htm.
Maldonado Jr., David. 1999. *Protestantes/Protestants: Hispanic Christianity Within Mainline Traditions.* Nashville, TN: Abingdon Press.
Mata, Michael. 1999. "Protestant Hispanics Serving the Community: Summary of Research Findings." Pew Charitable Trusts.
———. 1999b. "The Hispanic Family and Faith." Annie E. Casey Foundation. May 1999.
Tennant, Agnieszka. 2003. "Tallying Compassion." *Christianity Today* 47(2): 56.

U.S. LATINO/A CLERGY AND CHURCHES IN POLITICAL AND SOCIAL ACTION

Gastón Espinosa[1]

INTRODUCTION

Conventional wisdom holds that except on rare occasions, Hispanic religious leaders, churches and religious organizations have not been proactive in political or social action and indeed in some cases tacitly approved of the oppressive conditions under which Hispanics had to live and work (Acuña 1972: 148–149).[2] However, recent scholarship nuances and enlarges that story. For instance, the book *Latino Religions and Civic Activism in the United States*[3] shows that there has been a tradition of Hispanic political and social action over the past 150 years, especially in the southwestern United States.

---

[1] The author wishes to thank The Pew Charitable Trusts for funding the Hispanic Churches in American Public Life (HCAPL) research project, which generated the survey data for this analysis. Jesse Miranda of Vanguard University and Virgilio Elizondo of the University of Notre Dame co-directed the HCAPL project. The author also wishes to thank lead analyst So Young Kim and Han-Sun of Northwestern University for their assistance in analyzing the data for this publication and Edwin I. Hernández, Kenneth Davis, Milagros Peña and Ulrike Guthrie for their critical feedback on early drafts of this essay.

[2] I will use the terms "civic" action and "political" action interchangeably. I include under the category of "civic leaders" all public leaders. This includes civic, city, state, government, political and other leaders. By "religious leaders," I mean all ordained and non-ordained persons in churches or religious organizations that provide leadership to their constituencies or organizations in either a paid or voluntary capacity. I also use the terms Latino/a and Hispanic interchangeably. Rodolfo Acuña wrote: "The Catholic Church refused to promote social action and limited itself to meeting the minimal spiritual needs of the people . . . [It] was a missionary group that, by its silence, tacitly supported the oppressive conditions under which Chicanos had to live and work." Protestants were not much better as they were "not interested in championing rights or promoting brotherhood."

[3] Edited by Gastón Espinosa, Virgilio Elizondo and Jesse Miranda (Oxford University Press), in which portions of this essay are also published. The volume is one of two book projects to come out of the Hispanic Churches in America Public Life project (HCAPL), which seeks to examine the impact of religion on political and civic engagement in the Latino community.

In the early 1990s, Sidney Verba, Kay Lehman Schlozman, and Henry E. Brady argued in *Voice and Equality: Civic Voluntarism in American Politics* that Hispanic churches and faith-based organizations provided critical leadership and capacity-building skills that could be transferred into the political and social arena, even though Hispanics lagged behind Anglo-Americans and Blacks on almost every measure of political mobilization and participation. However, in campaign work and board membership (i.e., non-monetary forms of participation), Hispanic citizens matched Anglo-Americans' participation. Although in all categories of measurement Hispanic citizenship slightly increased the level of political participation, in no case did it surpass their Anglo-American and in only one case did it surpass their Black counterparts (Verba, Schlozman and Brady, 1995: 148–149).

Table 1. Political Activities by Race (percent active) in *Voice and Equality*

Political Event	Whites	Blacks	Hispanics
Voting	73%	65%	41%
Campaign Work	8%	12%	7%
Campaign Contributions	25%	22%	11%
Contacting Public Officials	37%	24%	14%
Protesting	5%	9%	4%
Board Membership	4%	2%	4%
Political Organization Affiliation	52%	38%	24%

Verba and his colleagues also found that Hispanic Protestants were more likely to engage in political participation and activities than Hispanic Catholics. In fact, Hispanic Protestants were just as likely to be politically active as their White and Black counterparts. The authors hypothesized that this was because Hispanic Protestants devoted twice as much time to religious and to non-religious activities (both inside and outside of the church) as Catholics. For this reason, they contended that Hispanic Protestants were more likely than Catholics to engage in skill-endowing activities that can be transferred into the political arena. They also found that churches and religious organizations (often unwittingly) provided critical capacity and leadership skills and opportunities (e.g., leading a Bible study or CCD class, leading a board, fundraising, youth, and/or women's committee meetings) that could also be transferred into the political arena (Verba, Schlozman, and Brady 1995: 230–235, 245, 320–333). In the 1990s, other researchers added important contributions to this research: Rudy de la Garza (1996), Louis DeSipio, Jongho Lee, Chris García (1997) and Peggy Levitt (2002) have all briefly referred to the role of clergy and/or churches in political and social action.

Although this small but growing revisionist historiography on the relationship between Hispanic clergy, churches and religious organizations and political and social action challenges our understanding of what has transpired over the past 150 years, scholars still know very little about the actual role such religious institutions play in the Hispanic community. Moreover, until recently, no study has examined whether or not Hispanic clergy, civic leaders and the general population believe that clergy, churches and religious organizations are presently engaging in political and social action.

The results of the Hispanic Churches in American Public Life (HCAPL) research project—consistent with the findings of other scholars in this book—indicate that Hispanic clergy, churches and religious organizations are engaging in political and social action at higher levels than hitherto realized. In fact, Latinos in general and civic leaders in particular report that clergy and churches are not only active in addressing educational, social and political issues, but that they need to become *more* involved. The following chapter examines the response of Hispanics to a battery of questions in the HCAPL national, civic and clergy surveys on church-sponsored political and social action among the general population and civic and religious leaders.[4] It next analyzes the level of church participation by political

---

[4] The HCAPL national survey has two batteries of questions about church participation in political and social action. The first is question number thirty-two. It reads as follows: "During the last five years, which of the following activities has your church or religious organization been involved in?" Helped in voter registration—1, Given people a ride to polls on election day—2, Handed out campaign materials—3, Advocated on behalf of a specific ballot issue, proposition, or referendum—4, Asked people to support certain political candidates—5, Organized and/or participated in protests or rallies—6, Don't know/Refused to answer—9. The second is question number thirty-three. It reads as follows: "During the last five years, which of the following activities has your church or religious organization been involved in?" Reached out to gangs in an effort to reduce community violence—1, Helped members of your community secure jobs, better wages or better working conditions—2, Helped newly arrived immigrants establish themselves—3, Started drug or alcoholic rehabilitation programs—4, Started English or citizenship classes—5, Started day-cares, food co-ops or child care centers—6, Started after school youth programs for teenagers—7, Don't know/refused to answer—9.

and social action and explores differences across various religious groups.[5] Finally, it looks at how Hispanics in general, and civic and religious leaders in particular, responded to a series of questions about the role of religious leaders and churches in educational, political and social issues. I also include data on alternative Christian traditions such as Jehovah's Witnesses and Mormons.

Before delving into the details, a brief word on methodology is merited. The findings in this chapter are based on the Hispanic Churches in American Public Life (HCAPL) research project and recent scholarship on Hispanic Catholic and Protestant faith-based political and social action. The HCAPL project was a three-year, non-sectarian study funded by a $1.3 million grant from The Pew Charitable Trusts from 1999 to 2003. The largest study in U.S. history on Hispanic religions and politics, it was managed by the author and directed by Virgilio Elizondo of the University of Notre Dame and Jesse Miranda of Vanguard University. We also collaborated with Harry Pachon, Rodolfo de la Garza and Jongho Lee of the Tomás Rivera Policy Institute (TRPI), who were commissioned to conduct three national surveys and eight community profiles as part of the project.

The findings in this chapter draw on secondary research on the subject and primary research from all five phases of the HCAPL project including: (1) a national random sample telephone survey of 2,310 Hispanics; (2) a total mail-out survey of 434 Hispanic civic [229] and religious leaders [205]; (3) community profiles of 266 religious clergy and laity in 45 congregations, representing 25 denominations and religious traditions in eight cities and urban locations in Los Angeles, San Antonio, rural southern Colorado, Chicago, rural Iowa, Miami, New York City, and San Juan, Puerto Rico; (4) seventeen commissioned scholarly papers on the history of Hispanic religions and faith-based political, civic and social action; and (5) three years of primary and secondary research on the topic (Espinosa, Elizondo, and Miranda, 2003: 13).

---

[5] I use self-definition and self-identification as "Christian" as the basis for this classification system.

HISPANIC CHURCHES AND POLITICAL ACTION

The data from the HCAPL project build on Verba, Schlozman and Brady's finding that Hispanics nationwide are not as active as Whites and Blacks on most measures of political action. The HCAPL survey found that, for example, 26 percent of Hispanics nationwide said that their churches or religious organizations gave people a ride to the polls on election day; 24 percent that they advocated on behalf of a specific ballot issue, proposition or referendum; 20 percent handed out campaign materials; 18 percent organized and/or participated in protests or rallies; and 16 percent asked people to support a certain political candidate. Somewhat exceptional was voter registration; 39 percent of all Hispanics said their churches and religious organizations were involved in voter registration.

Analysis of the findings by Protestant and Catholic religious affiliation found that Hispanic Protestants were somewhat more likely than Catholics to indicate that their churches and religious organizations engaged in political action such as giving people a ride to the polls (31 percent versus 24 percent), handing out campaign materials (23 percent versus 19 percent), and asking people to support certain political candidates (20 percent versus 14 percent).

Table 2. Political Mobilization by Catholic & Protestant Affiliation in the HCAPL

During the last five years, which of the following activities has your church or religious organization been involved with?

Question	Hispanic Catholic	Hispanic Protestant
1. Helped in voter registration	37%	39%
2. Given people a ride to the polls on election day	24%	31%
3. Handed out campaign materials	19%	23%
4. Advocated on behalf of a specific ballot issue, proposition or referendum	24%	23%
5. Asked people to support certain political candidates	14%	20%
6. Organized and/or participated in protests or rallies	18%	19%
7. None of the above		

These findings go beyond Verba, Schlozman and Brady's general hypothesis that Hispanic Protestants are more likely to participate in political action than their Catholic counterparts. They also identify the perceptions of civic leaders, as well as six kinds of political activities Hispanic churches and religious organizations engage in along with the percentage of churches that do so as well. Furthermore, these findings are broken down into a new five-point classification of U.S. Hispanic "Christian" traditions, and then cross-tabulated by percentage of Hispanics in these traditions who indicated that their churches are engaged in the above-mentioned six measures of political action. Analysis of religious family grouping by six measures of church-sponsored political action confirmed several widely held, but hitherto unsubstantiated stereotypes, and discovered several trends.

Table 3. Hispanic Political Mobilization by Religious Family Grouping

During the last five years, which of the following activities has your church or religious organization been involved with?

Question	Catholic	Mainline Protestant	Evangelical Protestant	Pentecostal Protestant	Alternative Christian
1. Helped in voter registration a	37%	50%	32%	41%	44%
2. Given people ride to the polls on election day	24%	36%	28%	31%	31%
3. Handed out campaign materials	19%	32%	20%	23%	25%
4. Advocated on behalf of a specific ballot issue, proposition or referendum	24%	21%	24%	24%	19%
5. Asked people to support certain political candidates	14%	25%	21%	15%	25%
6. Organized and/or participated in protests or rallies	18%	18%	21%	18%	13%

First, and consistent with some previously held stereotypes, Hispanic Mainline Protestants were as likely or more likely to indicate that their churches engaged in political action than their Catholic, Evangelical, Pentecostal or Alternative Christian counterparts. Second, and counter to certain sectarian and apolitical stereotypes, Alternative Christian traditions like the Jehovah's Witnesses and Mormons were

the second most likely self-described Christian religious family group
to indicate that their churches and religious organizations helped in
four out of six measures of political action. Third, and counter to
Catholic social teaching, liberation theology and farm worker union-
support stereotypes, Catholics scored their churches as low or lower than
the other four religious family groups on three out of six measures
of political mobilization. Fourth, and counter to various sectarian,
anomie, and apolitical stereotypes, Hispanic Pentecostals scored their
churches as high or higher than did their Catholic counterparts on
all six measures of political mobilization.[6] In fact, Pentecostals were
the only religious grouping that reported as high or higher scores
for all six measures of political action than their Catholic counterparts.

Factors in Hispanic Political and Social Action

Why are Hispanic Catholics generally less likely than Protestants to
say that their churches and religious organizations are engaged in
certain political actions? According to our analysis, at least four major
factors that help explain why: (1) immigration, (2) income, (3) education and (4) religious participation.

With regard to the first major factor, immigration, U.S. Hispanic
Catholics (54 percent) are more likely to be immigrants than their
Protestant counterparts (33 percent). The HCAPL national survey
found that immigrants are significantly less likely to be involved in
political or social action than their non-immigrant counterparts. Two
index variables containing six measures of political action and seven
measures of social action from the HCAPL national survey were
constructed.[7] When these two index variables are analyzed by immigrant status, there is a negative correlation between both political

---

[6] *Anomie* refers to the moral meaninglessness that uprooted immigrants, migrants
and other people experience in the process of social dislocation. Some have suggested that Pentecostal growth in Latin America is due to the social dislocation created by the changes in Latin American society which has created "refugees from
modernity" and "deprived searchers for some new form of psychological compen-
sation." Emilio Willems and Harvey Cox challenge this interpretation of Pentecostalism.
Harvey Cox, *Fire From Heaven: The Rise of Pentecostal Spirituality and the Reshaping of
Religion in the Twenty-First Century* (New York: Addison-Wesley, 1995), 171–177; Emilio
Willems, *Followers of the New Faith* (Nashville: University of Tennessee Press, 1967).

[7] The political and social indexes were created by indexing all of the possible
responses from question 32 and 33 from the HCAPL national survey on political
and social action.

(−0.141) and social action (−0.132). These relationships may indicate that Hispanic immigrants are less likely to attend churches that engage in political and social action than their non-immigrant counterparts.

A number of reasons influence why one's immigrant status may negatively affect a church's decision to become politically and socially active. First, immigrants are less likely to have had courses on U.S. civics and politics and thus are less likely to know how to engage in political and, to a lesser extent, social activities than non-immigrants. Second, almost one-third of all Hispanic Catholics are non-citizens and therefore cannot vote in elections. Third, a large number of immigrants may be reluctant to engage in these kinds of activities because they come from countries where political and social dissent was repressed. One Evangelical Baptist woman from war-torn El Salvador said, "I can't say that I've gotten involved in political issues. In social issues, yes. In my country there were so many things going on. There, politics is violence. When you come to this country you are afraid to get involved in political issues because you are not used to it. When I came here I saw a protest in front of my house, a protest by teachers, and I got scared, because in my country there would be police and even deaths."[8]

Fourth, immigrants (especially those from Central America, the Caribbean and South America) that arrived after 1980 are less likely to be aware of and draw upon the *de facto* tradition of Hispanic and especially Mexican American faith-based political and civic activism of the 1960s and 1970s (Espinosa, Elizondo, Miranda 2005; Gómez Quiñones 1990: 88–92; Gutiérrez 1998: 40–41, 331; Muñoz 1989: 50–55). Fifth, immigrants may have genuine philosophical objections (especially given their experiences in their home countries) to mixing religion and politics. David Vargas, for example, is a Catholic parishioner from Los Angeles who said, "No, [I don't support congregations getting involved in politics]. There should be a political organization for the laity. But clergy shouldn't intervene directly in politics because it's not their role. It's not [their] role to be political. [They] should be involved in such a way that it promotes and encourages the laity to become interested in politics, to fight for their rights, [so] that their petitions are respected. . . . In all these things clergy should make people aware."

---

[8] Unless otherwise noted, all of the quotes in this essay were taken from the HCAPL community profile interviews. The names have been omitted or changed to protect the anonymity of the interviewees.

María González, a member of a Hispanic Mormon Church in Chicago, said that she agreed with the separation of church and state because "in my country there was a time when they were not separated and it was bad because there was not religious freedom, there was only one religion [Roman Catholic]. If they are separated, then we all have religious freedom, we can believe in and pray to whomever we want." Carlos Segundo, a Pentecostal leader from Argentina now living in Miami concurred, "Separation of church and state? I agree with the separation. I come from a country where they are not separated, so I saw the other side of the coin. There, a Christian Evangelical is a second-class citizen. Until the 1960s, when an Evangelical died, there was no place to bury him. The cemeteries were Catholic."

Sixth, immigrants may have less money and expendable time to offer their churches for political and social activities. Seventh, some immigrants may fear that their political and social activities will lead to either their deportation or lack of visa renewal or that of a family member or friend.

Another major factor influencing political participation is income; that is, there is a direct correlation between high income, class standing and political or social action. The HCAPL national survey found that Hispanics who lived below the poverty line (with annual incomes below $24,999) were much less likely to say that their churches engaged in political and social action than Hispanics who were middle ($25,000–$64,999) or upper middle ($65,000+) class. Although the difference between the two groups is not statistically significant for political action (1.39 lower class versus 1.55 middle/upper class), the difference was statistically significant (2.46 versus 2.79 or 95 percent level) for social action. Why Hispanics living in poverty were less likely to attend churches that engaged in political and social action is uncertain, but we may hypothesize that Latino churches located in economically disadvantaged and underdeveloped neighborhoods do not have adequate staffing to prepare and lead Hispanics in political and social activities.

Hence, although significantly larger than their Protestant counterparts in numerical size, raw income, material resources and denominational support, Catholic churches may be handicapped precisely by their large size if only one or two priests and a handful of lay leaders must minister to a thousand or more families. This contrasts with the average Protestant church, which although it may only have one or two clergy, might only have 130 parishioners as well. Disparity in ratio of clergy (and lay leaders) to parishioners may be further exacerbated by other potential obstacles such as lack of clergy fluency in Spanish and/or understanding of Latin American history, popular traditions and culture.

This may speak to the Catholic situation since, as Froehle and Gautier have noted, there is a shortage of both Spanish-speaking and Hispanic priests. Although there are over 47,000 priests in the U.S. today, Hispanics—who make up 40 percent of all Catholics in the United States—are only 5 percent of all priests (See Chapter Three in this volume, "Latino/a Catholic Leaders in the United States").

This situation contrasts with Hispanic Protestant immigrant churches, which are are more likely to be led by Latin American and second- or occasionally third-generation U.S. Hispanic pastors. It would seem reasonable to hypothesize that Latin American and U.S. Hispanic clergy may be more likely to engage in political and social action than their Anglo-American, Hispanic-serving counterparts because they are more personally invested in the outcome. While clearly there are large numbers of dedicated Anglo-American priests and lay leaders that have worked selflessly to serve their Hispanic Catholic parishioners (and in a few cases more so than Latin American and U.S. Hispanic priests), on average it may be that they simply are not as committed to political and social engagement or at the very least have made it less of a priority.

Another factor worth noting is that there appears to be a relationship between the level of education and the likelihood that Hispanic Catholics and Protestants reported that their churches and religious organizations are engaged in political and social action.

The HCAPL national survey found that Hispanic Protestants are more likely than Catholics to have graduated from high school (27 percent versus 23 percent) or attended college (28 percent versus 21 percent). Catholics (19 percent) are more likely than Protestants (13 percent) to say that they have an elementary school level or less educational background. Thus we may conclude that some Hispanic Protestants are more likely to say they attend churches that engage in political and social activities because they are more likely to have attended or graduated from high school or have attended college. Other studies in this volume suggest that inadequate seminary education may also hinder or retard an otherwise politically and socially active priest or lay leader from equipping larger numbers of lay people for activism.

When Hispanic Catholics and Protestants are analyzed by the level of guidance that religion provides by their church's level of political and social action, Hispanic Protestants (67 percent) were significantly more likely than Catholics (48 percent) to say that religion provides a great deal of guidance for their day-to-day living. The HCAPL national survey found that Latinos who read their Bibles, lead a Bible study, and attend church are more likely to say that their churches engage in political or social action than those that never read their Bibles, never lead a Bible study, or never attend church. Latino Protestants were significantly more likely than Catholics to say that they read the Bible once a week or more (67 percent of Protestants versus 25 percent of Catholics), attend church every week or more than once a week (69 percent of Protestants versus 48 percent of Catholics), and to say that they had led a Bible study (42 percent of Protestants versus 21 percent of Catholics). Unlike the other three questions regarding religious participation, this particular question is not biased in favor of Protestants. All these factors, but especially religious guidance and leading a Bible study (a leadership skill that could be transferred to the political and social arenas), may help explain why Protestants were more likely to report that their churches engaged in political and social action.

To summarize, socioeconomic factors like immigration, income/class, education and religious participation are closely related to Hispanic involvement in church-sponsored political and social action. Although being Protestant is not significantly tied to all six measures of political activism in equal measure, it is nonetheless positively related to political activism in general. In addition, being Protestant is significantly related to social action overall but in varying degrees for each of the seven measures. In fact, Catholics have the lowest mean index for both political and social action. When analyzed further, Mainline Protestants (1.80 and 2.84 for political and social action respectively) and alternative Christians (1.55 and 2.83) have a higher mean of both political and social activism than Catholics (1.34 and 2.45), Pentecostals (1.53 and 2.66) and Evangelicals (1.46 and 2.76). In conclusion, Hispanic Protestants are more likely to be engaged in social activities than Hispanic Catholics because the latter are more likely to be immigrants, live in poverty, have lower levels of education and have lower levels of religious participation.

Hispanic Civic Leaders' Perception of Church Involvement in Political Mobilization

Hispanic civic and political leaders gave their Catholic and Protestant churches and religious organizations mixed reviews concerning their attempts at political mobilization. In fact, they gave them lower scores than did the general Hispanic population on four out of the six measures of political mobilization.

Table 4. Hispanic Political Mobilization by General Population, Civic Leaders, Clergy, Black Clergy

During the last five years, which of the following activities has your church or religious organization been involved with?

Question	Hispanic National	Hispanic Civic	Hispanic Clergy	Black Clergy
1. Helped in voter registration	39%	38%	60%	84%
2. Given people a ride to the polls on election day	26%	5%	11%	64%
3. Handed out campaign materials	20%	11%	19%	31%
4. Advocated on behalf of a specific ballot issue, proposition or referendum	24%	40%	43%	28%
5. Asked people to support certain political candidates	16%	14%	14%	
6. Organized and/or participated in protests or rallies	18%	25%	26%	17%
7. None of the above		38%	20%	
(Blank spaces indicate where data was not available)				

Further, although 40 percent of civic leaders surveyed said their churches or religious organizations advocated on behalf of a specific ballot issue, 38 percent helped in voter registration, and 25 percent said their churches or religious organizations organized and/or participated in protests or rallies, only 14 percent of civic leaders said their churches and religious organizations asked parishioners to support a certain political candidate, 11 percent handed out campaign materials, and 5 percent gave parishioners a ride to the polls on election day.

Hispanic religious leaders took a more positive view of their work than their civic counterparts. Like civic leaders, religious leaders tended to view their churches and religious organizations as more likely to help in voter registration, advocate on behalf of a specific ballot issues or proposition, or organize a protest or rally than hand-

ing out campaign materials, asking people to support certain political candidates, or giving people a ride to the polls on election day.
When comparing the HCAPL Hispanic clergy findings to their Black
counterparts in R. Drew Smith's study on the public influences of
African American churches, Black clergy were significantly more
likely than Hispanic clergy to say that they and their churches participated in voter registration (84 percent versus 60 percent), gave
people a ride to the polls on election day (64 percent versus 11 percent), and handed out campaign literature (31 percent versus 19 percent). However, Hispanic clergy were more likely than Black clergy
to report that they advocated on behalf of a specific ballot issue,
proposition or referendum (43 percent versus 28 percent) and organized and/or participated in protests or rallies (26 percent versus 17
percent).[9]

Hispanic Churches and Social Action

Much of the confidence that the Hispanic population in general and
civic leaders in particular afford clergy, churches and religious organizations may be due to the fact that they are perceived as providing badly needed social services and programs free of charge to the
Hispanic community, thus taking pressure off local city and state
governments. This seems to defy the stereotype in many Hispanic
studies programs that clergy, churches and religious organizations
are doing little to alleviate the suffering of the poor, and instead
preach a kind of naïve "pie-in-the-sky after you die" message of political and social complacency. Despite this stereotype, a high percentage of the Hispanic population reported that their churches were
starting daycare programs, food co-ops and child care centers (44
percent), reaching out to gangs in an effort to reduce community
violence (39 percent), helping newly arrived immigrants establish
themselves (35 percent), helping members of their community secure
jobs, better wages or better working conditions (34 percent), starting
drug and alcohol rehabilitation programs (32 percent), and starting

---

[9] The questions regarding voter registration, giving people a ride to the polls,
handing out campaign materials, advocating on behalf of a specific issue and participating in protests or rallies were taken directly from R. Drew Smith's national
survey of black clergy and thus can be used for comparisons. Smith, 9–10, 58–83.

English or citizenship classes (31 percent). This is wholly consistent with the observations outlined elsewhere in this volume.

As is true with Hispanic political mobilization, there were differences when Hispanic Catholics were compared to Protestants. Hispanic Protestant churches are more likely to provide social services than their Catholic counterparts in four out of the seven measures of social action such as reaching out to stop gang violence (44 percent versus 36 percent), helping immigrants establish themselves (39 percent versus 35 percent), starting day cares, food co-ops or child care centers (48 percent versus 43 percent), as well as starting after school programs (43 percent versus 35 percent). In five out of seven measures (Table 5), Latino Catholics consistently gave their churches lower marks than their Mainline Protestant, Evangelical, Pentecostal or Alternative Christian counterparts. This may be because they expect more out of their churches.

Table 5. Hispanic Social Services Provided by Religious Family Grouping in National Survey

During the last five years, which of the following activities has your church or religious organization been involved with?

Question	Catholic	Mainline Protestant	Evangelical Protestant	Pentecostal Protestant	Alternative Christian
1. Reached out to gangs in an effort to reduce community violence	36%	46%	44%	43%	52%
2. Helped members of your community secure jobs, better wages or better working conditions	33%	37%	36%	34%	40%
3. Helped newly arrived immigrants establish themselves	35%	42%	38%	37%	30%
4. Started drug or alcohol rehabilitation program	33%	35%	28%	34%	38%
5. Started English or citizenship classes	30%	38%	34%	30%	31%
6. Started daycare programs, food co-ops or childcare centers	43%	52%	50%	45%	49%
7. Started after school youth programs for teenagers	35%	35%	46%	43%	42%

Alternative Christian traditions like the Jehovah's Witnesses and Mormons reported that their congregations had a higher rate of social action on three out of seven measures than their Mainline Protestant, Pentecostal, Evangelical and Catholic counterparts. Mainline Protestants ranked highest on three out of six measures, and second or tied for second highest on six out of seven measures of social action. Evangelicals and Pentecostals ranked highest or tied for highest on two (helping newly arrived immigrants and starting youth programs) and one (starting youth programs) measure respectively.

While statistical evidence is lacking, one of the reasons churches were not more active may be due to lack of money. Although her assessment is only anecdotal, Rev. Julia Hernández, an associate pastor of an American Baptist Church in New York City, said that churches do not do more "because they do not have big budgets to develop community programs." This recalls Amy Sherman's observation in Chapter Five that Hispanic pastors may not consider their informal community ministries as social services because they do not have big budgets. Despite this fact, Rev. Hernández's church, like many others, still managed to offer some non-monetary-driven social services to the community such as counseling for victims of domestic violence and ESL classes for immigrants. Still other churches like one Hispanic Reform Church in America stated that they sponsored food pantry programs, "Kids with a Promise" tutoring classes, Boy and Girl Scouts troops, Alcoholics Anonymous, computer training classes for older people to enhance their professional skills, ESL classes, fundraising for community-based organizations and social worker advocacy for youth and the elderly. Similarly, several Pentecostal churches reported offering social programs, contacting politicians and contacting the police to let them know about the needs and problems facing their community. Juana García, vice president of her Pentecostal church's women's organization, said that although she does not get too involved with politics, she does fight for educational and social issues. Likewise, Jorge Sena of Chicago said that his Pentecostal church gave away 1,000 pairs of children's shoes, provided food for the poor, sponsored a food pantry and created after school programs for youth. Other denominations appear to be doing the same. Father José Valle from Chicago said that his church's primary social focus is aimed at gangs, the needs of youth, immigrants, providing ESL classes, addressing economic issues and fighting for labor rights. He found that reaching youth in gangs was challenging because "the ones that [were] not killed wound up in jail."

It is interesting to note that this commitment to social justice went beyond interviewees' respective denominational communities. A number of Hispanics from different Christian denominations said their congregations were actively involved in providing relief (especially food and clothing) and support (e.g., collecting funds) for victims of the September 11, 2001 terrorist attacks in New York City, the Vieques Struggle in Puerto Rico, Hurricane Mitch in Honduras, Hurricane Andrew in Florida, the terrible earthquake that devastated El Salvador and for Afghan refugees. One Seventh-day Adventist pastor from Miami said, "We have a department that is dedicated to meeting the needs of our community, people that have financial woes, or social issues . . . We have a disaster relief department that takes clothes and food; for example, we were very involved when Hurricane Andrew hit. . . . . The relief department works at an international level . . . [in] the floods and earthquakes in Central America . . . and right now our institution is helping in New York." Similarly, a Pentecostal leader from Miami stated regarding social programming, "The Church participates in all events, like 9/11—our members donated blood, and our children gave money to Afghanistan. We help Central American countries." Networking in order to maximize social capacity is a prominent theme in Latino faith-based activism.

In this respect, Hispanic Protestants and Catholics both share a common *de facto* social justice commitment that is community-based and yet national and international in vision and scope. The fact that 38 percent of all Hispanics were born outside of the U.S. and/or come from countries where poverty and right-wing dictators often functioned like terrorists may help contribute to this sense of collective identity.

Civic and Religious Leaders' Views on Churches Providing Social Services

How do civic and religious leaders view the church's role in providing social services? On three out of seven measures of social action, civic and religious leaders cited similar levels of involvement by their churches, as Table 6 illustrates.[10]

---

[10] Those three measures were: reaching out to gangs in an effort to reduce community violence (civic—33 percent vs. clergy—35 percent), starting day-care centers,

Table 6. Social Services by Hispanic Churches by National Population,
Civic Leaders and Clergy

*During the last five years, which of the following activities has your church or religious
organization been involved with?*

Question	National	Civic	Clergy
1. Reached out to gangs in an effort to reduce community violence.	39%	33%	35%
2. Helped members of your community secure jobs, better wages or better working conditions	34%	32%	55%
3. Helped newly arrived immigrants establish themselves	35%	33%	55%
4. Started drug or alcoholic rehab prog.	32%	16%	23%
5. Started English or citizenship classes	31%	36%	47%
6. Started day-cares, food co-ops or child-care centers	44%	35%	36%
7. Started after school youth programs for teenagers	37%	36%	35%
8. Serve as a site for labor organizing		4%	10%
9. Help your members get affordable housing		27%	43%
10. Organize international assistance		30%	36%
11. Organize disaster relief		39%	37%
12. None of the above		16%	10%

In contrast, on three out of the four remaining measures, there was significant disagreement. All three of the discrepancies share a common civic orientation and thus may help explain the low civic response. Conversely, the high religious response is noteworthy (if true) because of the previously mentioned stereotype that churches have not been civic-oriented in the Hispanic community. For example, when compared to their religious counterparts, civic leaders were less likely than clergy to report that their churches or religious organizations help members of their community secure jobs, better wages or better working conditions (32 percent versus 55 percent), help newly arrived immigrants establish themselves (33 percent versus 55 percent), start a drug or alcoholic rehabilitation program (16 percent versus 23 percent), or start English or citizenship classes (36 percent versus 47 percent).

---

food co-ops, or child-care centers (civic—35 percent vs. clergy—36 percent), and starting after school youth programs for teenagers (civic—36 percent vs. clergy—35 percent).

In addition to the significant work of churches, a growing number of faith-based organizations (FBOs) are providing social services. In 2002, Richard Wood noted that the vast majority of the 133 faith-based organizations that he studied and their 3,300 affiliated congregations were associated with a religious tradition. All combined, these FBOs were reaching an estimated 1.5 million people in just their own congregations. Twenty percent of the 3,300 congregations (660) were Hispanic and 16 percent of the 550 professionals employed in FBOs were Hispanic, 50 percent of whom are women. Thus Hispanics are represented in faith-based organizations at a slightly higher rate than their percentage (now nearly 14 percent) of the U.S. population. This may be due to the rich heritage of Catholic social teaching, liberation theology and largely Mainline Protestant faith-based organizing and social justice activism during the Mexican American and Black Civil Rights movements of the 1960s and 1970s. However, there are also a growing number of Pentecostal and Evangelical FBOs across the U.S. whose activism draws on other traditions.[11]

HISPANIC ATTITUDES ON CLERGY INVOLVEMENT IN EDUCATIONAL, POLITICAL AND SOCIAL ISSUES

Despite the fact that Hispanic churches and faith-based organizations are very active in voter registration but not in most other traditional forms of political mobilization and participation, they still enjoy the overwhelming support of Hispanic civic leaders. When asked how important Hispanic churches and religious organizations are in shaping current national discussions, 88 percent of Hispanic civic leaders and 82 percent of religious leaders indicated they were "very important" or "somewhat important." More than one-third (35 percent) of all Hispanic civic leaders said clergy input in national discussions was "very important." Civic leaders also gave religious leaders very high marks for shaping community affairs (75 percent)

---

[11] For example, there are large faith-based organizations like Pueblo Nuevo, My Father's House, and City Impact in southern California, Project Quest in San Antonio, Resurrection Project in Chicago, Nueva Esperanza in Philadelphia, the Latino Pastoral Action Center in the Bronx, and Nehemiah House in New York City, that are sponsoring a growing number of social programs.

as well as for addressing educational, social and political issues (73 percent).

This overwhelmingly positive support may be based on recognition of the critical role that Catholic and Protestant churches play in the daily lives (e.g., baptism, marriage, last rites, Eucharist and other church programs, for example) of ordinary Hispanics. Although difficult to determine, it may also be due to the influence of Catholic social teaching, liberation theology, popular Catholicism, Our Lady of Guadalupe, faith-based Catholic charities, faith-based organizations like COPS, UNO, EPISO, AMEN, LPAC, Nueva Esperanza, and the fundamental recognition that Hispanic culture and values are largely tied to Christian morality and a Judeo-Christian worldview. Given that 93 percent of all U.S. Hispanics self-identify as Christian, it would be unwise for an elected political official to offend or overlook Christian organizations (Espinosa, Elizondo and Miranda, 2003: 14–16).

Despite their general support for clergy, churches and religious organizations, civic leaders were less enthusiastic about the idea of Hispanic churches and religious organizations becoming *more* involved in educational, social and political issues. Even so, 62 percent of the general Hispanic population, 74 percent of civic leaders, and 82 percent of religious leaders surveyed indicated that religious leaders should become *more* involved.

Interestingly, this general support for greater Hispanic church and clergy participation in political, social and educational issues dropped off significantly when survey respondents were asked whether or not they believed that religious leaders should try to influence public affairs. Only 50 percent of Hispanics nationwide and 61 percent of civic leaders favored this notion. This contrasts with 92 percent of religious leaders. Finally, more than half (54 percent) of all Hispanic civic leaders surveyed indicated that they had seen an *increase* in the frequency of contacts by Hispanic religious leaders.

Despite the different levels of support for Hispanic church and clergy involvement in educational, political and social issues, Hispanics generally believe that their churches are taking positive steps to address social issues. For example, the HCAPL national survey found that 65 percent of the general Hispanic population believes that religious leaders and churches *are* talking about the pressing social and political issues of the day either "very often" (21 percent) or "fairly often" (44 percent). Clearly, as *Latino Religions and Civic Activism in the*

United States (Espinosa et. al, 2005) found, Hispanic religious leaders' involvement in the Sanctuary movement and the struggles over Proposition 187 in California, Elián González in Miami and Vieques in Puerto Rico indicate the commitment of at least some clergy, churches and religious organizations to faith-based social and political action.

Hispanic civic leaders recognize this; 63 percent believe that clergy or church parishioners do play an important role in shaping issues in their political jurisdiction. Furthermore, 78 percent indicated that churches and religious organizations were at least somewhat important in shaping community affairs. This may explain why 62 percent of the national Hispanic population and 71 percent of civic leaders surveyed wanted their churches or religious organizations to become *more* involved in educational, social and political issues. A Chicago Pentecostal reflected, "I think that from a social perspective we need to be more involved [in politics]. Politically, I think every Christian organization should have a voice and vote in what is going on politically. If we don't speak up, then people will speak for us. If we don't vote then they will vote for us. Then it will be our fault." Perhaps reflecting the influence of César Chávez, Catholic social teaching and/or liberation theology, María Sánchez said, "We are called through Jesus to do that because he was our main example of helping the poor and fighting any injustice that we saw in our society. And so through government, which is the dominant power in our country, we are called to be involved. This church is not separate from society; it's within society. We have to work with society and try to change it for the better."

Regardless of the widespread support that Hispanic churches, clergy and religious organizations enjoy, religious leaders have yet to capitalize on that confidence. For example, only 22 percent of all Hispanics said that their churches or religious organizations had asked them to engage in social activities. Only 19 percent of political and civic leaders said religious leaders routinely contacted them regarding specific political, civic or social issues. In fact, only 33 percent of all Latino civic leaders sought clergy support and input for their political campaigns and civic programs. It may be the case that some highly assimilated and secular-oriented second- and third-generation Latino political and civic leaders simply do not have the knowledge or connections to reach out to local Spanish-speaking congregations. Amy Sherman noted in the previous chapter that Latino/a religious leaders often lack the "know how" to be more socially active; perhaps some Hispanic political and civic leaders also simply do not have the knowledge or connections to reach out to local Spanish-speaking Catholic, Pentecostal, Evangelical, Mainline Protestant and Alternative Christian churches and/or congregations. Since Hispanic religious leaders, churches and religious organizations are highly valued, we would argue that they could do more to network with government officials.

SOCIAL SERVICES PROVIDED BY CHURCHES AND DIOCESES

The high level of confidence that civic leaders have in Hispanic Catholic and Protestant religious leaders and churches appears well founded. This is evident in the 2002 study of Hispanic ministry directed by Bryan T. Froehle and Mary L. Gautier at the Center for Applied Research in the Apostolate (CARA) at Georgetown University. The study found that a significant percentage of dioceses provide direct services as part of their social ministry to the Hispanic community. When asked "what is the most important resource that your [Diocesan Hispanic Ministry Office] provides to the Hispanic/Latino community?" one leader from the Grand Island diocese wrote, "Pastoral formation programs, awareness on social justice, multicultural ministry, sense of belonging and ownership, migrant ministry programs, collaboration among parishes." Still another from Youngstown, Ohio said, "Bilingual resources, prison ministry, care of migrant workers" (Froehle and Gautier, 2002: 49, 52).

Hispanic ministry offices appear to be meeting important needs. Three-fourths of the 106 Catholic dioceses (out of 176 nationwide) that responded to the Froehle and Gautier survey indicated that their Hispanic ministry offices collaborated with local Hispanic service agencies, with the diocesan office of religious education, and with Catholic Charities. They also found that seven in ten respondents from Western states provide naturalization assistance (versus 27 percent from the Northeast, 36 percent from the Midwest and 42 percent from the South) and more than six in ten from the West provide legal advocacy, although only half from the Northeast and South do the same. Further, more than two-thirds of those working in parish churches serving more than 9,000 Hispanics said they provided legal advice. However, the report did not state what percentage of smaller

Hispanic-serving ministry offices provided support, although it would probably be considerably less and this could, in part, help explain their lack of participation in the survey (Froehle and Gautier, 2002: 1–3, 5, 11, 49, 52).

Despite this possibility, a significant percentage of Catholic diocesan ministry offices reported that they provide free legal advice (47 percent), naturalization assistance (42 percent), financial assistance (39 percent), food or clothing (37 percent), and health services (20 percent) to the Hispanic community. At the parish level, a number of churches offer financial assistance to immigrants (78 percent), legal advocacy (66 percent), food or clothing (65 percent), social gatherings/events (64 percent) and health services (59 percent). Diocesan churches are not trying to provide these social services alone, however. Approximately 81 percent of diocesan Hispanic ministry offices collaborate with local Hispanic faith-based organizations and secular social service agencies. For example, they collaborate with Catholic Charities (77 percent), immigrant/migrant/refugee services (72 percent), and health care ministries (31 percent). Such broad involvement in social services that includes collaboration and networking is evident in virtually all the denominations examined in this book.

The critical role that the Catholic Church plays in providing social services to Hispanics through such collaboration and networking was evident in the finding that the most important resource that the diocesan office provides for Hispanic ministries are "services and advocacy." More than half (53 percent) of all diocesan offices said that this was the single most important ministry their office provided the Hispanic community, followed by "collaboration" with outside social service agencies (47 percent) and "leadership formation" (33 percent).

Given the fact that a significant percentage of Hispanic Catholics are immigrants (54 percent), it is not surprising that "advocacy" on behalf of those not able to advocate for themselves is the single most important social service the Church provides its parishioners. When asked what advice Hispanic ministry offices should give to a diocese seeking to expand Hispanic programs, leaders from Oklahoma City said, "One must get to know the needs and cultural customs of each community [and visit] parishioners, hospitals, prisons [and] jails. They also encouraged them to visit the poor and form their own local Pastoral Parish Plan" (Froehle and Gautier, 2002: 9, 14, 25, 32–33, 56).

The findings in Froehle and Gautier's study challenge the widely held stereotype that the Catholic Church is not providing social services and programs for Hispanics. In fact, the Catholic Church annually provides millions of dollars worth of social services to the Hispanic community free of charge. The growing number of Catholic Hispanic ministry offices has directly shaped these services and increased support (Froehle and Gautier, 2002: 9, 14, 25, 32).

Although the long and rich tradition of Hispanic Catholic social teaching and faith-based activism make the findings about Catholic social work somewhat predictable, contributors to this book such as Adair Lummis and Amy Sherman note a similar level of social service among Hispanic Protestants. Today there are 8 million Hispanic Protestants in the United States, 88 percent (7 million) of whom self-identify with an Evangelical denomination or say they are "born-again" Christian. There are now more Hispanic Protestants in the United States than Jews or Muslims.

Sherman's research found that Protestants are providing social services in the Latino community; indeed 72 percent of the 452 Protestant congregations she surveyed offered social service programs. The average congregation provided six social services to the community. Over 55 percent of churches said that they partnered with other churches, social service non-profits, schools, the police, courts/probation/parole officers and local government, and 38 percent indicated that they partnered with secular social service providers. The most common reason why 28 percent of Latino churches were not sponsoring social service programs was lack of "know how" (55 percent) and their small size and lack of money (46 percent). Only eight percent said they were philosophically opposed to offering social programs. In short, despite their conservative theology and moral positions, 92 percent of Latino Protestant religious leaders indicated that they already sponsored or were open to sponsoring social service programs (Espinosa, Elizondo, and Miranda, 2003: 14, 28, endnote 21).

Conclusion: Interpreting the Significance of Hispanic Faith-based Activism

What can we conclude about the importance of Hispanic clergy, churches and religious organizations in shaping political and social action? First, the findings in this chapter nuance and enlarge the perceptions of scholars like Rodolfo Acuña. Indeed, Hispanic churches and religious organizations are much more politically and socially active than researchers have noted in the past. They appear to be becoming more active with each passing decade. Given the fact that the vast majority of Hispanics are Roman Catholic, Pentecostal or non-Charismatic Evangelical and that neither Hispanic Pentecostalism nor Evangelicalism has had a reputation for political or social action, we expected our own research to reveal much lower levels of participation and support. Instead, almost four out of ten (39 percent) Hispanics nationwide indicated that their churches helped in voter registration and one in four (26 percent) said that their churches had given people a ride to the polls on election day and advocated on behalf of a specific ballot issue, proposition or referendum.

Second, the findings of our study confirm and go beyond some of the findings in the Verba, Schlozman and Brady study. Hispanic Protestants are as active or more politically active than their Catholic counterparts on all six HCAPL measures of political action. As noted earlier in this chapter, four key socio-religious factors—immigrant status, income/class, education and religious participation—help explain why Hispanic Protestant churches are more active than their Catholic counterparts.

Third, the Hispanic population in general and civic leaders in particular gave churches and clergy high marks for addressing educational, social and political issues. However, Latino church leaders' efforts still lag behind those of their Anglo-American and Black counterparts, especially when it comes to political activism.

Fourth, and perhaps not surprising in light of this finding, 62 percent of Hispanics nationwide and 74 percent of civic leaders surveyed want religious leaders to become more involved in educational, social and political issues. Given the lack of regular contact between Hispanic civic and religious leaders, it was surprising to find that Hispanic civic leaders gave churches and religious leaders consistently higher levels of support than the general population. However, this support dropped off when civic leaders were asked whether or not they think that religious leaders should try to influence public affairs.

Fifth, Hispanics are much more likely to get involved in social than political issues. Many factors may explain this finding, including the political attitudes of refugees who fled military dictatorships in Central and South America in the 1980s and 1990s or the fact that many Latin American immigrants and U.S. Hispanics simply do not have sufficient leisure time or information to become more politically active.

Sixth, this helps to explain why Hispanics are less likely than their African American counterparts to become involved in political mobilization. However, Hispanics are actually as likely or, in some cases, slightly more likely to become involved in providing certain social services for their community than their African American counterparts.

Seventh, Hispanic Protestants not only tend be more engaged in political (and social) issues because they are more involved in their churches—as Verba, Schlozman and Brady point out—but also because they are less likely to be immigrants, live in poverty, have low levels of education, and are more likely to attend church, lead a Bible study, and say that religion provides "some" or a "great deal" of meaning for their day-to-day living.

Eighth, and perhaps somewhat predictably given the long tradition of Anglo-American political and social activism, Hispanic Mainline Protestants indicated that their churches and religious organizations were more politically and socially active than their Catholic, Evangelical or Pentecostal counterparts.

Ninth, generally-speaking, Hispanic Christians that have higher (although not necessarily the highest) levels of church attendance, Bible reading, and leading Bible studies were more likely than those who never attended church, never read the Bible, and never led a Bible study to say that their churches engaged in political or social action. Thus, there does appear to be a correlation between religious participation and political and social action.

Lastly, Alternative Christians (i.e., Jehovah's Witnesses, Mormons and Christian Scientists) were the second most likely religious grouping to indicate that they were involved in political mobilization and in providing social services—more so than their Catholic, Evangelical or Pentecostal counterparts. By including Alternative Christian traditions, this study adds an important dimension to traditional analyses of Hispanic Christianity in the United States.

All of these findings point to the general conclusion that Hispanic clergy, churches and religious organizations are actively engaged in political and social action, and have the widespread support of both the Hispanic population in general and civic leaders in particular. The emerging evidence presented in this book indicates that this trend in Hispanic faith-based political and social action is likely to continue well into the twenty-first century.

REFERENCES

Acuña, Rodolfo. 1973. *Occupied America: A History of Chicanos*. New York City, NY: Harper & Row.
Cox, Harvey. 1967. *Fire from Heaven: The Rise of Pentecostal Spirituality and the Reshaping of Religion in the Twenty-First Century*. New York City, NY: Addison-Wesley.
De la Garza, Rodolfo. 1996. *Ethnic Ironies: Latino Politics in the 1992 Elections*. Boulder, CO: Westview Press.
—— Louis DeSipio, F. Chris García, John A. García, and Angelo Falcón. *Latino Voices: Mexican, Puerto Rican, and Cuban Perspectives on American Politics*. Boulder, Colorado: Westview Press.
Espinosa, Gastón, Virgilio Elizondo, and Jesse Miranda, 2003. *Hispanic Churches in American Public Life: Summary of Findings*. Notre Dame: IN: Institute for Latino Studies at the University of Notre Dame.
——, Virgilio Elizondo, and Jesse Miranda, eds. 2005. *Latino Religions and Civic Activism in the United States*. New York City, NY: Oxford University Press.
Froehle, Bryan T. and Mary L. Gautier. 2002. *Ministry in a Church of Increasing Diversity: A Profile of Diocesan Hisapnic/Latino Ministry*. Washington, D.C.: Georgetown University: Center for Applied Research in the Apostolate.
Gómez Quiñones, Juan. 1990. *Chicano Politics: Reality & Promise 1940–1990*. Albuquerque: University of New Mexico Press.
Gutiérrez, José Ángel. 1998. *The Making of a Chicano Militant: Lessons from Crystal*. Madison, WI: University of Wisconsin Press.
Levitt, Peggy. 2002. "Two Nations under God? Latino Religious Life in the United States," in Marcelo M. Suárez-Orozco and Mariela M. Páez, *Latinos Remaking America*. Berkeley: University of California Press.
Muñoz, Carlos Jr. 1989. *Youth, Identity, and Power: The Chicano Movement*. New York City, NY: Verso Books.Smith, R. Drew. 2003. *New Day Begun: African American Churches and Civic Culture in Post-Civil Rights America*. Durham, NC: Duke University Press.
Verba, Sidney, Key Lehman Schlozman, and Henry F. Brady. 1995. *Voice and Equality: Civic Voluntarism in American Politics*. Cambridge, MA: Harvard University Press.
Willems, Emilio. 1967. *Followers of the New Faith*. Nashville, TN: University of Tennessee Press.
Wood, Richard. 2002. *Religion in Action: Religion, Race, and Democratic Organizing in America*. Chicago: University of Chicago Press.
——. 2004. Fe y Acción Social: Hispanic Churches in Faith-Based Community Organizing," in Espinosa, Gastón, Virgilio Elizondo, and Jesse Miranda, eds., 2005. *Latino Religions and Civic Activism n in the United States*.

IF THE PASTOR SAYS "LET'S DO IT," IT GETS DONE: SUCCESS STORIES IN LATINO SOCIAL MINISTRY[1]

Edwin I. Hernández, Rebecca Burwell, Marciana Popescu, Milagros Peña and Juan Carlos Rivera

INTRODUCTION

One of the most important tasks facing U.S. religious bodies, social movements, para-church organizations, faith-based nonprofits and ministerial education centers is the need to train Latino and Latina leaders for the unique challenges of Hispanic ministry.[2] In this chapter, we seek to better understand the experiences, needs, aspirations and challenges that Latino religious leaders face, whether clergy or laypersons. We also derive lessons and practices from exemplary organizations and leaders that others can apply in their own contexts. Our exploration draws upon various sources of information including national databases on the Latino general population, clergy, and seminarians,[3] focus group interviews with Hispanic clergy,[4] and

---

[1] The research summarized here was made possible through grants from the Annie E. Casey Foundation, Louisville Institute and The Pew Charitable Trusts. We thank their staff, especially Carole E. Thompson and Stephanie C. Boddie, for permission to share the research findings in this book and for their commitment to strengthening Latino pastoral leadership. We also thank the pastors, leaders and volunteers from St. Pius, San Lucas and Women's Shelter of Hope. Finally we thank Luis Cortes and Danny Cortes from Nueva Esperanza, Inc. who graciously allowed us to showcase the results of the Hispanic Capacity Project.

[2] An Annie E. Casey Foundation report by Helene Slessarev-Jamir titled *Sustaining Hope, Creating Opportunities: The Challenge of Ministry among Hispanic Immigrants*, chronicled the immense challenges that the dramatic growth of the Latino population poses to those ministering in the United States. A key finding was that the Latino faith-based serving infrastructure is rather weak and thus increased resources need to be secured to enhance the serving capacity of Latino religious organizations.

[3] *2004 Latino Political Survey* conducted by the Pew Hispanic Center; *1995 National Survey of Hispanic/Latino Theological Education*, for more information see Edwin I. Hernández and Kenneth Davis, *Reconstructing the Sacred Tower*, 2003; and the *2004 Latino/a Seminarian Survey*, conducted by the Center for the Study of Latino Religion at the University of Notre Dame.

[4] Nine focus groups were conducted throughout 2003 in the following cities: Boston, Massachusetts; Chicago, Illinois; Forth Worth, Texas; Los Angeles, California; New York City; Raleigh, North Carolina; and San Antonio, Texas. These cities

ethnographic case studies of two Latino churches and a Latino faith-based organization.[5]

The chapter is divided into four parts. Part One discusses broadly the role that churches play in building social capital. We describe key background characteristics of practicing Latino clergy and present their own reflections about their sense of calling to ministry and the challenges and opportunities they face. We also present critical information on the next generation of Latino clergy in order to explore how they are currently involved in community ministry and the sort of training they think would most increase their effectiveness. Part Two presents two case studies of socially engaged churches—a mainline Protestant and a Catholic parish in the city of Chicago. The case studies examine how the congregations are involved in the community, their best practices and challenges for their clergy and lay leaders. Similarly, in Part Three we narrate the story of a Latino owned-and-operated faith-based organization that has participated in an unprecedented training initiative called the Hispanic Capacity Project (HCP) through Nueva Esperanza, Inc. Funded by a 2002 capacity-building grant under the Compassionate Capital Fund,[6] this initiative provides training and technical assistance to Latino faith-based organizations in six cities. Finally, in Part Four we give recommendations for strengthening the community-serving capacity of Latino organizations and churches.

---

were chosen because they represent the ethnic diversity of Hispanics in the U.S., and the shifting demographic trends in both long-standing Latino communities (e.g., San Antonio and Los Angeles), and in areas of the country that have only recently experienced rapid growth in their Latino populations (e.g., North Carolina). The participants were selected by seminary Hispanic faculty in collaboration with the research team of Dr. Milagros Peña and Dr. Edwin I. Hernández. Each group was comprised of 6 to 7 participants, and all together 24 women and 36 men were interviewed, representing the following traditions: 26 percent Pentecostal, 21 percent Roman Catholic, 16 percent Methodist, 13 percent from Independent Churches, 10 percent Southern Baptist, 5 percent Disciples of Christ, 5 percent Presbyterian, 2 percent United Church of Christ and 2 percent Mennonite.

[5] The two congregational case studies in Chicago were conducted by Dr. Rebecca Burwell and Juan Carlos Rivera, a doctoral student at Loyola University, as part of the Chicago Latino Congregations Study. The case study of the Latino faith-based organization was conducted by Dr. Marciana Popescu.

[6] Initial grant competition under the Faith-based and Community Initiative.

PART ONE: LATINO RELIGIOUS LEADERS AND THE CALL TO
STRENGTHEN SOCIAL CAPITAL

Scholars have identified churches as a rich resource for civic involvement (Putnam 2000; Verba, Sidney and Schlozman 1995) and religion—particularly through the Catholic faith—permeates Latino/a culture and identity. Churches are usually the frontline institutions providing social welfare assistance to immigrant communities (Cnaan 1999, 2002; Ebaugh and Chafetz 2000). For Latinos/as and others, churches are dynamic institutions that nurture spiritual beliefs and cultural and civic values, and serve as channels for community involvement. Recent research has shown that the mere presence of churches in blighted neighborhoods has a significant effect on improving life opportunities for church members and their neighbors, most particularly for young people (Sikkink and Hernandez 2003).

Another way in which religious institutions contribute to community well-being is by mobilizing volunteers. According to Harvard researcher Robert Putnam (2000), church-related volunteering represents as much as 50 percent of all of the volunteering that takes place in the United States, and is the primary source of volunteers in the poorest communities. However, there are marked differences in the social, civic and political mobilization of churches according to their racial and ethnic demographics. Latino/a churches are significantly depoliticized when compared to African-American churches (Harris 2003). This is partly due to the large immigrant character of the Latino community, a lack of organized efforts at the local and national levels, and the fact that many clergy interested in civic engagement often lack the skills or imagination to be effective, or they are not part of a larger network engaged in such efforts.

While Latinos/as have higher church attendance rates than Anglo Whites, they participate significantly less frequently in church social outreach programs. Compared to Anglo and African American churches in the city of Philadelphia, for example, Latino churches are significantly less likely to provide social services (Cnaan, Hernandez and McGrew 2005). This is primarily because these churches are more newly established and poorer, and for the most part do not have highly educated clergy. Thus, while Latinos are the largest and fastest growing population in this country and are protagonists of the largest demographic shift in U.S. history, the social service-providing potential among Latino congregations is relatively weak compared to other faith communities.

A recent survey of Latino and Latina seminarians shows differences between religious groups in their levels of community service activity (Table 1).[7] The Evangelical respondents in the study were more likely to be involved in congregations that are active in efforts to reduce community and family violence than their mainline and Catholic counterparts.[8] They were also more involved in providing community sports groups and/or recreational excursions and counseling services. The churches of the Catholic and Evangelical respondents were more involved in efforts to bring the community together (e.g. cultural holiday commemoration, community festivities) than were the mainline churches.

Table 1. Social Service Activities of Churches as Reported by Latino
Seminarians by Denominational Family
*Question: In the last five years, in which of the following activities has your
church been involved?*

	Catholic (n = 125)	Mainline (n = 137)	Evangelical (n = 178)
1. Efforts to reduce community violence (*)	12%	10%	22%
2. Efforts to reduce incidences of family violence (*)	14%	18%	27%
3. Job training and/or helping members of the community secure jobs, better wages or working conditions	10%	13%	16%
4. Helping newly arrived immigrants to establish themselves	21%	17%	22%
5. Drug/alcoholic rehabilitation programs	13%	13%	21%
6. English or citizenship classes	15%	7%	16%
7. Day-cares or child care centers	7%	16%	13%
8. Food co-ops, soup kitchens	25%	26%	27%
9. After school youth programs for teenagers	12%	9%	14%
10. Church/community sports groups and/or recreational excursions (*)	13%	17%	26%
11. Organizing senior citizen programs	16%	13%	10%

---

[7] 2004 Latino Seminarian Survey.

[8] However, the lower number of social services provided by Catholic parishes can be accounted for by the fact that organizations like Catholic Charities play an important role in providing social services across America among Catholics. Also, Catholic parishes often create networks with other parishes and establish and support an FBO to provide social services. For example, in Chicago, the Resurrection Project is a Latino FBO supported by a network of Catholic parishes (see www.resurrectionproject.org).

Table 1. (*cont.*)

	Catholic (n = 125)	Mainline (n = 137)	Evangelical (n = 178)
12. Helping in the provision of shelter for the homeless	12%	11%	12%
13. Helping members to have better access to basic social services (health programs, Medicaid)	14%	9%	14%
14. Counseling services (*)	23%	35%	40%
15. Voter registration	6%	5%	7%
16. Organizing international disaster relief/ humanitarian assistance	11%	9%	10%
17. Efforts to bring the community together (e.g. cultural holiday commemoration, community festivities) (*)	32%	19%	31%
18. Other community outreach	6%	4%	10%

* Differences of 10% or more significant at .05 or less; + significant at .01

Regardless of denomination, pastors and others who serve, facilitate, organize, motivate and inspire their communities are central for mobilizing their communities to expand their sense of mission. As one participant in this study's 2003 focus groups with Latino pastors said,

> The pastor is . . . key in any church, no matter which. If the pastor says 'it does not interest me,' it won't get done. But if the pastor says 'let's do it,' it gets done (Focus group, *Male Baptist Pastor*).

Time and time again research has shown that the critical needs of the people are a daily concern for many men and women in Hispanic ministry, as in this example:

> The community where I serve [is] a community of many, many ethnic groups and it's constantly receiving dozens of new immigrants . . . [We] have a lot of members from like 15 different countries, but the families are fragmented . . . They have to survive in this country, but also they have to feed their families—wherever they have left them . . . They're always constantly in the tension between immigration, housing and education. Many of the parents would love to learn English, but they have to keep at least two jobs in order to survive and do something— even pay the money where they have borrowed money to come (Focus group, *Evangelical Female Pastor*).

A corresponding theme among the Latino/a ministers in focus groups was the demand to perform a wide range of roles in order to respond to the array of needs within their communities. As one Evangelical male pastor described:

> There are great demands on the pastor as a person. A lot of the time, we notice that the leadership does not have the preparation or the knowledge to be able to effectively help the pastor . . . And we find the pastor and a lot of our colleagues acting as social workers, or taxis, or lawyers, painters, etc. This is a *pueblo* that is in a completely different socioeconomic and political situation from the rest. And they have very tangible needs and very few places to go. So, it comes to the church to get help with all of that (Focus group participant).

Giving and financial management in poor immigrant congregations are constant sources of tension and concern in many Latino churches, as attested by a Latina Lutheran pastor:

> I'm no financial genius . . . When you have a poor congregation . . . how do you survive without developing a survival mentality and how do you . . . get what you need to do ministry without agonizing too much over the difficulty of finances? . . . Our council president lost his job a few months ago. He was . . . a victim of the economy. . . . He just recently found a temporary contract job, but I told him we were really praying for him to get a job . . . When you're small one crisis could have an impact and turn into two or three crises in your congregation which can have a major impact on your normal survival situation (Focus group participant).

While being called to minister in distressed communities, many Latino/a clergy and lay-people have benefited from education and training through seminaries and other institutions. The level of education and training differs by denominational affiliation and tradition, however. While the Catholic Church and most mainline Protestant denominations require a seminary graduate degree for their ordained pastors, seminary education is less common among Pentecostal and Evangelical denominations and independent churches. The data from the *National Survey of Hispanic/Latino Theological Education* found that the most formally educated Latino clergy were pastors from Mainline denominations,[9] followed by Roman Catholics[10] and then Evangelicals[11] (Table 2).

---

[9] Episcopalians, Lutherans, Methodists, Presbyterians, United Church of Christ, Disciples of Christ.

[10] Of the 103 Catholics in the sample, 64 percent were Diocesan priests, 33 percent religious order priests, 2 percent lay persons, and 1 percent woman religious.

[11] Baptists, Pentecostals, Seventh-day Adventists, and Non-denominational.

Table 2: Denominational Family by Highest Level of
Education of Clergy (N = 613)

	Roman Catholics (n = 94)	Mainline (n = 178)	Evangelicals (n = 341)
Bible Institute or Diocese Training Program		1%	8%
Some College	7%	7%	11%
College	15%	3%	21%
Master's	56%	70%	46%
Doctorate	16%	18%	12%

Source: *National Survey of Hispanic/Latino Theological Education*

The majority of the Evangelical Latino pastors who participated in this survey were Pentecostals who are more likely to have attended a non-formal theological education institution like a Bible Institute than a seminary or school of theology. Yet despite this, there is an increasing expectation and demand for more formal theological education among this religious sector. Forty-four percent of the Latino/a population now enrolled in ATS institutions have Evangelical backgrounds, of which half come from Pentecostal traditions.[12] The increased emphasis on graduate theological education among Pentecostals is well illustrated by the leading Pentecostal Latino theologian in the United States, Dr. Eldin Villafañe, who states:

> It is imperative that Pentecostal ministers receive higher levels of theological education in order to be more effective in their ministry. A seminary education allows these leaders to move beyond the local congregation, to engage the complexities of the society more effectively. Pentecostal leaders need to be challenged to move beyond their anti-intellectual roots, to discover the ways that education can be useful without threatening their spiritual roots.[13]

In addition to theological training, many pastors feel that other areas of training are increasingly needed to serve the Latino community. The *2004 Latino/a Seminarian Survey* asked students to identify from a list of 12 non-theological skills the three areas in which they would most like to receive additional training. Listed below, by level of

---

[12] 2004 Latino/a Seminarians Survey.
[13] From a consultancy document prepared for The Pew Charitable Trusts, 2000.

importance, are the skill areas that the respondents (n = 523) indicated were important to them.

Seminarians' Training Priorities:

1) Most important skill
   a. Assessing community needs
   b. Managing conflict within the congregation
   c. Leading strategic planning for the church
2) Second most important skill
   a. Starting a community-serving ministry (day care, food pantry etc.)
   b. Managing the financial aspects of the church
   c. Networking with social service providers
3) Third most important skill
   a. Proposal writing skills to support community ministry services
   b. Managing the work of paid staff and volunteers
   c. Risk management (legal aspects of church)

As the evidence indicates, although theological education is critical for Latinos and Latinas, increased training in particular skill areas is also needed and desired. The list of training topics outlined above provides concrete ideas that seminaries, non-profit training centers and the philanthropic community could develop to improve the applicability of theological education and grassroots training.

Still other factors inhibit Latino/a religious leaders from receiving adequate seminary education. A Latino religious denominational leader who participated in one of focus group pointed out how the broader culture in which these leaders serve does not necessarily value or support such formal education:

> We have to realize that we are working with a culture [Hispanic] that basically does not value education in the same way that we [denominational leaders] obviously consider it. So . . . making them jump from where they are to . . . seminary, is similar to saying, "do you want to jump the Grand Canyon?" (Focus group, *Male Baptist Pastor*).

In addition to this kind of resistance to theological education, a lack of an undergraduate degree, finances and other barriers keep many Latino/a leaders from pursuing formal theological education.[14] But

---

[14] For an extensive discussion of these issues see, Reconstructing the Sacred Tower by Edwin I. Hernández and Kenneth Davis.

in a credentialed society, diplomas, certifications and degrees do matter, and provide a critical entrée for employment consideration within denominational structures and for community and philanthropic support. As one Pentecostal pastor put it, "If you don't have your credentials you are invisible to the power structures in your denomination and society."

One of the long-standing successful programs that provides training in non-profit management to religious leaders recently expanded its reach to include the Latino religious community in Minneapolis/St. Paul, Minnesota.[15] In an interview with a group of eight Latino religious leaders who had participated in an eight-week, once-a-week non-profit management certificate program provided by the University of St. Thomas, there was overwhelming consensus about the important value of having a certificate of completion from a recognized university. As one interviewee put it:

> Having that piece of paper saying that I completed the program hanging on my wall and written in my vita—a certificate of completion from a reputable known institution here in town even though it is not a formal degree—has helped open doors to funders and other community organizations. And for someone who doesn't have a college degree that certificate means a lot.

In summary, the church is playing a central role in building stronger neighborhoods in the Latino community. By providing the majority of the volunteering workforce to community, educational and ethnic organizations, congregations and their leaders contribute significantly to the overall civic health of poor immigrant neighborhoods. Yet due to a lack of congregational resources and leadership training the Hispanic religious community is not realizing its full potential. Many leaders lack adequate theological training and those who do attend seminary indicate the need for additional training in community development and nonprofit management.

In the face of such challenges and promise, many Latino churches and faith-based organizations exemplify best practices that have led to the creation of vibrant and transformative social ministries. The

---

[15] Faith Communities Project in Minneapolis/St. Paul, a capacity building program for faith-based organizations working in such areas as housing, day care, education, health care and prison ministries, formed through a partnership of TURN Leadership Foundation, and the University of St. Thomas.

following sections look at two Latino churches and a Latino faith-based organization that stand as such models in order to highlight how their examples might inspire and be replicated in other communities.

PART TWO: ENGAGED CHURCHES IN CHICAGO'S *COMUNIDAD*

Chicago is home to over 750,000 Latinos, who make up 26 percent of the city's population. Though most are of Mexican origin, the city also has large communities of Puerto Ricans, Guatemalans, Salvadorans and other Latin Americans.[16] According to the 2000 census, Chicago Latinos have an average income of $41,000 and about 35 percent of their population is under the age of 18. Moreover, Latinos comprise 27 percent of people living in poverty in the city of Chicago (Paral, Ready, Chun and Sun 2004).

Since Latinos are a growing proportion of Chicago's population, how does religious life in the Latino community affect everyday life in the city? To explore this question, we will profile two churches that have not incorporated into a 501c(3), but whose primary functions are worship *and* service. Though very different from one another, these churches are equally engaged in serving their communities in Chicago.

The Humboldt Park neighborhood lies about 15 minutes west of Chicago's north loop, between Western and Hamlin Avenues. Two impressive Puerto Rican flags flank Division Street as cars pass between Western to California Avenues. Sitting unobtrusively on the north side of the neighborhood is a former dance hall that now houses San Lucas United Church of Christ. Through these church doors, people who need food, clothing, help with heating their homes or support obtaining fair wages can find some respite.

South and east of Humboldt Park is the Pilsen neighborhood, often considered the epicenter for the Mexican and Mexican-American communities in Chicago. Crossing under the numerous railroad tracks that cut diagonally across the southwest side of the city, one emerges in a neighborhood full of stores, restaurants and billboards with signs written in Spanish; street vendors amble down sidewalks. Rising impressively amidst the din of city living is the spire of St. Pius

---

[16] US Census Bureau, 2000.

Church, a Roman Catholic parish near 16th Street and South Ashland Avenue. Many recent immigrants from Latin America come through St. Pius' doors seeking help in finding jobs, housing, or counseling, and a general orientation to the city.

As part of the Chicago Latino Congregations Study, we studied the congregations of San Lucas and St. Pius for nearly six months by interviewing parishioners, pastors, volunteers and lay-leaders at each place and conducting participant observation. Both of the parishes confront similar issues: unemployment, a lack of affordable housing in the neighborhoods that pushes church members outside of *el barrio*, and general help with material needs such as access to food, clothing and energy assistance. The following sections describe the work that these churches do by highlighting how they serve their communities, their leadership and the challenges they confront. It also explores in detail how San Lucas developed one of its community-serving ministries.

San Lucas United Church of Christ

With a three-decade long history of social activism in the mostly Latino neighborhood of Humboldt Park, San Lucas United Church of Christ is a respected and vital presence in the area. While it is composed of about 75 members, the number of people that participate in the church's social services and organizing activities is impressive. San Lucas' committed workers and volunteers are able to serve and mobilize hundreds of people around different social justice causes.

San Lucas houses works of charity and justice in different ways. Workers' rallies and open meetings with elected officials, soup kitchens and food pantry programs, and educational lectures on AIDS, drugs and birth control are part of the array of services and advocacy activities that take place within the walls of San Lucas Church. Serving an average of 475 people per month through their hot meal program, 72 families in the Food Pantry program, and referring 10 families a month to social service agencies, San Lucas Church is an important branch of a broader network of institutions that enable the physical and social survival of the many marginalized men, women and children in Humboldt Park.

By providing space to such programs, San Lucas not only grants other organizations access to its building, but in important symbolic ways it lends legitimacy to the activities those groups promote and practice. Their open doors give a vote of confidence to the actions of those who meet there. Amy Garvin, the director of the San Lucas Workers Center (note that it bears the church's name) says that the support of the local faith community has been critical:

> Without the churches in Chicago, the day labor movement would not move . . . it's important to bring members and leaders from the faith community to this movement. They are not seen as enemies and are not afraid to confront the labor agencies. They help get the different players involved to the negotiating table (*Interview, February 17, 2005*).

San Lucas is also an ecumenical space. A United Church of Christ congregation, its pastor comes from the Methodist tradition, its program coordinator is a Puerto Rican member of a black Pentecostal church on the South Side of Chicago, and two Catholics and a Seventh-day Adventist are among the most committed volunteers in the hot meal program. San Lucas is also an example of active ecumenism in the social justice causes that affect Latinos in Chicago. An ethnographic description of a protest organized by the workers' center gives an idea of this collaboration:

> *A crowd of women, men, children and members from St. Pius Church was already gathered at the corner of 25th Avenue and Central Park. Some of the adults present were wearing t-shirts from the San Lucas Workers Center. Some time later a cameraman from Telemundo arrived to cover the event . . . At 12:30 p.m. the priest from St. Pius arrived, wearing a priest's collar. The director of the San Lucas Workers Center was also there, with two workers and board members from the Center. People were passing signs emblazoned with protest slogans to those present. At 1 p.m. the crowd of more than fifty people walked to 26th Avenue, the main strip of the neighborhood, in order to enter the Day Labor Agency . . . Some of the children who had come with their mothers were carrying signs; one read (in Spanish), "pay our mother so that we can eat" (Participant Observation, August 6, 2004).*

St. Pius Catholic Parish

Together with San Lucas, St. Pius in Pilsen is one of a number of Latino churches and community organizations that form a web of solidarity that, if not powerful enough to stop the structural forces that threaten the already precarious social reality of Latino communities, is strong enough to challenge these issues through their social, material and spiritual support.

Like San Lucas, St. Pius Church offers numerous services for parishioners and community members alike: a youth center—Casa Sor Juana—which offers after school tutoring, computer classes and youth support; a domestic violence counseling program; assistance with workers' issues; voter registration drives; and social service provision. The church also lends its space to numerous community causes: HIV/AIDs information fairs, seminars about human rights in the Americas and immigration forums. The church is the faith home for thousands of Latinos in the Pilsen neighborhood. Led by two Spanish-speaking Anglo priests, St. Pius also has a large staff of lay-leaders from the community who routinely help develop and lead many programs.

One issue that sets St. Pius apart from other Catholic Latino churches is its work to address domestic violence in its community. The church decided to create a counseling and advocacy program for women experiencing abuse after many women came to the church looking for help and support. Through counseling, referrals, drama and education, the program is helping women and children confront this issue, as well as assisting them in seeking employment, economic security and safety.

While this is just a brief overview of the work done by San Lucas and St. Pius, the following sections discuss the development of one of the programs at San Lucas and illuminate the themes that clergy and lay-leaders have expressed as strengths and challenges to building community serving ministries.

Building Community Ministry: How One Program Works

On most weekdays, the small offices of San Lucas United Church of Christ are filled with people: families lined up waiting to fill out forms to get assistance with heating bills, men and women waiting for the Tuesday hot meal, mothers looking for food and clothing donations, and workers asking for help in addressing workplace grievances.

On one wintry day, the director of the Workers Center is talking to several day laborers that have come in complaining that they have not received paychecks from the temporary work agency that employs them. The San Lucas Workers Center[17] helps contingent

---

[17] See Jobs with Justice-Chicago website for more information (www.chicago-jwj.org).

laborers—those who obtain "day jobs" through temporary job agencies—gain access to safe, affordable jobs and forces companies to treat laborers fairly. Their work involves lobbying, direct action and education around workers' issues. They also help connect workers with legal assistance, and work to craft legislation that protects and supports day laborers.

The center started as a cooperative of several groups in the city that were working on labor issues: the Chicago Coalition for the Homeless, Chicago Jobs with Justice, the Chicago Interfaith Committee on Workers' Issues, and the Center for Urban and Economic Development at the University of Illinois-Chicago. At that time they called themselves the "Day-Labor Collective." As a church, San Lucas had been involved in helping people who had been abused by these day labor agencies and had worked with the other organizations in the collective. The pastor and parishioners were supportive of the issue, going to rallies and speaking out about labor issues in the church and in the wider community.

Eventually, San Lucas decided to donate its space to help develop a more permanent organization focused on day labor issues. The collective then became known as the San Lucas Workers Center, and it is no longer a cooperative but a 501c(3) organization. Being located in Humboldt Park is particularly important since many day laborers and day labor agencies are located in the surrounding neighborhoods. Thus, having a presence there was and has been important to giving the issue visibility.

The church helped establish the center by volunteering materials and labor, and assisting board and staff development. The director stated that:

> The church has given us low-cost rent and cheap utilities . . . they also let us use the church van sometimes, or have donated food for some events . . . we've also used church facilities for activities or sometimes we'll get administrative support from them, such as use of the fax machine (*Interview, February 17, 2005*).

The church has further supported the center's work by helping get people out to rallies, discussing labor issues as theological and moral issues during Sunday services, and conducting joint fund-raising efforts with the pastor.

The work that the church does and has done around labor issues has been almost entirely in partnership with community groups and other churches. San Lucas already had a number of lay-leaders engaged in other community issues. Consequently, the engaged clergy and laity recognized workers' issues as theological and moral issues worthy of attention. Out of this framework of understanding workers' issues as religious issues, San Lucas was willing to work in collaboration with these community groups on day labor issues and helped give birth to the San Lucas Workers Center.

What Works: Strengths in Program Development

The previous descriptions illuminate the different types of work that Latino churches are doing in Chicago: helping the homeless, providing material and emotional assistance to low-income families, addressing domestic violence and challenging labor policies. However, there are many limitations that churches experience in doing this work. Both San Lucas and St. Pius do a lot with little money and small numbers of volunteers and paid staff.

Before discussing the obstacles they face, it is worthwhile to highlight areas that capture the strengths of these two churches as they work to develop economic survival strategies for low-income people. Their success strategies include engaged and participatory leadership, collaboration, theological frameworks that promote justice and engagement, and connection to funding and material resources.

1. Leadership: Lay-women in Church and Community Work

San Lucas is an important example of the central role of women in ministry, not just in the everyday work of church maintenance and service provision, but also the charismatic and efficient leadership essential to the development of community ministries. Women hold all of the leadership positions in the ministries at San Lucas. Of these, three are Puerto Rican and one is Anglo. Likewise, even though women cannot be ordained in the Catholic tradition, many of St. Pius' most engaged lay-leaders are women who coordinate base communities, run youth programs and advocate on behalf of domestic violence survivors.

Although other institutions in the city often marginalize Latinas, work in churches' community-serving ministries gives women a chance to develop leadership skills that they might not otherwise have learned. Involvement in these church ministries allows women to hone their leadership skills and deepen their knowledge of community needs.

Furthermore, these churches rely on the work and leadership of lay-people; pastoral care and work are not the sole jurisdiction of members of the clergy. Both of the churches profiled here, perhaps because their clergy are already time-strapped, have to rely on the work of lay-people. Further, their leadership is not hierarchical but egalitarian and participatory; at San Lucas it is often Cristina, the church council leader, who directs volunteers, organizes outreach events and leads meetings. She does so with the blessing and assistance of the pastor, who encourages the leadership of others.

2. *Collaboration*

At both San Lucas and St. Pius, collaboration is essential to developing community ministries, leveraging funding, establishing relationships with political allies and sharing resources. This collaboration takes several forms: interdenominational connections, relationships with non-religious groups and inter-ethnic and racial collaboration. For example, the hot meal program at San Lucas runs smoothly with the consistent help from Seventh-day Adventist, Catholic, Pentecostal and UCC volunteers recruited through their respective churches.

One vehicle for the development of the San Lucas Worker Center was collaboration with other churches including neighborhood Catholic, UCC and Methodist churches. Pastors at each of these churches helped to get people out to rallies. Collaboration also happens with non-Latino churches: San Lucas receives a lot of its funds for ministries from Anglo UCC churches in the suburbs that commit to funding San Lucas programs in Chicago.

Furthermore, collaboration with foundations is important for establishing a funding base. For example, the San Lucas Workers Center became its own fiscal agent through collaboration between already-established community groups and stable, active churches. The center's relationships with foundations came through other community groups who already had connections or had received funds from Chicago-based foundations.

Finally, collaboration with non-religious groups is also important for such efforts. The Workers Center came out of this collaboration with community-based groups. As Amy, the Center's director, says:

> The Chicago Coalition for the Homeless (CCH) was working to get a program out in Humboldt, where a lot of the day labor agencies

are located . . . San Lucas had supported CCH's work in the neighborhood. So, the church became a partner [leading to the development of the center] (*Interview, February 17, 2005*).

Churches that are willing to partner with non-religious groups develop
important relationships to help fund, build and sustain their programs. San Lucas offered what they could to community groups that
wanted to build a workers center: low-rent space, an identity tied to
a historically active church, and participation by church leaders in
promoting workers' issues as religious issues.

3. *Theology and Calling*
Theological frameworks can also provide an incentive for engaging
in social justice work and service provision. At San Lucas, all segments of the work are understood theologically, from preparing the
hot meal to engaging day labor agencies in fair labor practices.
Indeed, the pastor's sermons on Sunday morning often reflect the
biblical call to justice.

In a similar vein, homilies at St. Pius often focus on justice. For
example, in a homily based on the parable of the rich young man,
the priest illustrated the gospel reading with the example of real
estate developers who buy cheap land from the city, then move low-
income residents from this property to make way for developing
expensive condos for the wealthy.

Consequently, the theological framework of the church and its
leaders can enable the development of these programs. Leaders who
suggest that caring for the dispossessed and questioning the power
of the wealthy are matters of theological concern provide the impe-
tus for agitating for the oppressed.

4. *Connecting to Resources*
While St. Pius and San Lucas run many programs with little outside money, their institutional connections enable them to leverage
the support that they do receive. For example, San Lucas' hot meal
program functions solely on money donated from Anglo UCC
churches. Thus an independent church without ties to some institutional structure might have difficulty raising money for a program.
In addition, San Lucas' work with community groups has put them
in contact with private foundations that fund these types of ministries, illustrating how networking with non-religious groups and
other churches is important for connecting with funding sources.

St. Pius also thrives in part because of its connections to an institutional body—in its case, the Catholic Archdiocese of Chicago. This relationship can help provide access to monies for program development and implementation. However, all of these resources are limited, which leads to some of the challenges that these two churches face in developing their ministries.

Challenges: Barriers to Program Development

Although they come from two distinct religious traditions, both of the churches we have profiled encounter similar barriers to creating community serving ministries: the time constraints and multiple roles of ministers, denominational barriers and a lack of technical assistance with tasks such as grant writing and program evaluation. Even though some of these issues are also strengths—for example, the church's theology or support from larger religious bodies can help grow programs—they can also be barriers to serving the community. The sections below elaborate on these issues.

1. Multiple Roles: Bi-vocational Pastors

It is difficult to exaggerate the amount of work required from a pastor committed to social justice in her community. Poverty, lack of affordable housing, immigrant rights, gang violence, domestic violence and HIV/AIDS are just a few of the issues in a litany of challenges faced by many Latino communities. Numerous meetings, logistics, preaching and emails (for those who have a computer and a connection) are just part of the "to-do list" of social activism and pastoral care. Particularly when a pastor has two jobs, the situation can become extremely burdensome. This is often the case for the pastor of San Lucas.

When asked what she thinks is lacking or needed in order to improve some of the programs in the church, Lisa Jimenez, the social service coordinator at San Lucas, said:

> I wish a pastor could be here [during the week's hot meal program] . . . people might be more respectful if that presence were here. There are some things that a pastor could help them with, too (*Participant Observation, February 1, 2005*).

For Lisa, the spiritual dimension of the program, while not totally absent, could be much stronger with the pastor's presence. According to her, the mere presence of a pastor could impose a feeling of respect and order to their soup kitchen program. Interestingly, based on our field observations, the lack of a pastor's presence in this program has allowed for Lisa's impressive leadership skills to fill that supposed vacuum, as is evident from the following field notes that document this:

> *Before starting to serve food, Lisa tells everyone to be silent in order to pray and welcome the presence of God. She does not allow the meal to begin until the men have taken off their hats and everyone has bowed their heads. She directs the prayer, and some follow, murmuring their "Amens" and thanking God for the food. One must see how more than one hundred people, mostly men, become silent and, if not pray, at least wait with respect, until she has pronounced the last words . . . She tells them to keep their heads up, that God loves them, and that things will get better for them. Soon after the prayer is done, she is firmly relaying instructions to a kitchen-full of volunteers, stirring soup with one hand while directing the activities of the kitchen so that she can feed 150 people in a matter of an hour (Participant Observation, February 1, 2005).*

Lisa's charisma and active engagement flourish in the hot meal program, where she is both the coordinator and the *de facto* "pastor." In this case an institutional need and "weakness" becomes a "capacity building" possibility for a lay leader.

2. *Institutional Constraints: Denominational Structures and Traditions*

One of the founders of San Lucas Church, Reverend Jose Villa, argues that:

> The struggles of the present church today [have] much to do with the kind of leadership that it develops . . . it is a matter of whether or not leadership is transformative [or just focused on] soul saving and cultivating people's individual spirituality (*Interview, February 23, 2005*).

Shaped by the social and political experiences of the 1960s and 1970s, Reverend Villa promotes a theology of liberation that sees God as "an empowering God, an historical, political . . . and liberating God." Villa's work has been marked by his engagement with community organizations and social activists that he would characterize as among the "best leaders in Chicago."

For Villa there are two main challenges for mainline Protestants churches today. One of these is the lack of commitment and resources dedicated to the formation of "transformative" leadership (or leadership that is socially and politically engaged in social justice work). The second challenge is the absence of support for the Latino community and its religious leaders. This absence of support is expressed in the dearth of training facilities and programs targeting Latinos. Seminaries, religious studies programs and ministry resources show a glaring lack of Latino presence and attention to Latino community needs. Reverend Villa argues that this lack of institutional support in turn discourages the emergence of Latino/a religious leaders in the church.

Consequently, mainline Protestant churches in Chicago must engage in pastoral "lending" in order to survive and continue their religious work. For example, one may find a Methodist pastor ministering in a United Church of Christ, or a Presbyterian minister leading a Methodist Church. A barrier to building community serving ministries in Latino neighborhoods is the real lack of Latino leadership in these denominations.

However, one can also see an interesting opportunity in this "weakness." For example, the possibility of a truly ecumenical religious and social engagement in denominations that lack leaders of their same faith tradition is illustrated in the case of San Lucas, where a Methodist pastor serves her United Church of Christ congregation. An important challenge is increasing new Latino/a denominational leadership while at the same time maintaining and developing existing ecumenical collaboration. The case of the San Lucas Workers Center illustrates the importance of collaboration between UCC, Methodist and Catholic churches.

In addition, the denomination or tradition can constrain the development of a community ministry through its theology. For example, a staff member at St. Pius who works in the domestic violence program claims that more conservative church members accuse the counselors of "promoting divorce." In this case, the faith tradition's view of marriage as a sacrament affects and influences the support (or lack of support) that they receive in this particular program. Thus, this understanding of marriage limits the support that some churches might receive for a domestic violence program or other programs in general.

3. Lack of Program Evaluation and Grant Writing Skills

According to a staff member, one issue that the domestic violence program at St. Pius confronts is accessing funds from private foundations and finding someone to write grant proposals for the church's programs. She claims that foundations are more interested in "results and exit numbers." Foundations that are concerned with program evaluation and "maximizing efficiency" in programs do not understand that "the women who use the program at St. Pius stay in the program for support and leadership, not co-dependence." She suggests that just because their program does not exit participants "quickly," does not mean that they are not successful in assisting women who live in violent homes. She interprets the emphasis on program evaluation as something that can hamper the work of some churches, given differing understandings of "success."

Consequently, it is hard to gain access to private funding when there is a disconnection between the understood priorities of foundations and the philosophy of a particular church program. Foundations could do more to help church programs understand the merits of program evaluation and how it might be used constructively, and they could support efforts to training more lay-people in grant writing.

PART THREE: LEADERSHIP IN LATINO FAITH-BASED ORGANIZATIONS

The Role of Intermediary Organizations—The Case of Nueva Esperanza and the Hispanic Capacity Project

Now more than ever, Latino organizations and churches dot the horizon of many large U.S. cities in the United States. Both for their numbers and contributions, the Latino community has caught the attention of churches, community groups and politicians who are taking note of the important work that Latinos are doing in their communities. In this section, we explore the critical role of intermediary organizations in strengthening grassroots Latino faith community organizations; in particular we describe the capacity building efforts of one intermediary organization and present a case study of a Latino faith-based organization that has been transformed by its efforts.[18]

In 1987, a network of more than 80 clergy in the Philadelphia area representing over 20 religious denominations took shape under the leadership of Reverend Luis Cortés, Jr. This so-called "Hispanic

---

[18] We define "Latino faith-based organizations" as organizations whose leadership and primary serving population are majority Latino. In order to be "faith-based," these groups also grew out of religious organizations and/or churches and have a faith component as part of their mission.

Clergy" network in turn formed Nueva Esperanza, Inc., which would eventually become the nation's largest Hispanic faith-based community development corporation. Nueva Esperanza's mission statement calls for the establishment of Hispanic owned-and-operated institutions that lead to the familial, economic and spiritual development of the community.[19]

Today, Nueva Esperanza is a leading Latino-led community organization primarily serving the northeastern section of the city of Philadelphia, while Esperanza USA—its national subsidiary—operates nationwide programs such as the Hispanic Capacity Project (HCP). HCP emerged as a faith-based response to the complexity of the Hispanic experience in the United States. Funded by the U.S. Department of Health and Human Services, HCP has provided a total of 140 organizations in six cities across the country (Los Angeles, Miami, New York, Orlando, Philadelphia and Seattle) with training in non-profit management and thousands of dollars' worth of technical assistance.

Through its three main interventions—training, technical assistance and small grants—the Hispanic Capacity Project aims to strengthen the organizational capacity and the leadership of churches and faith-based community organizations. As the following case study of a HCP participating organization attests, training and technical assistance can have a major impact on the leadership development and organizational growth of a faith-based organization.

Responding to a Higher Call: Women's Shelter of Hope

Women's Shelter of Hope is a faith-based organization in Hialeah, Florida that serves survivors of domestic violence. The organization started in 1996 when its founder, Norma Rodriguez, moved to Florida after leaving an abusive home. Rodriguez now considers that move as "part of God's plan for her ministry." She recently graduated from college with a bachelor's degree in Christian Ministry and has an associate degree in business.

Women's Shelter of Hope was officially incorporated in 2001, and received its 501c(3) status in August of 2002. Initially, it had no budget or space and worked as a volunteer-only organization for two

---

[19] See http://www.esperanza.us for further information.

and-a-half years. All funds obtained during this time were small monetary grants and in-kind donations of food and clothing.

In the spring of 2003, Rodriguez' mentor from the University of Florida referred her to the Hispanic Capacity Project. Women's Shelter of Hope was one of the 25 organizations initially selected for training and capacity building through the HCP in the Miami area. Just two years later, the shelter that began with an annual budget of $6,000 and no paid staff now operates a budget of about $300,000, has three full-time employees, two office spaces, and three on-going grants funding its ever-expanding programs.

As a direct outcome of the training provided within the Hispanic Capacity Project, Rodriguez's grant-writing skills improved considerably, which consequently increased the organization's funding capacity. Women's Shelter of Hope obtained an initial capacity development grant as a sub-award for Hispanic Capacity Project participants for a total of $5,000. In the second year, the organization was awarded another capacity development grant of $6,800.

Soon after, Norma Rodriguez started networking with local stakeholders. She applied for and received two contracts: a county contract for three years worth $45,000 per year, and a district contract of $25,000 per year that is annually renewable. After receiving both contracts, she contacted city officials to request space for her organization and was given two offices free of charge. Understanding the benefits of leveraging funds and applying her newly obtained skills, she submitted a third proposal to Nueva Esperanza and was awarded a strategic leverage grant for year three for a total amount of $30,000.

Women's Shelter of Hope now has seven beds and a referral network with the other shelters in the area. They provide emergency food and clothing through a network established with churches, businesses in the community, and faith-based support groups. They also assist clients in getting legal support to address matters like restraining orders, child support and residency issues.

The organization serves a total of 300 to 350 people annually, with 200 new clients added since receiving the county and district contracts. As it has grown, Women's Shelter of Hope has had to consider developing new programs to meet the emerging needs of the community. Changes in the population it assists have also precipitated a broadening of its organizational vision, since 23 percent of the people they now serve are male victims of domestic violence, and 63 percent are undocumented immigrants.

When asked about her vision for the future, Norma listed three grant proposals that will allow the organization to increase services in the crucial areas of education, legal and social services. The ultimate dream is to establish a holistic center for victims of domestic violence that will include a 40-bed shelter, social services that address physical and psychological needs, educational services for women and children, legal advice and support for independent living through job training and job placement.

The services that Women's Shelter of Hope offers to Latina women who are domestic violence survivors provide a critical alternative to the English-only services available, thus addressing the language barriers that can prevent women from even asking for help. Norma's deep faith has compelled her to create a safe haven for undocumented immigrant women who are abused by their partners and of a system that does not offer them many options. Her efforts to pursue funding and convince donors to support her mission are fueled by her conviction that she has been called to do this work, and thus cannot do otherwise. As she expressed it, "sometimes even I don't know how I will do all that I set up to do, but I go by faith, and I cannot stop!" (*Norma Rodriguez, interview, 2005*).

Best Practices in Leadership Development in Latino Faith-Based Organizations

What can leaders of Hispanic faith-based organizations learn from groups like Women's Shelter of Health? What best practices does this case study illustrate? The following list identifies areas in which leadership and program development, in the case of Women's Shelter of Hope, contributed to overall growth of the organization. These lessons are representative of the information learned from other HCP case studies, and include the following:

- THEOLOGY AND CALLING: A sense of "calling" derived from deep faith is a key leadership characteristic of effective service. In most of the successful Latino FBOs that we have studied, a sense that the work derives from a spiritual call to a particular community sustains the vision and the commitment of such efforts. Another important element of effective Latino religious leadership is having a theology that promotes civic engagement and understands social ministry as an essential aspect of the call of the Gospel.
- ENTREPRENEURSHIP: Another characteristic of effective leadership is

having an entrepreneurial spirit. In our case study the leader demonstrated an extraordinary ability to identify needs and mobilize people and resources to create a program to meet those needs.

- NETWORKING AND COLLABORATION: Networking capacity is a key factor to the success of Latino faith-based organizations. Women's Shelter of Hope pursued relationships with local authorities and other groups to secure concrete resources (e.g.: building space), volunteers and referrals for a variety of needs (e.g.: legal matters, housing, food).

- NEEDS ASSESSMENT: The ability to accurately identify the needs in one's community and to comprehend their underlying causes and potential solutions is critical for effective leadership. Norma Rodriguez was able to identify needs through her personal experience and knowledge, as well as by paying attention to the changes in the shelter's clientele in order to adapt the services offered to meet the needs of the population.

- INTERMEDIARY ORGANIZATIONS: Women's Shelter of Hope attributes its recent success in organizational growth to the impact of Nueva's HCP. Through the training, technical assistance, grants program, networking and mentoring received through the HCP, the organization's leader gained expertise, guidance and inspiration that resulted in significant organizational growth, and positioned the organization for future funding and sustainability.

Challenges to Leadership and Program Development

The barriers and challenges that affect program development and effective community ministry as described by the leader profiled in the case study are as follows:

- STAFF STABILITY: While volunteer laborers are committed to serving the community, other external factors and circumstances (such as professional and personal life demands) affect their long-term commitment. The presence of paid, designated employees does increase the effectiveness and sustainability of such programs.

- LEVEL OF TRAINING/EXPERTISE: Organizational growth is highly dependent upon the increased skills of the leaders. Faith-based organizations are frequently understaffed, which leads to individuals multi-tasking without the accompanying level of expertise. This is particularly true in the areas of financial management and accounting.

- MOTIVATION AND LONG-TERM COMMITMENT: Successful leaders of the FBOs we have studied are highly motivated individuals with a strong sense of commitment to serve their communities. They persist in their efforts despite a lack of financial support, and identify their deep faith and love of service as that which sustains their long-term efforts.
- LANGUAGE BARRIERS: Though the ability to offer services in Spanish is absolutely critical, Latino leaders who are not proficient in English recognize the need to improve their English language skills and/or surround themselves with a team of leaders who are proficient in English in order to network with individuals and organizations outside of the Latino community, and to help the people they serve negotiate English-dominant services and systems. In response to this reality, Nueva made sure that all instructors/trainers were bilingual and used a combination of materials and presentation techniques in both English and Spanish.

Though this list of strengths and challenges is not exhaustive, it does point to some concrete examples of where training and technical assistance can develop and strengthen the serving capacity of Latino community and faith based organizations. Part Four will give specific recommendations for strengthening leaders and the social service programs in Latino community-serving congregations and faith-based organizations.

PART FOUR: RECOMMENDATIONS FOR STRENGTHENING EFFECTIVE
COMMUNITY MINISTRY

In this last part we provide a list of actions steps and recommendations that, if implemented, can significantly help Latino churches and faith-based organizations to more effectively serve vulnerable populations. These recommendations are presented in the order of the group to whom they are directed: churches and faith-based organizations; denominations, seminaries, colleges and universities; foundations; and city or government agencies.

A. LATINO CHURCHES AND FAITH-BASED ORGANIZATIONS: Through interviews, case studies, focus groups with participants in the HCP and our observations with exemplary community serving churches, we recommend the following steps to Latino churches and faith-based organizations and their leadership.

1. ASSESS YOUR CHURCH'S STRENGTHS AND WEAKNESSES: What human skills and talents can you count on as you begin or expand your social ministry? Understanding the abilities of your congregants and mobilizing church volunteers to use their gifts for the benefit of the church's ministry is key to effective community ministry.

2. IDENTIFY AND ASSESS COMMUNITY NEEDS: Excellent community ministry efforts begin with a thorough assessment of the actual needs of your community. This can be accomplished through interviews, surveys and contact with key community figures (Ammerman, Caroll, Dudley and McKinney 1998).

3. INCREASE FUND-RAISING CAPACITY: The most common need expressed by both churches and faith-based organizations is strengthening and expanding fundraising capacity. Leaders should consult with local organizations dedicated to supporting fundraising efforts and network with intermediaries on a given social ministry to access other resources.

4. INCREASE NETWORKING CAPACITY: Latino religious leaders who network with other churches and/or community organizations are more likely to succeed in their community serving efforts. Thus, establishing relationships with other churches, faith-based organizations, non-profits agencies or government services is critically important for any successful community serving effort.

5. INCREASE TRAINING: Despite limited opportunities to access and finance formal education, Latino pastors need to do all that they can to access training and educational opportunities. English language skills, formal theological education and non-profit management training are all critical areas to develop.

6. LEADERSHIP STYLE AND LAY-LEADERSHIP FORMATION: Latino leaders need to adopt a participatory style of leadership with increased involvement of lay-people, particularly women. Since churches are the primary sources for the volunteering work force in the Latino community, Latino leaders have an urgent responsibility to train, inspire and delegate responsibilities to lay men and women who share a passion for service.

7. ESTABLISHING A SEPARATE LEGAL ENTITY: Churches who want to increase their social service impact, professionalize their programs and expand their funding base should seriously consider establishing a separate 501c(3) entity.

B. DENOMINATIONS, SEMINARIES AND UNIVERSITIES: Though Latinos are the fastest growing demographic group in all of the major Christian denominations in the United States, Latinos lag significantly behind other groups in educational access and training opportunities.

1. INCREASED EDUCATIONAL SUPPORT: Denominations in collaboration with seminaries, colleges/universities and other relevant groups need to develop programs, facilitate access and provide financial support to make higher levels of formal theological education available to Latino religious leaders. This includes developing Latino-focused studies at seminaries, ministry centers and Bible Institutes, with particular attention to the needs of urban Latino communities.

2. LATINO THEOLOGY OF SOCIAL ENGAGEMENT: Clearly articulating a theology of social engagement and responsibility rooted in and relevant to the Latino reality is of extreme importance in mobilizing congregations and their leaders to embrace ministries to assist the most vulnerable populations.

3. INCREASED COLLABORATION BETWEEN EDUCATIONAL INSTITUTIONS: Seminaries, schools of religion, Bible institutes and Diocesan training programs particularly in cities with major concentrations of Latinos need to embrace the task of educating Latinos. Specific attention needs to be given to creating a pipeline that moves candidates from lower levels of educational attainment to graduate levels of formal theological education and other non-profit management training.

4. COLLABORATION WITH COLLEGES AND UNIVERSITIES: Christian colleges and universities have an important role to play in identifying and training Latino leaders. Educational institutions with business and non-profit training academic programs should collaborate with intermediaries or other grassroots networks to organize training programs specifically geared towards developing non-profit management skills necessary to carry out effective social ministries.

C. FOUNDATIONS AND DONORS: Latino churches have an untapped potential for affecting social good that is often unrecognized by the philanthropic community. At the same time, Latino churches and faith-based organizations lack access to private financial resources to carry out their community ministries. Many foundations are not familiar with the Latino religious community or with the work that they are doing. Thus in many places throughout this country the philanthropic community and the Latino religious community are not at all connected. To address this we recommend that they:

1. CREATE OPPORTUNITIES TO GET ACQUAINTED WITH THE LATINO FAITH COMMUNITY: Foundations should work through established networks of seminaries, pastoral associations, Bible institutes and diocesan training programs to gain access to the grassroots leaders and establish listening sessions in order for both groups to get better acquainted.

2. ESTABLISH SMALL GRANTS PROGRAM: Foundations should establish small grants programs together with technical assistance to help build organizational capacity in Latino faith communities.

3. DEVELOP TRAINING PROGRAMS: Local foundations in collaboration with other intermediaries or educational institutions should develop leadership training and organizational capacity building programs in the basic skill areas of managing social service programs, and particularly in the area of fund development, grant writing and outcome assessment.

D. CITY AND GOVERNMENT SOCIAL SERVICE AGENCIES: Many cities and states are establishing offices of faith-based and community initiatives in recognition of the key role that religious organizations play in providing services to the community. However, in many immigrant communities with limited English language skills a greater degree of social distance exists between government and grassroots religious organizations. Only intentional efforts can build a bridge between these two sectors.

1. INCREASE OUTREACH EFFORTS TO THE LATINO RELIGIOUS COMMUNITY: Government social service outreach efforts should intentionally seek opportunities to network with Latino religious leaders. Understanding the key role that churches play in providing the majority of the volunteering work force to the civic and non-profit sector should alert agencies of the need to strengthen relationships with the religious community. This is particularly true for the health and educational systems where the religious community could be potential partners in health prevention efforts and helping young people stay educationally on track.

2. INCREASE CAPACITY BUILDING EFFORTS: Government agencies
in partnership with foundations and other non-profit organizations could facilitate increased opportunities to provide technical assistance and training to Latino religious leaders.

CONCLUSION

While these steps are not exhaustive, they enumerate practical and
realistic action that can significantly assist Latino churches and faith-
based organizations in their community-serving ministries. Without
the material and spiritual assistance of churches like St. Pius and
San Lucas and faith-based organizations like Women's Shelter of
Hope, many vulnerable people, literally, might not survive. Their
work has also fostered the coincidental development of important
community leaders, many of whom are women.

The leadership practices in the case studies presented above highlight the importance of engaged, transformative clergy and lay-people
faithfully responding to the needs of those around them. As one
focus group respondent declared, "community-based organizations
exist as long as there is funding; faith-based organizations exist with
or without funding, as long as there are needs to be addressed, and
wounds to be healed" (Focus group, *HCP 2003*).

The United States is facing one of the greatest demographic shifts
in its history due in large measure to the unprecedented growth of
the Latino community, which is significantly affecting the educational, health, civic and political sectors of our country. Latino
churches and faith-based organizations are the first-response organizations providing basic services to vulnerable populations, particularly immigrants with limited English language skills. Finding ways
to enhance the leadership and the organizational capacity of these
organizations by leveraging support from denominations, seminaries,
colleges and universities, foundations and government agencies are
important steps to ensure the future health of America's neighborhoods.

REFERENCES

Ammerman, Nancy T., Jackson W. Carroll, Carl S. Dudley, and William McKinney,
     eds. 1998. *Studying Congregations: A New Handbook.* Nashville, TN: Abingdon Press.

Cnaan, Ram A. 1999. *The Newer Deal: Social Work and Religion in Partnership.* New York: Columbia University Press.

———. 2002. *The Invisible Caring Hand.* New York: New York University Press.

Cnaan, Ram A., Edwin Hernández, and Charlene C. McGrew. 2005. "Latino Congregations in Philadelphia." Unpublished paper. Center for the Study of Latino Religion at the University of Notre Dame.

Ebaugh, H. R., and J. Chafetz. 2000. *Religion and the New Immigrants: Continuities and Adaptations in Immigrant Congregations.* Walnut Creek: Altamira Press.

Harris, Fredrick. 2003. "Ties That Bind and Flourish: Religion as Social Capital in African-American Politics." In *Religion as Social Capital: Producing the Common Good*, pp. 121–138. Waco, Texas: Baylor University Press.

Paral, Rob, Timothy Ready, Sung Chun, and Wei Sun. 2004. "Latino Demographic Growth in Metropolitan Chicago." In *Research Reports: A Series of Papers by the Institute for Latino Studies and Research Associates.* December, 2004, vol. 2.

Putnam, Robert D. 2000. *Bowling Alone.* New York: Simon and Schuster.

Sikkink, David, and Edwin I. Hernández. 2003. "Religion Matters: Predicting Schooling Success Among Latino Youth." Interim Reports (1). Notre Dame: Institute for Latino Studies, University of Notre Dame.

Verba, Sidney, Kay Lehman Schlozman, and Henry E. Brady. 1995. *Voice and Equality: Civic Voluntarism in American Politics.* Cambridge, MA: Harvard University Press.

CONCLUSION

Taken together, the chapters of this book provide a detailed and compelling portrait of Hispanic ministry today and make a unique, significant contribution to scholarly literature on the topic. The sociology of religion in the United States has yet to examine the Latino experience with anything like the kind of attention given to many other ethnic communities in the past. This book's primary contribution is that it helps to fill that lacuna. In particular, it is one of the few to give equal consideration to the experiences of U.S. Hispanics from Catholic, Protestant and Evangelical faith traditions. As the Latino population continues to grow—and Hispanics' religious preferences and practices shift or show continuity—such ecumenical studies will be increasingly needed and helpful.

COMMON THEMES

As the introduction mentioned, our contributors worked independently and used varying methodologies, yet arrived at very similar conclusions. While their research uncovered rich detail and many differences, common themes also emerged from their findings. Both anecdotally and through rigorous empirical work, for example, our authors discovered that Latinos describe good ministry as joining head and heart, church and community, spiritual and worldly concerns and aptitudes. And contrary to previous scholarly assessments of Hispanic churches as politically and social inactive, these studies show that Latino churches and their leaders are delivering an amazing breadth of social ministries throughout the country, with a tremendous value for the communities they serve.

Far from being unaware of or unengaged in the social and political life of their surrounding communities, Hispanic congregations are reaching out to make a difference. At the same time, our authors concur that Hispanic churches cannot yet draw upon the strong infrastructure for social service provision that the Anglo-American and African American communities enjoy. Especially among Protestant denominations, there is growing recognition that churches must work harder to attract, retain and train Latino pastors. They are also investing varying levels of resources and attention in recruiting Hispanic lay leaders and congregation members. Similarly, Latinos are under-represented among Catholic clergy (especially in proportion to the number of Latinos who are Catholic), but the percentage of Hispanics in lay ministry formation programs and diaconate programs is growing.

It's a hopeful sign, yet the bulk of these Catholic lay leaders are involved in non-formal theological education programs, better known as certificate training programs. While this training is very helpful and in most instances the only option available, such programs do not guarantee access to leadership positions at the parish or diocesan levels, which often require formal graduate degrees. Thus, one of the greatest challenges facing the Catholic Latino church is the training and development of leadership with formal degrees.

Around the country, our authors found that faith leaders are tremendously committed to community service but need support, resources, training and networking opportunities to avoid burnout and to gain practical skills. Across denominations, leadership development requires an immediate and significant investment. Future Latino and Latina church leaders need better access to formal seminary education; those who are already heading congregations need affordable, short-term training opportunities to become more effective. Support for Hispanic women in ministry is of utmost importance. Latinas are under-represented in seminaries and other training programs and among clergy in general, despite their obvious (and potential) contributions to church and community. As one author observed, equally important to increasing Latinas' access to seminary education is making sure that educational curricula in every setting are relevant to the real needs of the communities that Hispanic men and women serve.

As this book has repeatedly noted, a concrete barrier that Latino/a ministers confront daily is the lack of financial assets available to their communities and to them as individuals. Latinos who wish to enter ministry start out with lower incomes and this situation doesn't change as they become pastors; it is common for them to be bivocational and earn their principal income in a setting other than their churches. Despite these difficulties, they confront challenges creatively and collaboratively. Indeed, this book shows time and again that an outstanding strength of Hispanic church leaders is their collaborative style, whether it means partnering with other churches, with congregation members or with local government to get things done.

Independently, the chapters also confirm that the young age of the growing U.S. Latino population represents a challenge and an opportunity for faith leaders. More than one-third of U.S. Latinos are 18 years old or younger and across denominations, churches are increasingly aware that they should do more to minister to Latino youth. These young people have tremendous potential for leadership but at the same time, fewer educational opportunities than non-Latinos. How pastors, churches and faith-based organizations deal with this reality will have a major impact on U.S. society in the future.

Despite demographic and denominational differences, Hispanics share important commonalities when it comes to religion. According to various surveys they are more likely than non-Hispanics to see religion as an important part of their daily lives; they have a greater trust in clergy; they face common obstacles to leadership; they are devout and attend church fairly regularly. Yet while commonalities are important, our studies repeatedly prove that awareness of differences can increase understanding of how Hispanic churches respond uniquely and effectively to community needs. As we have seen, Protestant versus Catholic affiliation and socioeconomic factors like immigration, income/class, education and church attendance are closely related to the types and levels of Hispanic involvement in church-sponsored political and social action. These issues merit further study.

If the past is any guide, Hispanic faith leaders' social and political engagement with their communities will only increase in the coming decades. Research shows that Latino citizens and civic leaders support this trend, although the degree and style of church leaders' involvement will no doubt vary by location and faith tradition. Scholars have begun to explore how religion shapes political attitudes and behaviors in communities across the United States, and as their findings come to light it should further enrich understanding of this important dimension of religious life.

FUTURE DIRECTIONS

These conclusions, like any which are based on solid and thought-provoking research, lead to further questions. What directions should research on Hispanic ministry take in the future? We gather our suggestions in three sections: first, we offer questions related to

methodological issues; second, we recommend avenues for study that
relate to specific denominations; third, we list more general areas
that deserve further attention.

METHODOLOGICAL QUESTIONS

- The methodological challenge for those wanting to conduct a
  national study of Latino churches or their leaders is clearly enormous, given that no national list of Latino churches and their
  leaders exists, that denominations have gathered only limited information on Latino churches, and that information on the independent churches is almost nonexistent. How does one generate
  a representative list of Latino churches and/or pastors?
- Given the enormous growth of youth in the Latino population,
  how can scholars conduct research that examines the religious life
  of Latino youth from first and second generation?

DENOMINATIONAL QUESTIONS

- To what extent do Latino Catholics and Protestants show similarities and differences in their involvement in politics and social
  causes? How may their differences and similarities be related to
  their leaders' education, ethnicity and language proficiency?
- Given the scarcity of Latino candidates for the priesthood within
  the Catholic Church, what are the likely pathways, experiences
  and recruitment strategies that can help increase the number of
  candidates for the clergy?
- What are the key factors contributing to Latino churches' getting
  involved in social ministries? How does the level of involvement
  differ by denomination?
- Given the need for the development of Latino religious leadership, particularly among Catholics priests, what is the role of
  Catholic colleges and seminaries in attracting and retaining Latinos
  to the priesthood? In each denomination, what incentives draw
  Hispanics to education that prepares them for the clergy?
- To what extent are Alternative Christian faiths attracting U.S. Hispanics?
  Why? How does such attraction differ by generation, country of
  origin, socio-economic background or previous religious affiliation?
- To what extent are U.S. Hispanics embracing Islam? Why?

GENERAL QUESTIONS

- Women play an increasingly important role in the leadership of churches across denominations. Aside from the theological barriers to full inclusion in ministry, why aren't more Latina women in positions of leadership?
- How might the greater optimism and satisfaction of Hispanic immigrants in relation to their economic future be related to their religious beliefs and practices? How, concretely, does faith serve as a source of strength for Latinos?
- As more Hispanics move from Catholic to Protestant churches, what are the factors contributing to religious switching among Latinos?
- What is the relationship between Latino ethnic identity and the conversion/switching process? Are Latino Protestants/Evangelicals as likely to maintain strong ethnic identification as Latino Catholics?
- In what ways does the church contribute to the development of civic and cultural incorporation of Latino immigrants?
- Are Latinos who are closely connected to religious organizations more or less likely to be civically engaged? And if so, why?
- Hispanic Catholics are less likely to register at a congregation or attend church service than Latino Protestants. Yet the vast majority of Catholic Latinos say religion is a very important aspect of their daily lives. What do these and other apparent contradictions say about uniquely Catholic Hispanic ways of expressing faith?
- If around the United States Latino churches are less involved in providing certain types of social services than non-Latino churches, what are the reasons? Does it have to do with a traditional expectation that the family will care for the elderly, for example, with the stigma attached to certain problems like drug addiction, with Hispanic churches' relatively fewer resources and staff, or other reasons?
- Given the important role that Latino parishes/churches play in providing social services to their local communities, how can they be encouraged or trained to improve and expand their services?

Beyond their interest for scholars of Latino religion, the answers to these questions will have a major impact on the strength and vitality of Hispanic communities and U.S. society as a whole. Similarly, how churches rise to the challenge of serving Latino communities will have an impact on their own survival. Indeed, as theologian Justo González has remarked, "to survive as a viable agent of mission, the Church must be bilingual . . . It will be necessary to move across the various social divides in our emerging society, and to witness to Christ in myriad different contexts."[1] It is our hope that researchers and church leaders will respond to the emerging needs these questions represent—and to the voices of this book—just as faith leaders, by God's grace, will act upon the urgent choices they continue to identify.

---

[1] Quoted in Edwin I. Hernández, et al., "Strengthening Hispanic Ministry Across Denominations: A Call to Action," Durham, NC: Pulpit and Pew Research on Pastoral Leadership, 2004.

CONTRIBUTORS

Rebecca Burwell, Ph.D. is a Research Fellow at the Center for the Study of Latino Religion, Institute for Latino Studies at the University of Notre Dame.

Jackson W. Carroll, Ph.D. is the Director of *Pulpit & Pew* and the Ruth W. and A. Morris Williams Professor Emeritus at Duke University Divinity School.

Kenneth G. Davis, O.F.M., Conv. is associate professor of pastoral studies at Saint Meinrad School of Theology. Visit his website at http://kennethgdavis.com.

Gastón Espinosa, Ph.D. is assistant professor of religious studies at Claremont McKenna College. He recently managed the $1.3 million Pew Charitable Trusts-funded Hispanic Churches in American Public Life research project. He is coauthoring with Virgilio Elizondo and Jesse Miranda the forthcoming *Latino Religions and Civic Activism in the United States* and *Latino Religions and Politics in American Public Life.*

Mary L. Gautier, Ph.D. is a senior research associate at CARA, the Center for Applied Research in the Apostolate at Georgetown University. A sociologist, Mary specializes in Catholic demographic trends in the United States, manages CARA databases on Church information, and conducts demographic projects and computer-aided mapping. She also edits *The CARA Report*, a quarterly research newsletter, and other CARA publications.

Mark M. Gray, Ph.D. is a Research Associate at the Center for Applied Research in the Apostolate (CARA) at Georgetown University. His research is focused on lay ministry and lay persons serving parishes without resident priest pastors and national-level polls of lay Catholics.

Andrew Hernández is the Executive Director of the 21st Century Leadership Center at St. Mary's University in San Antonio, Texas. The former president of the Southwest Voter Registration Project, he is the co author of the *Almanac of Latino Politics 2002–2004.*

Edwin I. Hernández, Ph.D. became director of the Center for the Study of Latino Religion at the Institute for Latino Studies, University of Notre Dame, in 2002. He was previously a program officer for religion at The Pew Charitable Trusts. He also served as vice president for academic affairs at Antillian Adventist University, Mayaguez, Puerto Rico, and as a faculty member at Andrews University, Berrien Springs, Michigan.

Philip E. Lampe, Ph.D. is Professor of Sociology at University of the Incarnate Word. His primary areas of interest in research and publications are U.S. Hispanics, religion and family.

Adair T. Lummis, Ph.D. is a Faculty Associate in Research at the Institute for Religion Research, Hartford Seminary. She is a sociologist of religion who for over twenty years has been engaged in studies on clergy and ethnic groups in Christian and other faiths.

Melissa D. Mauldin, M.A. is a doctoral student in the Department of Sociology at the University of Florida. She studies issues related to Latino/as, Latin America and inequalities in health and health care.

Milagros Peña, Ph.D. is Associate Professor of Sociology and Women's Studies at the University of Florida. She received her doctorate from the State University of New York-Stony Brook. The author of several books and articles, in 1995 she was awarded a Fulbright Research Fellowship to Mexico.

Marciana Popescu, Ph.D. is an Associate Professor of Social Work at Andrews University in Berrien Springs Michigan.

Juan Carlos Rivera is a **Ph.D.** candidate in sociology at Loyola University, Chicago.

Amy L. Sherman, Ph.D. is a senior fellow of the Sagamore Institute for Public Policy, where she directs the Faith in Communities initiative. She is the author of four books, most recently *Reinvigorating Faith in Communities* (Hudson Institute, 2002). She also serves as Editorial Director for the Faith and Service Technical Education Network (FASTEN), an initiative of The Pew Charitable Trusts.

Elizabeth Station, M.A. is a freelance writer, editor and translator specializing in higher education and the nonprofit sector. A frequent collaborator with the Institute for Latino Studies at the University of Nortre Dame, her work has appeared in national and international publications.

SUPPLEMENTAL BIBLIOGRAPHY

Articles

Agosto, Efraín. 1998. "Social Analysis of the New Testament and Hispanic Theology: A Case Study." *Journal of Hispanic/Latino Theology* 5 (May): 6–29.

Alexander, Bobby C. 1998. "A Pentecostal-Styled Mexican Mission in Dallas: An Illustration of Religious Diversity Among New Latino Immigrants." *Listening* 33 (Fall): 175–187.

Alicea Lugo, Benjamín. 1998. "Salsa y Adobo: Latino/Latina Contributions to Theological Education." *Union Seminary Quarterly Review* 52(1–2): 129–144.

Alvarez, Carmelo. 2002. "Hispanic Pentecostals: Azusa Street and Beyond." *Encounter* 63(1–2): 13–26.

Amberg, Marion. 2001. "From the Ground Up, a Church on the Rise!." *Extension* 96(8): 10–11,14–19.

Amuchástegui Herrera, Ana. 2001. "The Hybrid Construction of Sexuality in Mexico and its Impact on Sex Education." *Sex-Education* 1(3): 259–277.

Anderson, Kim Renay. 1998. "Church-Affiliated Group Aims at Neighborhood Revitalization." *National Mortgage News* (October 19): 78.

Anonymous. 1998. "McCarrick Dedicates First US Diocesan-Run Facility for Training Lay Hispanic Leaders." *National Catholic Reporter* 35 (December 25): 7.

———. 1998. "Survey Finds Greater Ethnic Mix Choosing Consecrated Life." *National Catholic Register* 74 (January 25–31): 2.

———. 1999. "Fordham University's Graduate School of Social Service to have Research Center Devoted to Studying Mental Health of Hispanics." *National Catholic Reporter* 35 (September 3): 8.

Arasa, Daniel. 2000. "The Challenge of the Hispanic Wave." *Our Sunday Visitor* 89 (November 5).

Atkinson, Ernest E. 1997. "Hispanic Baptists in Texas: A Glorious and Threatened History." *Apuntes* (Summer): 41–44.

Badillo, David A. 1997. "Between Alienation and Ethnicity: The Evolution of Mexican-American Catholicism in San Antonio, 1910–1940." *Journal of American Ethnic History* 16(4): 62–83.

Bannon, Anne Louise. 2000. "Political Prisoners Thank MARCHA; Caucus Looks to Future." *Christian Social Action* 13(1): 35–37.

———. 2001a. "Christian Hispanics: Same Politics, Culture." *Christian Century* 118(17): 12.

———. 2001b. "Hispanic/Latino Faith Strong, Diverse." *CARA Report* 6(4): 4.

———. 2001c. "Latino Catholics and Protestants Compared." *CARA Report* 7(1): 1,11.

———. 2001d. "Seventy Percent of Latino Identify as Catholic, Says Survey." *America* 184(18): 4.

———. 2001e. "Survey Profiles Diocesan Directors of Hispanic Ministry." *CARA Report* 7(1): 11.

———. 2002a. "Demographic Changes to Impact Church in Europe and USA." *CARA Report* 7(3): 10.

———. 2002b. "Encouraging Hispanic Vocations." *CARA Report* 7(3): 11.

———. 2002c. "Hispanic Catholics and Protestants Compared on Social Attitudes." *CARA Report* 7(4): 9.

———. 2002d. "Hispanic Catholic Leadership Development." *CARA Report* 8(1): 11.

———. 2002e. "Hispanic Ministry" *CARA Report* 8(1): 12.

——. 2002f. "Hispanic Voice in Religious and Public Life." *CARA Report* 8(2): 10.

——. 2002g. "Image of Religious Life Positive, Little Understood." *CARA Report* 7(4): 3.

Berryman, Phillip. 1999. "Churches as Winners and Losers in the Network Society." *Journal of Interamerican Studies and World Affairs* 41(4): 21–34.

Bell, Daniel M, Jr. 2001. "Crossing the Postmodern Divide: Hispanic and Latin American Liberation Theologians in the Struggle for Justice." *Apuntes* 21(1): 4–14.

Blake, Deborah D. 2001. "'We Wanted to Include Him': Personhood in One Family's Experience of the Genetic Illness and Loss of Their Son." *Illness, Crisis and Loss* 9(4): 323–335.

Bono, Agostino. 2002. "Hispanics Seek Voice in Religious, Public Life." *National Catholic Reporter* (May 17): 11.

Bowey, James A. 2001. "Waiting for Water on the Tex-Mex Border." *Extension* 96(6): 6–12.

Bravo, Benjamín. 1999. "La Parroquia Urbana." *Journal of Hispanic/Latino Theology* 6 (May): 19–56.

Burger, John. 2002. "Pro-abortion Governor Won with Pro-life Hispanic Votes." *National Catholic Register* 78(46): 1,7.

Burke, John Francis. Summer 1998. "U.S. Hispanic Theology and the Politics of Border Crossings: 'We Hold these Truths' from La Frontera." *Review of Politics* 60(3): 563–74.

Burnside, Gordon. 1999. "Ministry Hails US Decision on Immigrants: Catholic Providers Hope the Move will ease Enrollment of Hispanic Children in Medicaid and CHIP." *Health Progress* 80 (July-August): 16–17.

Cabassa, Leopoldo J. 2003. "Measuring Acculturation: Where We Are and Where We Need to Go." *Hispanic Journal of Behavioral Sciences* 25(2): 127–146.

Cardoza-Orlandi, Carlos. 1998. "'Now You See It, Now You Don't': Mission and Ecumenism in a Hispanic/Latino Perspective." *Theology Today* 54 (January): 499–506.

Carnes, Tony. 1998. "King's College Resurrection Signals Big Apple's Renewal." *Christianity Today* (February 9): 90–91.

Carrasco, Rodolpho. 1997. "Quadruple Consciousness." *Urban Mission* 14 (June): 31–41.

——. 1999a. "Reaching Out to Latinos: Church Networks are Cooperating to Launch Congregations in Unlikely US Locations." *Christianity Today* 43 (September 6): 32,34,36.

——. 1999b. "Wanted: Young, Dedicated Leaders." *Christianity Today* 43 (October 4): 19.

——. 2001. "Catching Up with Hispanics: New Census Data on the Latinos in our Midst Presents a Reality Check for Cross-cultural Outreach." *Christianity Today* 45 (November 12): 66–69.

Casas, Ralph. 2001. "'Making-Face, Making-Heart': The Spiritual Foundations of an Indigenous Pedagogy." *Journal of Hispanic/Latino Theology* 9(2): 17–47.

Cassese, Giacomo. 2000. "De La iglesia y El Estado Omnipotente: Como Debemos Vivir La Fe En El Imperio?" *Apuntes* 20(3): 104–117.

Castelo, Daniel. 2003. "Resident and Illegal Aliens." *Apuntes* 23(2): 65–77.

Castuera, Ignacio. 2000. "Justice Ministries and the Hispanic Community: A Call to 'Radically Contemplate' Justice Issues." *Christian Social Action* 13(2): 16–25.

Caulfield, Brian. 2002. "Reaching Out to Hispanic Catholics [Hispanic Catholic Men Finding Home for their Faith, Family and Values in the Knights of Columbus]." *Columbia* 82(12): 20–22.

Center for Applied Research in the Apostolate (US). 2002. "Diocesan Leadership in Hispanic Ministry [graph]." *CARA Report* 8(2): 10.

Chavez, Linda. 1998. "Our Hispanic Predicament." *Commentary* 105 (June): 47–50.

Chignoli, C. William. 1999. "Cultural Differences: The Silent Language." *Apuntes* 19(2): 21–31.

Climie, Jeff, Janet Davison, J. D. Dueck, and Sally Rose. 1998. "Doing Good in the 'Hood." *Urban Mission* 15(4): 7–17.

Collins, Bradley, and Rosalinda Gandara. 2000. "Carolinians Finally Find 'Room at the Inn.'" *Extension* 94 (February): 16–20.

Cnaan, Ram A. 2000–1. "Keeping Faith in the City: How 401 Urban Religious Congregations Serve Their Neediest Neighbors." CRRUCS Report 2000–1.

Cook, Kaye V. 2000. "'You Have to Have Somebody Watching Your Back, and if that's God, then that's Mighty Big': The Church's Role in the Resilience of Inner-city Youth." *Adolescence* 35(140): 717–730.

Cruz, Ronaldo. 1998. "Hispanic Ministry in the United States." *Osservatore Romano* 1524 (January 14): 11.

Csordas, Thomas J., and Elizabeth Lewton. 1998. "Practice, Performance, and Experience in Ritual Healing." *Transcultural Psychiatry* 35(4): 435–512.

Daly, Les. 1999. "Get Muddy, Save a Church: Regular Mudding Events Keep Church and Tradition Intact for the Hispanic Communities of Northern New Mexico." *Smithsonian* (December): 122+.

Davis, Kenneth G. 1997a. "A New Catholic Reformation?" *Chicago Studies* 36(3): 216–223.

———. 1997b. "A Survey of Contemporary U.S. Hispanic Catholic Theology." *Theology Digest* 44(3): 203–212.

———. 1997c. "Challenges to the Pastoral Care of Central Americans in the United States." *Apuntes* 17(2): 45–56.

———. 1999a. "Cursillo de Cristiandad: Gift of the Hispanic Church." *Chicago Studies* 38(3): 318–328.

———. 1999b. "Still Gringo After All These Years." *Quarterly Review* (Spring): 83–91.

———. 2002a. "Architects of Success: the Promise of Young Hispanic Catholic Leadership." *America* (April 29): 6–8.

———. 2002b. "Naturalismo." *AAR Abstracts* (November): 123.

———. 2004a. "Annoying the Sick?: Cultural Considerations for the Celebration of a Sacrament." *Worship* 78(1): 35–50.

———. 2004b. "Hispanic Ecumenism: An Unlikely mix of Churches Adopts a Shared Strategy and a Common Agenda." *America* (April 19–26): 22–25.

De Genova, Nicholas. 1998. "Race, Space, and the Reinvention of Latin America in Mexican Chicago." *Latin American Perspectives* 25 (September): 87–116.

Diaz, César. 2002. "To Mend Rift, US Church Needs to Embrace Gifts of Latinos." *National Catholic Reporter* 38 (March 22): 30–33.

Díaz-Stevens, Ana María. 1998. "Syncretism, Popular Religiosity, and Communitarian Spirituality among Puerto Ricans and Hispanics in the United States." *Listening* 33 (Fall): 162–174.

———. 1999. "Memory, Imagination, and Tradition: Diasporic Latino Spirituality." *Union Seminary Quarterly Review* 53(1–2): 1–18.

DiIulio, Jr., John J. 2002. "The There Faith Factors." *The Public Interest* 149 (Fall): 50–64.

———. 2003 "Government by Proxy: A Faithful Overview." *Harvard Law Review* 116(5): 1271–1284.

Dudley, Roger L., Duane C. McBride, and Edwin I. Hernández. 1997. "Dissenting Sect or Evangelical Denomination: The Tension Within Seventh-day Adventism." *Research in the Social Scientific Study of Religion* 8: 95–116.

Dutwin, David et al. (2005). "Latinos and Political Party Affiliation." *Hispanic Journal of Behavioral Sciences.* 27 (2): 135–160.

Dukes, Richard L. and Jennifer Valentine. 1998. "Gang Membership and Bias Against Young People who Break the Law." *Social Science Journal* 35(3): 347–360.

Ellison, Christopher G, Xiaohe Xu, and Chris D. Grayson. 2002. "Religion and Norms of Filial Obligation among U.S. Elders." *Southern Sociological Society* (SSS).

Escobar, Samuel. 2003. "Migration: Avenue and Challenge to Mission." *Missiology* 31(1): 17–28.

Espin, Orlando O. 1999. "La Experiencia Religiosa en el Contexto de la Globalización." *Journal of Hispanic/Latino Theology* 7(2): 13–31.

——. 2000. "Immigration, Territory, and Globalization: Theological Reflections." *Journal of Hispanic/Latino Theology* 7(3): 46–59.

——. 2002. "Toward the Construction of an Intercultural Theology of Tradition." *Journal of Hispanic/Latino Theology* 9(3): 22–59.

Espinosa, Gastón. 2004. "Latino Voice Emerging in US political and Civic Life." *CARA Report* 9(4): 1, 10.

Falicov, Celia J. 2001. "The Cultural Meanings of Money: The case of Latinos and Anglo-Americans." *American Behavioral Scientist* 45(2): 313–328.

Fernandez, Eduardo C. 2001. "Latinos and Ecumenism: Compelling Servants in a New Era." *Journal of Hispanic/Latino Theology* 9(2): 5–16.

Figueroa Deck, Allan. 1997. "Latino Religion and the Struggle for Justice: Evangelization as Conversion." *Journal of Hispanic/Latino Theology* 4 (February): 28–41.

——. 2002. "The Latino Catholic Ethos: Ancient History or Future Promise?" *Journal of Hispanic/Latino Theology* 9 (February): 5–21.

——. 2004. "A Latino Practical Theology." *Theological Studies* 65(2): 275–297.

Flores, Gilberto. 2001. "Hispanic Mennonites in North America." *Mennonite Life* (Online) 56 (3). Retrieved Nov. 12, 2004 (http://www.bethelks.edu/mennonitelife).

Ford, John T. 2002. "Hispanic Ecumenism: New Findings and Possibilities." *Ecumenical Trends* 31(10): 145–149.

Frisbie, W. Parker, and Seungeun Song. 2003. "Hispanic Pregnancy Outcomes: Differentials Over Time and Current Risk Factor Effects." *Policy Studies Journal* 31(2): 237–252.

García, Albert L. 2000. "Christian Spirituality in Light of the US Hispanic Experience." Ed. Frederick J. Gaiser. *Word and World* 20(1): 52–60.

García, Ismael. 1997. "Theological and Ethical Reflections on the Church as a Community of Resistance." *Journal of Hispanic/Latino Theology* 4 (February): 42–73.

García, Mario T. 2000. "The Chicano Southwest: Catholicism and its meaning." *U.S. Catholic Historian* 18(4): 1–24.

García, Sixto J. 1999. "Hispanic Theologians as Actors, Poets and Prophets of Their Communities." *Journal of Hispanic/Latino Theology* 6 (May): 5–18.

Garrard-Burnett, Virginia. 1998. "Identity, Community and Religious Change among the Maya of Chiapas and Guatemala." *Journal of Hispanic/Latino Theology* 6 (August): 61–79.

Gloria, Alberta M., et al. 2005. "Perceived Educational Barriers, Cultural Fit, Doping Responses, and Psychological Well-Being of Latina Undergraduates." *Hispanic Journal of Behavioral Sciences*. 27 (2): 161–183.

Goizueta, Roberto S. 2004. "The Symbolic Realism of US Latino/a Popular Catholicism." *Theological Studies* 65(2): 255–274.

Gratton, Brian, and Myron P. Gutmann. 2000. "Hispanics in the United States, 1850–1990: Estimates of Population Size and National Origin." *Historical Methods* 33(3): 137–153.

Greenberg, Anna. 2000. "The Church and the Revitalization of Politics and Community." *Political Science Quarterly* 115 (Fall): 377–394.

Groody, Daniel G. 2004. "Crossing the Line: A Spiritual View of the US/Mexican Border." *The Way* 43(2): 58–69.

Guntzel, Jeff. 2004. "Pastoral Challenges Differ among Groups of Young Hispanics." *National Catholic Reporter* (Jan. 30): 12–13.

Hanagan, Michael P. 1998. "Labor History and the New Migration History: A Review Essay." *International Labor and Working Class History* 54 (Fall): 57–79.

Haney, Patrick J. and Walt Vanderbush. 1999. "The Role of Ethnic Interest Groups in U.S. Foreign Policy: the Case of the Cuban American National Foundation." *International Studies Quarterly/Oxford* 43(2): 341–361.

Harknett, Kristen. 2001. "Working and Leaving Welfare: Does Race or Ethnicity Matter?" *Social Service Review* 75(3): 359–385.

Harris, Joseph C. 2002. "The Future Church: a Demographic Revolution." *America* 186 (March 18): 7–9.

Hernández, Edwin. 2001. "A Call for the Renewal of Adventism's Communal Consciousness." *Journal of Research on Christian Education* 10 (Fall): 285–307.

Hernandez, Edwin I., and Kenneth G. Davis. 2001. "The National Survey of Hispanic Theological Education." *Journal of Hispanic/Latino Theology* 8(4): 37–59.

———. 2002. "From Sacred Tower to Beacon of Hope: Opening Institutional Doors to Foster Hispanic Theological Education." *Perspectivas* (Spring): 29–39.

Hernández, Edwin I., Kenneth G. Davis, and Catherine Wilson. 2002. "The Theological Education of U.S. Hispanics." *Theological Education* 38: 2.

Hernández, Edwin, and Roger L. Dudley. 2002. "Education and the Latino Seventh-day Adventist Church." *Journal of Adventist Education* (October-November): 17–21.

Hernández, Edwin I., Roger Dudley, and Duane McBride. 1996–97. "Church Leaders Select Priorities for Education." *Journal of Adventist Education* (December-January): 8–13.

Hernández, Elizabeth. 1997. "International Ministry: An Interview with Elizabeth Hernandez." *Journal of Biblical Counseling* 16(1): 20–24.

Hudson, Deal Wyatt. 2001. "The Political Enigma of Catholic Minority Groups." *Crisis* 19(6): 8.

Hunt, Larry L. 1998. "The Spirit of Hispanic Protestantism in the United States: National Survey Comparisons of Catholics and Non-Catholics." *Social Science Quarterly* 79(4): 828–845.

———. 2000. "Religion and Secular Status among Hispanics in the United States: Catholicism and the Varieties of Hispanic Protestantism." *Social Science Quarterly*, 81(1): 344–362.

———. 2001. "Religion, Gender, and the Hispanic Experience in the United States: Catholic/Protestant Differences in Religious Involvement, Social Status, and Gender-Role Attitudes." *Review of Religious Research* (December): 139–160.

Hunt, Matthew O. 2000. "Status, Religion, and the 'Belief in a Just World': Comparing African Americans, Latinos, and Whites." *Social Science Quarterly* 81(1): 325–343.

———. 2002. "Religion, Race/Ethnicity, and Beliefs about Poverty." *Social Science Quarterly* 83 (September): 810–831.

Huntington, Samuel. 2004. "The Hispanic Challenge." *Foreign Policy* 141 (March/April): 1–12.

Icaza, Rosa María. 2002. "Council a Vital Boost to Hispanic Identity." *National Catholic Reporter* 38 (October 4): 11–12.

Isasi-Díaz, Ada Maria. 2002. "Lo Cotidiano: a Key Element of Mujerista Theology." *Journal of Hispanic/Latino Theology* 10(1): 5–17.

———. 2004. "*Burlando al Opresor*: Mocking/Tricking the Oppressor." *Theological Studies* 65(2): 340–363.

Irvine, Andrew. 2000. "Mestizaje and the Problem of Authority." *Journal of Hispanic/Latino Theology* 8(1): 5–37.

Jiménez, Pablo A. 1997. "The Laborers of the Vineyard (Matthew 20:1–16): A Hispanic Homiletical Reading." *Journal for Preachers* 21(1): 35–40.

Johnson, Byron R. 2000. "A Better Kind of High: How Religious Commitment Reduces Drug Use Among Poor Urban Teens." *CRRUCS Report 2000–2*.

Johnson Byron R., and David B. Larson. 1998. "The Faith Factor: Studies Show Religion is Linked to the Mental and Physical Health of Inmates." *Corrections Today* 60(3): 106–109.

Johnson-Mondragón, Ken. 2002. "Hispanic Young People Have Unique Needs." *CARA Report* 8(2): 1,9.

Jones, Arthur. 1999. "Faith of Hispanic Catholics Rooted in Family." *National Catholic Reporter* 35 (August 27): 5.

———. 2000. "Wide Variations in Ministry to Hispanics." *National Catholic Reporter* 36 (February 11): 3.

Jones, Melissa. 2002. "INS Targeting Immigrant Rights Groups, Minnesota Hispanic Activists Say." *National Catholic Reporter* 38 (April 5): 7.

Jones-Correa, Michael A., and David L. Leal. 2001. "Political Participation: Does Religion Matter?" *Political Research Quarterly* 54(4): 751–770.

Kaufmann, Karen M. 2003. "Black and Latino Voters in Denver: Responses to Each Other's Political Leadership." *Political Science Quarterly* 118(1): 107–125.

Kelly, Nathan J., and Jana Morgan Kelly. 2005. "Religion and Latino Partisanship in the United States." *Political Research Quarterly* 58(1): 87–95.

Keysar, Ariela, et al. 2004. "Religious identification of US adult Hispanics." *CARA Report* 9(3): 4.

Kim, Hyoun K., and Patrick McKenry. 1998. "Social Networks and Support: a Comparison of African Americans, Asian Americans, Caucasians, and Hispanics." *Journal of Comparative Family Studies* 29(2): 313–334.

Krokos, Mike. 1999. "INS Responds to Hispanic Concerns in Minnesota." *National Catholic Reporter* 35 (March 12): 3.

Kus, Robert J. 2004. "Registering Hispanics in the Parish: the St. Catherine Story [Parish Bulletin]." *Church* 20(2): 25–27.

Lasalle Klein, Robert. 1998. "The Body of Christ: The Claim of the Crucified People on US Theology and Ethics." *Journal of Hispanic/Latino Theology* 5 (May): 48–77.

Lawson, Ronald. 1999. "Internal Political Fallout from the Emergence of an Immigrant Majority: The Impact of the Transformation of Seventh-Day Adventism in Metropolitan New York." *Review of Religious Research* 41 (Summer): 21–47.

León, Luís. 1999. "Metaphor and Place: The US-Mexico Border as Center and Periphery in the Interpretation of Religion." *Journal of the American Academy of Religion* 67 (September): 541–571.

Levine, Elana. 2001. "Constructing a Market, Constructing an Ethnicity: US Spanish-Language Media and the Formation of a Syncretic Latino/a Identity." *Studies in Latin American Popular Culture* 20: 33–50.

Liaugminas, Sheila G. 2002. "The Parish that Rose from the Ashes." *Catholic Digest* 66 (March): 66–73.

Llanes, Eduardo. 1998. "Learning from Other Cultures: Hispanic-American Culture." *Brethren in Christ History and Life* 21 (April): 172–177.

Machado, Daisy L. 1997. "From Anglo-American Traditions to a Multicultural World." *Discipliana* 57 (Summer): 47–60.

———. 1999. "Abre Mis Ojos a la Realidad de la Mujer Hispana." *Apuntes* 19 (Summer): 35–41.

MacHarg, Kenneth D. 1998. "Hispanic Christian Radio Grows by Blocks and Blends: New information-age strategy enables stations to compete with secular counterparts." *Christianity Today* 42 (May 18): 19.

Marquez, Benjamin. "Choosing Issues, Choosing Sides: Constructing Identities in Mexican-American Social Movement Organizations." *Ethnic and Racial Studies* 24(2): 218–235.

Martínez, Christopher D. 1996–97. "African-Americans, Hispanics Move to Bridge Bitter Divide." *National Catholic Register* (Dec. 29–Jan. 4): 1+.

Martínez, Demetria. 1999a. "Latinos Need to Know Their Rights." *National Catholic Reporter* 35 (July 16): 16.

——. 1999b. "Segregation in Catholic Intellectual Life." *National Catholic Reporter* 36 (December 3): 18.

Matovina, Timothy M. 1998. "San Fernando Cathedral and the Alamo: Sacred Place, Public Ritual, and Construction of Meaning." *Journal of Ritual Studies* 12(2): 1–13.

Maynard-Reid, Pedrito U. 2003. "Diverse worship: African-American, Caribbean and Hispanic Perspectives." *Apuntes* 23(4): 156–158.

McCord, H. Richard. 1999. "Where is Hispanic Ministry in Parishes Headed?" *Origins* 29 (July 29): 145–148.

Medina, Lara. 2001. "Transformative Struggle: The Spirituality of Las Hermanas." *Journal of Feminist Studies in Religion* 17(2): 107–126.

Medinger, Jessica A. 2000. "Building on God's Kingdom in Texas." *Extension* 94 (November): 6–10, 18–19.

Mendieta, Eduardo. 2002. "Making Hombres: Feo, Fuerte, Formal. On Latino Masculinities." *Journal of Hispanic/Latino Theology* 9(4): 41–51.

Mejido, Manuel J. 1998. "Moribundity and Metanoia: A Sociological Perspective on the Catholic Church in Socialist Cuba." *Journal of Hispanic/Latino Theology* 6 (August): 32–60.

——. 1999. "Theoretical Prolegomenon to the Sociology of US Hispanic Popular Religion." *Journal of Hispanic/Latino Theology* 7 (August): 27–55.

——. 2002. "Propaedeutic to the Critique of the Study of U.S. Hispanic Religion: a Polemic Against Intellectual Assimilation." *Journal of Hispanic/Latino Theology* 10(2): 31–63.

Miller, John J. 2001. "How Hispanics Help the GOP." *Crisis* 19(4): 44–45.

Mohl, Raymond A. 2002. "Latinization in the Heart of Dixie: Hispanics in Twentieth-Century Alabama." *Alabama Review* 55(4): 243–274.

Moore, Philip S. 2004. "Death in the Desert [on Immigrant Needs and Sovereignty Clash at Mexican Border]. *Register* 80(2): 1, 7.

Murphy, Caryle. 2002. "Latinos Take Their Faith Door to Door." *Catholic Digest* 66 (March): 79–83.

Nesch-Olver, Delia. 2001. "Immigrant Clergy in the Promised Land." *Missiology* 29(2): 185–200.

Odem, Mary E. 2004. "Our Lady of Guadalupe in the New South: Latino Immigration and the Politics of Integration in the Catholic Church." *Journal of American Ethnic History* 24(1): 26–57.

O'Rourke, David K. 1998. "Our War with Mexico." *Commonweal* 125 (March 13): 8–9.

Pagan, Samuel. 1999. "Bienaventurados los Pobres en Espíritu: Jesús y los Manuscritos del Mar Muerto." *Apuntes* 19 (Summer): 42–50.

Pantoja, Segundo. 2002. "Church, Community and Identity: Latinos' Experiences with Religious New York." *Apuntes* 22(2): 64–79.

Peña, Milagros. 1997. "Border Crossings: Sociological Analysis and the Latina and Latino Religious Experience." *Journal of Hispanic/Latino Theology* 4(3): 13–27.

——. 2002. "Devising a Study on Religion and the Latina Experience." *Social Compass* 49(2): 281–294.

Peña, Milagros, and Lisa M. Frehill. 1998. "Latina Religious Practice: Analyzing Cultural Dimensions in Measures of Religiosity." *Journal for the Scientific Study of Religion* 37 (December): 620–635.

Pineda, Ana María. 2004. "*Imagenes de Dios en el Camino*: Retablos, Ex-votos, *Milagritos*, and Murals." *Theological Studies* 65(2): 364–379.

Pistone, John. 2004. "Embracing Diversity [Deacons and Priests]." *Priest* 60(5): 32.

Potapchuk, William R., Jarle P. Crocker, and William H. Schechter, Jr. 1997.

"Building Community with Social Capital: Chits and Chums or Chats with Change." *National Civic Review* 86(2): 129–139.

Raijman, Rebeca and Marta Tienda. 2000. "Immigrants' Pathways to Business Ownership: a Comparative Ethnic Perspective." *International Migration Review* 34(3): 682–706.

Ramírez, Daniel. 1999. "Borderlands Praxis: The Immigrant Experience in Latino Pentecostal Churches." *Journal of the American Academy of Religion* 67 (September): 573–596.

Ramírez, Ricardo. 1998. "Stewardship Tradition in US Hispanic Communities." *Origins* 28 (October 15): 308–312.

Ravuri, Evelyn. 2003. "Changes in Asian and Hispanic Population in the Cities of the Great Plains, 1990–2000." *Great Plains Research* 13(1): 75–96.

Recinos, Harold J. 1997. "Politics, Martyrdom, and Life Story: Salvadoran Refugees Speak a Word of Life to the United States." *Journal of Hispanic/Latino Theology* 5 (November): 5–21.

Riebe-Estrella, Gary. 1997. "Latinos and Theological Education." *Journal of Hispanic/Latino Theology* (February): 5–12.

——. 2004. "A Youthful Community." *Theological Studies* 65(2): 298–316.

Rivera Pagán, Luis N. 1998. "Polifonía Étnico-Cultural y la Crisis de la Cristiandad Colonial." *Journal of Hispanic/Latino Theology* 6 (August): 6–31.

Robeck, Cecil M., Jr. 1997. "Evangelization or Proselytism of Hispanics? A Pentecostal Perspective." *Journal of Hispanic/Latino Theology* 4 (May): 42–64.

Rodriguez, Daniel A. 2002 "Victory Outreach International: a Case Study in Holisitc Hispanic Ministry." *Apuntes* 22(4): 136–148.

——. 2003. "No Longer Foreigners and Aliens: toward a Missiological Christology for Hispanics in the United States." *Missiology* 31(1): 51–67.

Rodriguez, Jeanette. 2004. "Mestiza Spirituality." *Theological Studies* 65(2): 317–339.

Rodríguez, Jesús. 1999. "Chaplains' Communications with Latino Patients: Case Studies on Non-verbal Communication." *Journal of Pastoral Care* 53(3): 309–317.

Rosaria Rodriguez, Ruben. 2002. "A Voice for the Voiceless: Discussing Abortion from a Hispanic Perspective." *Apuntes* 22(3): 107–118.

Royal, Robert. 2004. "Hispanic Peril—or Promise? [Seeing Things]." *Crisis* (May): 44–45.

Ruiz, Jean Pierre. 1998. 2001. "Immigrants and Illegal Aliens in the US." *Journal of Hispanic/Latino Theology* 8 (February): 3–5.

Ruiz, Pedro. 1998. "The Role of Culture in Psychiatric Care." *American Journal of Psychiatry* 155(12): 1763–1765.

Sánchez Walsh, Arlene. 1998. "Latino Pentecostalism—A Bibliographic Introduction." *Evangelical Studies Bulletin* 15 (Spring): 1–5.

——. 2000. "Workers for the Harvest: The Latin American Bible Institute and the Institutionalization of a Latino Pentecostal Identity." *Journal of Hispanic/Latino Theology* 8 (August): 54–79.

——. 2001. "'Normal Church Can't Take Us': Re-creating a Pentecostal Identity among the Men and Women of Victory Outreach." *Journal of Hispanic/Latino Theology* 9 (November): 48–78.

Schaeffer, Pamela. 1999. "Latino, Black Scholars Protest Exclusion." *National Catholic Reporter* 36 (November 5): 9.

——. 2000. "Scholars Say Religious Institutions Ignore Growing 'Latino Reality'." *National Catholic Reporter* 36 (March 17): 4.

Schneider, Jo Anne. 1999. "Trusting That of God in Everyone: Three Examples of Quaker-Based Social Service in Disadvantaged Communities." *Nonprofit and Voluntary Sector Quarterly* 28(3): 269–295.

Siems, Larry. 1999. "Loretta Sanchez and the Virgin." *Aztlán* 24(1): 153–173.

Sikkink, David, and Edwin I. Hernandez. 2004. "Family Religiosity Important to Latino School Success." *CARA Report* 9(3): 11.

Smith, James P. 2003. "Assimilation Across the Latino Generations." *American Economic Review* 93(2): 315–319.

Smith, Steven Rathgeb and Michael R. Sosin. 2001. "The Varieties of Faith-Related Agencies." *Public Administration Review* 61(6): 651–670.

Stevens Arroyo, Antonio M. 1998. "The Latino Religious Resurgence." *The Annals of the American Academy of Political and Social Science* 558 (July): 163–177.

———. 2003. "Correction, 'Sí'; defection, 'No': Hispanics and US Catholicism." *America* 189 (July 7–14): 16–18.

———. 2004. "Characteristics of Latino Lay Ministers." *CARA Report* 9(4): 9.

Stout, Robert Joe. 1997. "Caught in the Middle: Millions of Mexican Adults, Caught Between Poverty in their Homeland and Legal Restrictions in the US, are Struggling to Survive on the Border." *Christian Social Action* 10 (October): 4–7.

Suro, Roberto, and Jeffrey S. Passel. 2004. "U.S. Hispanic Births Outpace Gains Through Immigration [tables]." *CARA Report* 9(3): 11.

Sylvest, Edwin Edward, ed. 2000. "The Mexican-American Program: Twenty-fifth Anniversary Celebration." *Apuntes* 20(2): 42–78.

Tapia, Andrés. 1997. "Candor, Repentance, Mark PK Latino Summit." *Christianity Today* 41 (June 16): 58–59.

Teaford, Jon C. 2003. "Life and Politics in Suburban Southern California." *Journal of Urban History* 29(6): 811–819.

Tombs, David. 2002. "Honor, Shame, and Conquest: Male Identity, Sexual Violence and the Body Politic." *Journal of Hispanic/Latino Theology* 9(4): 21–40.

Torre, Miguel A. de la. 1999. "Masking Hispanic Racism: A Cuban Case Study." *Journal of Hispanic/Latino Theology* 6(4): 57–74.

United States Conference of Catholic Bishops. 2002. "Encuentro and Mission: a Renewed Pastoral Framework for Hispanic Ministry." *Origins* 32(26): 425, 427–439.

United States Conference of Catholic Bishops and Conferencia Del Episcopado Mexicano. 2003. "Strangers No Longer: Together on a Journey of Hope."

USCC Hispanic Affairs Committee. 2000. "Hispanic Ministry at the Turn of the New Millennium." *Origins* 29 (April 27): 725,727–731.

Valle, David Del. 1998. "A Caveat for El Barrio." *Apuntes* 18 (Summer): 51–55.

Vélez-Ibáñez, Carlos G. 2004. "Regions of Refuge in the United States: Issues, Problems, and Concerns for the Future of Mexican-Origin Populations in the United States." *Human Organization: Journal of the Society for Applied Anthropology* 63(1): 1–20.

Vuola, Elina. 2001. "Sor Juana Ines de la Cruz: Rationality, Gender, and Power." *Journal of Hispanic/ Latino Theology.* 9(1): 27–45.

Wallis, Allan, Jarle P. Crocker, and William H. Schechter, Jr. 1998. "Social Capital and Community Building, Part 1." *National Civic Review* 87(3): 253–271.

Warren, Mark R. 1998. "Community Building and Political Power." *American Behavioral Scientist* 42(1): 78–92.

Weiss, Rhoda. 2003. "Boosting Organ Donation among Hispanics." *Health Progress* 84(1): 13–14.

Wilcox, W. Bradford. 2002. "Then Comes Marriage?: Religion, Race, and Marriage in Urban America." *CRRUCS Report 2002*.

———. 2001–4. "Good Dads: Religion, Civic Engagement, and Paternal Involvement in Low-Income Communities." *CRRUCS Report 2001–4*.

Wilson, Norman G. 1997. "Pedagogical Expectations of Hispanic Americans: Insights for Leadership Training." *Christian Education Journal* 1(1): 65–81.

Wirpsa, Leslie. 1998. "Hispanic Trends Create Pastoral Puzzles." *National Catholic Reporter* 34 (December 26–January 2): 6.

Wood, Susan Carlson 2000. "Do Latino Covenant Churches Need to Be Bilingual." *Covenant Quarterly* 58(3): 45–58.

Yocum, Glenn E., and Otto Maduro, eds. 1999. "Articles on the Theme of 'Latino Religion.'" *Journal of the American Academy of Religion* 67 (September): 541–636.

Chapters in Edited Books

Ainslie, Ricardo C. 1998. "Cultural Mourning, Immigration, and Engagement: Vignettes From the Mexican Experience." Pp. 285–300 in *Crossings: Mexican Immigration in Interdisciplinary Perspective*. Edited by Marcelo M. Suárez-Orozco. Cambridge, MA: Harvard University Press.

Anijar, Karen. 2001. "Selena—Prophet, Profit, Princess: Canonizing the Commodity." Pp. 83–101 in *God in the Details*. Edited by Eric Michael Mazur and Kate McCarthy. New York: Routledge.

Aponte, Edwin David. 1998. "Hispanic/Latino Protestantism in Philadelphia." Pp. 381–403 in *Reforming the Center: American Protestantism, 1900 to the Present*. Edited by Douglas Jacobsen and William Vance Trollinger. Grand Rapids, MI: Eerdmans.

Aris-Paul, María Marta. 1998. "Latin American and Caribbean Immigrants in the USA: The Invisible and Forgotten." Pp. 31–45 in *Revolution of Spirit: Ecumenical Theology in Global Perspective: Essays in Honor of Richard Shaull*. Edited by Nantawan Boonprasat Lewis Grand Rapids, MI: Eerdmans.

Aymerich, Ramón. 1998. "The Evangelization of Hispanic Young People." Pp. 86–94 in *Disorganized Religion: The Evangelization of Youth and Young Adults*. Edited by Sheryl A. Kujawa-Holbrook. Boston, MA: Cowley Publications.

Balmer, Randall Herbert. 2003. "Crossing the Borders: Evangelicalism and Migration." Pp. 53–60 in *Religion and Immigration: Christian, Jewish, and Muslim Experience in the United States*. Edited by Yvonne-Yazbeck Haddad, Jane Smith, and John Esposito. New York: AltaMira Press.

Cook, David A. 2002. "Forty Years of Religion Across Borders: Twilight of a Transnational Field?" Pp. 51–74 in *Religion Across Borders: Transnational Immigrant Networks*. Edited by Helen R. F. Ebaugh and Janet Saltzman Chafetz. New York: AltaMira Press.

Curry, Mary Cuthrell. 2001. "The Yoruba Religion in New York." Pp. 74–87 in *New York Glory: Religions in the City*. Edited by Tony Carnes and Anna Karpathakis. New York: New York University Press.

Díaz-Stevens, Ana María. 1998. "The Hispanic Challenge to US Catholicism, Colonialism, Migration, and Religious Adaptation." Pp. 157–179 in *El Cuerpo de Cristo: The Hispanic Experience in the U.S. Catholic Church*. Edited by Peter J. Casarella and Raul Gomez. New York: Crossroad.

——. 2003. "Colonization versus Immigration in the Integration and Identification of Hispanics in the United States." In Haddad, *Religion and Immigration: Christian, Jewish, and Muslim Experience in the United States*, 61–84.

Durand, Jorge. 1998. "Migration and Integration: Intermarriages among Mexicans and Non-Mexicans in the United States." In Suárez-Orozco, *Crossings: Mexican Immigration in Interdisciplinary Perspective*, 209–221.

Elizondo, Virgilio P. 1999. "Theology's Contribution to Society: the Ministry of the Theologian." Pp. 49–53 in *From the Heart of Our People: Latino/a Explorations in Catholic Systematic Theology*. Edited by Orlando O. Espin and Miguel H. Díaz. Maryknoll, NY: Orbis Books.

Empereur, James L. 1999. "The Cultural Bodies of Worship." Pp. 85–104 in *Bodies of Worship: Explorations in Theory and Practice*. Edited by Bruce T. Morrill. Collegeville, MN: Liturgical Press.

Espinosa, Gastón. 2002. "'Your Daughters Shall Prophesy': A History of Women in Ministry in the Latino Pentecostal Movement in the United States." Pp. 25–48 in *Women and Twentieth-Century Protestantism*. Edited by Margaret Lamberts Bendroth and Virginia Lieson Brereton. Urbana, IL: University of Illinois Press.

Falicov, Celia J. 1999. "Religion and spiritual folk traditions in immigrant families: therapeutic resources with Latinos." Pp. 104–120 in *Spiritual Resources in Family Therapy*. Edited by Froma Walsh. New York: Guilford Press.

Figueroa Deck, Allan. 1998. "Latino Leaders for Church and Society: Critical Issues." In Casarella, *El Cuerpo de Cristo: The Hispanic Experience in the U.S. Catholic Church*, 180–196.

———. 2004. "Evangelization as Conceptual Framework for the Church's Mission: The Case of US Hispanics." Pp. 85–110 in *Evangelizing America*. Edited by Thomas P. Rausch. New York. Paulist Press.

García, John A. 1997. "Political Participation: Resources and Involvement Among Latinos in the American Political System." Pp. 44–71 in *Pursuing Power: Latinos and the Political System*. Edited by F. Chris García. Notre Dame: University of Notre Dame Press.

García, Mario T. 1998. "Catholic Social Doctrine and Mexican American Political Thought." In Casarella, *El Cuerpo de Cristo: The Hispanic Experience in the U.S. Catholic Church*, 292–311.

Goizueta, Roberto S. 1997. "Catholic Theological Education and U.S. Hispanics." Pp. 340–350 in *Theological Education in the Catholic Tradition: Contemporary Challenges*. Edited by Patrick W. Carey and Earl C. Muller. New York: Crossroad.

———. 2000. "'There You Will See Him': Christianity Beyond the Frontier Myth." Pp. 171–193 in *The Church as Counterculture*. Edited by Michael L. Budde and Robert W. Brimlow. Albany, NY: State University of New York Press.

González, Justo L. 1998. "A Hispanic Perspective: By the Rivers of Babylon." Pp. 80–97, 162–163 in *Preaching Justice: Ethnic and Cultural Perspectives*. Edited by Christine M. Smith. Cleveland, OH: United Church Press.

Gros, Jeffrey. 1998. "Ecumenism in the US Hispanic/Latino Community: Challenge and Promise." In Casarella, *El Cuerpo de Cristo: The Hispanic Experience in the U.S. Catholic Church*, 197–212.

Guardiola Sáenz, Leticia A. 2002. "Minorities in the Midst of Affluence." Pp. 86–92 in *The Many Voices of the Bible*. Edited by Seán Freyne and Ellen van Wolde. London: SCM Press.

Gutiérrez, David G. 1998. "Ethnic Mexicans and the Transformation of 'American' Social Space: Reflections on Recent History." In Suárez-Orozco, *Crossings: Mexican Immigration in Interdisciplinary Perspective*, 309–355.

Hernández, Eli V. 2003. "Ministering to Hispanic-American Youth and Families." Pp. 58–65 in *City Lights: Ministry Essentials for Reaching Urban Youth*. Edited by Scott Larson and Karen Free. Loveland, CO: Group Publishing.

Hurtig, Janise D. 2000. "Hispanic Immigrant Churches and the Construction of Ethnicity." Pp. 29–55 in *Public Religion and Urban Transformation: Faith in the City*. Edited by Lowell W. Livezey. New York: New York University Press.

Isasi Díaz, Ada María. 1999. Mujerista Narratives: Creating a New Heaven and a New Earth. Pp. 227–243 in *Liberating Eschatology: Essays in Honor of Letty M. Russell*. Edited by Serene Jones and Margaret A. Farley. Louisville, KY: Westminster John Knox Press.

———. 2001. Creating a Liberating Culture: Latinas' Subversive Narratives. Pp. 122–139 in *Converging on Culture: Theologians in Dialogue with Cultural Analysis and Criticism*. Edited by Delwin Brown, Sheila Greeve Davaney, and Kathryn Tanner. New York: Oxford University Press.

Jensen, Carol L. 1997. "Roman Catholicism in Modern New Mexico: A Commitment to Survive." Pp. 1–26 in *Religion in Modern New Mexico*. Edited by Ferenc M. Szasz and Richard W. Etulain. Albuquerque, NM: University of New Mexico Press.

Juárez, José Roberto. 2001. "Hispanics, Catholicism, and the Legal Academy." Pp. 163–75 in *Christian Perspectives on Legal Thought*. Edited by Michael W. McConnell, Robert F. Cochran Jr., and Angela C. Carmella. New Haven, CT: Yale University Press.

Keller, Roger R. 2002. "Religious Diversity in North America." Pp. 27–55 in *Handbook of Psychotherapy and Religious Diversity*. Edited by P. Scott Richards and Allen E. Bergin. Washington, DC: American Psychological Association.

León, Luis. 1998. "Born Again in East LA: The Congregation as Border Space." Pp. 163–196 in *Gatherings in Diaspora: Religious Communities and the New Immigration*. Edited by Stephen R. Warner and Judith G. Wittner. Philadelphia: Temple University Press.

Livezey, Lowell W. 2000. "The New Context of Urban Religion." In Livezey, *Public Religion and Urban Transformation: Faith in the City*, 2–25.

Lucas, James W. 2001. "Mormons in New York City." In Carnes, *New York Glory: Religions in the City*, 196–211.

Maloney, Thomas J. 1999. "GC 34 and the Jesuit Political Scientist." Pp. 273–284 in *Promise Renewed: Jesuit Higher Education for a New Millennium*. Edited by Martin R. Tripole. Chicago: Loyola Press.

Marquez Marinas, Gelasia. 1998. "Hispanic Family Life Ministry." In Casarella, *El Cuerpo de Cristo: The Hispanic Experience in the U.S. Catholic Church*, 251–257.

Martínez, Marcos. 1998. "Community and the Sacred in Chicano Theater." In Casarella, *El Cuerpo de Cristo: The Hispanic Experience in the U.S. Catholic Church*, 312–324.

Matovina, Timothy M. 1999. "Representation and the Reconstruction of Power: The Rise of PADRES and Las Hermanas." Pp. 220–237 in *What's left?* Edited by Mary Jo Weaver. Bloomington, IN: Indiana University Press.

McGuire, Brian and Duncan Scrymgeour. 1998. "Santeria and Curanderismo in Los Angeles." Pp. 211–222 in *New Trends and Developments in African Religions*. Edited by Peter B. Clarke. Westport, CN: Greenwood Press.

Meyer, David S. 2002. "Opportunities and Identities: Bridge-building in the Study of Social Movements." In *Social Movements: Identity, Culture, and the State*. Edited by David S. Meyer, Nancy Whittier, and Belinda Robnett. New York: Oxford University Press.

Pantoja, Segundo. 2001. "Religious Diversity and Ethnicity among Latinos." In Carnes, *New York Glory: Religions in the City*, 162–173.

Pedraja, Luis. 2001. "Building Bridges Between Communities of Struggle: Similarities, Differences, Objectives, and Goals." Pp. 205–219 in *Ties that Bind: The African-American and Hispanic-American/Latino(a) Theologies in Dialogue*. Edited by Anthony B. Pinn and Benjamin Valentin. London: Continuum.

Peña, Milagros. 2002. "Encountering Latina Mobilization: Lessons From Field Research on the U.S./Mexico Border." Pp. 113–124 in *Personal Knowledge and Beyond Reshaping the Ethnography of Religion*. Edited by James V. Spickard, J. Shawn Landres, and Meredith B. McGuire. New York: New York University Press.

———. 2003. "Latinas, Border Realities, Empowerment, and Faith-based Organizations." Pp. 400–411 in *Handbook for the Sociology of Religion*. Edited by Michele Dillon. New York: Cambridge University Press.

Pérez y González, María E. 2001. "Latinas in the Barrio." In Carnes, *New York Glory: Religions in the City*, 287–296.

Recinos, Harold J. 2001. "Popular Religion, Political Identity, and Life-Story Testimony in an Hispanic Community." In Pinn, *Ties that Bind: The African-American and Hispanic-American/Latino(a) Theologies in Dialogue*, 116–128.

Rodriguez, Nestor. 2000. "Hispanic and Asian immigration waves in Houston." Pp. 29–42 in *Religion and the New Immigrants: Continuities and Adaptations in Immigrant Congregations*. Edited by Helen Ebaugh and Janet Saltzman Chafetz. Walnut Creek, CA: AltaMira Press.

Rosaldo, Renato and William V. Flores. 1997. "Identity, Conflict, and Evolving Latino Communities: Cultural Citizenship in San Jose, California." Pp. 57–96 in *Latino Cultural Citizenship: Claiming Identity, Space, and Rights*. Edited by William V. Flores and Rina Benmayor. Boston: Beacon Press.

Ruiz Baia, Larissa. 2001. "Rethinking Transnationalism: National Identities among Peruvian Catholics in New Jersey." Pp. 147–164 in *Christianity, Social Change, and Globalization in the Americas*. Edited by Anna L. Peterson, Manuel A. Vásquez, and Philip J. Williams. Brunswick, NJ: Rutgers University Press.

Sánchez Walsh, Arlene M. 2000. "Slipping into Darkness: Popular Culture and the Creation of a Latino Evangelical Youth Culture." Pp. 74–91 in *GenX Religion*. Edited by Richard W. Flory and Donald E. Miller. New York: Routledge.

Sandoval, Efren. 2002. "Catholicism and Transnational Networks: Three Cases from the Monterrey-Houston Connection." In Ebaugh, *Religion Across Borders: Transnational Immigrant Networks*, 93–110.

Solivan, Samuel. 1998. "Interreligious Dialogue: An Hispanic American Pentecostal Perspective." Pp. 37–45 in *Grounds for Understanding: Ecumenical Resources for Responses to Religious Pluralism*. Edited by S. Mark Heim. Grand Rapids, MI: Eerdmans.

Sullivan, Kathleen. 2000a. "St. Mary's Catholic Church: Celebrating Domestic Religion." In Ebaugh, *Religion and the New Immigrants: Continuities and Adaptations in Immigrant Congregations*, 125–140.

———. 2000b. "Iglesia de Dios: An Extended Family." In Ebaugh, *Religion and the New Immigrants: Continuities and Adaptations in Immigrant Congregations*, 141–151.

Torre, Miguel A. de la. 2000. "Cubans in Babylon: Exodus and Exile." Pp. 73–91 in *Sacred Texts and Human Experience in Caribbean Cultures and Traditions*. Edited by N. Samuel Murrell. New York: St. Martin's Press.

Traverzo Galarza, David. 1998. "Historical Roots of the Contemporary US Latino Presence: a Latino Protestant Evangelical Contribution." In Casarella, *El Cuerpo de Cristo: The Hispanic Experience in the U.S. Catholic Church*, 228–243.

Valentin, Benjamin. 2001. "Strangers No More: an Introduction to, and an Interpretation of, U.S. Hispanic/Latino/a Theology." In Pinn, *Ties that Bind: The African-American and Hispanic-American/Latino(a) Theologies in Dialogue*, 38–53.

Vásquez, Manuel A. 2001a. "Battling Spiritism and the Need for Catholic Orthodoxy." Pp. 449–461 in *Religions of the United States in Practice*. Edited by Colleen McDannell. Vol. II. Princeton, NJ: Princeton University Press.

———. 2001b. "Charismatic Renewal among Latino Catholics." In McDannell, *Religions of the United States in Practice*, 346–354.

Whalen, Carmen Teresa. 1998. "Bridging Homeland and Barrio Politics: The Young Lords in Philadelphia." Pp. 107–123 in *The Puerto Rican Movement: Voices From The Diaspora*. Edited by Andrés Torres and José E. Velázquez. Philadelphia: Temple University Press.

Zald, Mayer N., and John D. McCarthy. 1998. "Religious Groups as Crucibles of Social Movements." Pp. 24–49 in *Sacred Companies: Organizational Aspects of Religion and Religious Aspects of Organizations*. Edited by N.J. Demerath III, Peter Dobkin Hall, Terry Schmidt, and Rhys H. Williams. New York: Oxford University Press.

Zea, María Cecilia, Michael A. Mason, and Alejandro Murguía. 2000. "Psychotherapy with Members of Latino/Latina Religions and Spiritual Traditions." In Richards, *Handbook of Psychotherapy and Religious Diversity*, 397–419.

Books

Bendroth, Margaret Lamberts, and Virginia Lieson Brereton, eds. 2002. *Women and Twentieth- Century Protestantism*. Urbana, IL: University of Illinois Press.

Boonprasat Lewis, Nantawan, ed. 1998. *Revolution of Spirit: Ecumenical Theology in Global Perspective: Essays in Honor of Richard Shaull*. Grand Rapids, MI: Eerdmans.

Brown, Delwin, Sheila Greeve Davaney, and Kathryn Tanner, eds. 2001. *Converging on Culture: Theologians in Dialogue with Cultural Analysis and Criticism*. New York: Oxford University Press.

Budde, Michael L., and Robert W. Brimlow, eds. 2000. *The Church as Counterculture*. Albany, NY: State University of New York Press.

Campoamor, Diana, William Diaz, and Henry Ramos, eds. 1999. *Nuevos Senderos: Reflections on Hispanics and Philanthropy*. Houston, TX: Arte Publico Press.

Carey, Patrick W., and Earl C. Muller, eds. 1997. *Theological Education in the Catholic Tradition: Contemporary Challenges*. New York: Crossroad.

Carnes, Tony, and Anna Karpathakis, eds. 2001. *New York Glory: Religions in the City*. New York: New York University Press.

Casarella, Peter J., and Raul Gomez, eds. 1998. *El Cuerpo de Cristo: the Hispanic Presence in the U.S. Catholic Church*. New York: Crossroad.

Cenkner, William, ed. 1996. *The Multicultural Church: A New Landscape in US Theologies*. Mahwah, NJ: Paulist Press.

Clarke, Peter B., ed. 1998. *New Trends and Developments in African Religions*. Westport, CN: Greenwood Press.

Cnann, Ram A., and Stephanie C. Boddie. 2002. *The Invisible Caring Hand: American Congregations and the Provision of Welfare*. New York: New York University Press.

Cnann, Ram A., Robert J. Wineburg, and Stephanie C. Boddie. 1999. *The Newer Deal: Social Work and Religion in Partnership*. New York: Colombia University Press.

Connors, Michael. 2001. *Inculturated Pastoral Planning, The U.S. Hispanic Experience*. Rome: Pontificia Univ Gregoriana.

Cortina, Regina, and Mónica Gendreau, eds. 2003. *Immigrants and Schooling: Mexicans in New York*. Staten Island: Center for Migration Studies.

Coutin, Susan Bibler. 2000. *Legalizing Moves: Salvadoran Immigrants' Struggle for U.S. Residency*. Ann Arbor: University of Michigan Press.

Crahan, Margaret, and Alberto Vourvoulias Bush, eds. 1997. *The City and the World: NewYork's Global Future*. New York: Council on Foreign Relations.

Dahm, Charles P. 2004. *Pastoral Mninistry in a Hispanic Community*. New York: Paulist Press.

Dalton, Frederick John. 2003. The Moral Vision of César Chávez. Maryknoll, NY: Orbis Books.

Darder, Antonia, and Rodolfo D. Torres, eds. 1998. *The Latino Studies Reader: Culture, Economy, and Society*. Madlen, MA: Blackwell.

Davis, Kenneth G., Eduardo C. Fernández, and Verónica Méndez. 2002. *United States Hispanic Catholics: Trends and Works, 1990–2000*. Scranton, PA: Scranton University Press.

Davis, Kenneth G., and Jorge L. Presmanes. 2000. *Preaching and Culture in Latino Congregations*. Chicago: Liturgy Training Publications.

Davis, Kenneth G., and Yolanda Tarango, eds. 2000. *Bridging Boundaries: The Pastoral Care of U.S. Hispanics*. Tonawanda, NY: University of Toronto Press.

Demerath III, N.J., Peter Dobkin Hall, et. al, eds. 1998. *Sacred Companies: Organizational Aspects of Religion and Religious Aspects of Organizations*. New York: Oxford University Press.

Díaz-Stevens, Ana María, and Anthony M. Stevens-Arroyo. 1998. *Recognizing the Latino Resurgence in U.S. Religión: The Emmaus Paradigm*. Boulder, CO: Westview Press.

Dillon, Michele, ed. 2003. *Handbook for the Sociology of Religion*. New York: Cambridge University Press.

Ebaugh, Helen, and Janet Saltzman Chafetz, eds. 2000. *Religion and The New Immigrants: Continuities and Adaptations in Immigrant Congregations*. Walnut Creek, CA: AltaMira Press.

———. 2002. *Religion Across Borders: Transnational Immigrant Networks*. New York: AltaMira Press.

Elizondo, Virgilio P., and Timothy M. Matovina. 1998a. *Mestizo Worship: A Pastoral Approach to Liturgical Ministry.* Collegeville, MN: Liturgical Press.

———. 1998b. *San Fernando Cathedral: Soul of the City.* Maryknoll, NY: Orbis Books.

Espin, Orlando O., and Miguel H. Díaz. 1999. *From the Heart of Our People: Latino/a Explorations in Catholic Systematic Theology.* Maryknoll, NY: Orbis Books.

Espinosa, Gastón, Virgilio Elizondo, and Jesse Miranda, eds. 2005. *Latino Religions and Civic Activism in the United States.* New York: Oxford University Press.

Flores, William V., and Rina Benmayor, eds. 1997. *Latino Cultural Citizenship: Claiming Identity, Space, and Rights.* Boston: Beacon Press.

Flory, Richard W., and Donald E. Miller, eds. 2000. *GenX Religion.* New York: Routledge.

Foner, Nancy, ed. 2001. *New Immigrants in New York.* New York: Columbia University Press.

Freyne, Seán, and Ellen van Wolde. 2002. *The Many Voices of the Bible.* London: SCM Press.

García, F. Chris, ed. 1997. *Pursuing Power: Latinos and the Political System.* Notre Dame: University of Notre Dame Press.

Gittell, Ross, and Avis Vidal. 1998 *Community Organizing: Building Social Capital as a Development Strategy.* Thousand Oaks, CA: Sage Publications.

Gracia, Jorge J. E., and Pablo DeGreiff, eds. 2000. *Hispanics/Latinos in the United States: Ethnicity, Race, and Rights.* New York: Routledge.

Haddad, Yvonne-Yazbeck, Jane Smith, and John Esposito, eds. 2003. *Religion and Immigration: Christian, Jewish, and Muslim Experiences in the United States.* New York: AltaMira Press.

Harper, Nile. 1998. *Urban Churches, Vital Signs: Beyond Charity Toward Justice.* Grand Rapids, MI.: Eerdmans.

Harris, Margaret. 1998. *Organizing God's Work: Challenges for Churches and Synagogues.* New York: St. Martin's Press.

Heim, S. Mark, ed. 1998. *Grounds For Understanding: Ecumenical Resources for Responses to Religious Pluralism.* Grand Rapids: Eerdmans.

Jacobsen, Douglas, and William Vance Trollinger. 1998. *Reforming the Center: American Protestantism, 1900 to the Present.* Grand Rapids, MI: Eerdmans.

Jones, Serene, and Margaret A. Farley. 1999. *Liberating Eschatology: Essays in Honor of Letty M. Russell.* Louisville, KY: Westminster John Knox Press.

Kujawa-Holbrook, Sheryl A., ed. 1998. *Disorganized Religion: the Evangelization of Youth and Young Adults.* Boston: Cowley Publications.

Larson, Scott, and Karen Free, eds. 2003. *City Lights: Ministry Essentials for Reaching Urban Youth.* Loveland, CO: Group Publishing.

Levitt, Peggy. 2001. *The Transnational Villagers.* Berkeley, CA: University of California Press.

Livezey, Lowell W., ed. 2000. *Public Religion and Urban Transformation: Faith in the City.* New York: New York University Press.

Maldonado, David, Jr., ed. 1999. *Protestantes/Protestants: Hispanic Christianity within Mainline Traditions.* Nashville: Abingdon Press.

Matovina, Timothy M., ed. 2000. *Beyond Borders: Writings of Virgilio Elizondo and Friends.* Maryknoll, NY: Orbis Books.

Matovina, Timothy M., and Gerald Poyo. 2000. *Presente!: U.S. Latino Catholics from Colonial Origins to the Present.* Maryknoll, NY: Orbis Books.

Matthiessen, Peter. 2000. *Sal si puedes = (Escape if you can): Cesar Chavez and the New American Revolution.* Berkeley: University of California Press.

Maynard-Reid, Pedrito U. 2000. *Diverse Worship: African-American, Caribbean and Hispanic Perspectives.* Downers Grove: InterVarsity Press.

Mazur, Eric Michael, and Kate McCarthy, eds. 2001. *God in the Details.* New York: Routledge.

McConnell, Michael W., Robert F. Cochran Jr., and Angela C. Carmella, eds. 2001. *Christian Perspectives on Legal Thought*. New Haven, CT: Yale University Press.

McDannell, Collen, ed. 2001. *Religions of the United States in Practice*. Vol. II. Princeton, NJ: Princeton University Press.

Meyer, David S., Nancy Whittier, and Belinda Robnett, eds. 2002. *Social Movements: Identity, Culture, and the State*. New York: Oxford University Press.

Morales, Ed. 2002. *Living in Spanglish: The Search for Latino Identity in America*. New York: St. Martin's Press.

Morgan, David, and Sally M. Promey, eds. 2001. *The Visual Culture of American Religions*. Berkeley, CA: University of California Press.

Morrill, Bruce T., ed. 1999. *Bodies of Worship: Explorations in Theory and Practice*. Collegeville, MN: Liturgical Press.

Murrell, N. Samuel, ed. 2000. *Sacred Texts and Human Experience in Caribbean Cultures and Traditions*. New York: St. Martin's Press.

Nabhan-Warrend, Kristy. 2005. *The Virgin Of El Barrio: Marian Apparitions, Catholic Evangelizing, and Mexican American Activism*. New York: New York University.

Orsi, Robert, ed. 1999. *Gods of the City: Religion and the American Urban Landscape*. Bloomington, IN: Indiana University Press.

Peterson, Anna L., Manuel A. Vásquez, and Philip J. Williams, eds. 2001. *Christianity, Social Change, and Globalization in the Americas*. New Brunswick, NJ: Rutgers University Press.

Pinn, Anthony B., and Benjamin Valentin, eds. 2001. *Ties that Bind: The African-American and Hispanic-American/Latino(a) Theologies in Dialogue*. London: Continuum.

Putnam, Robert D. 2000. *Bowling Alone: The Collapse and Revival of American Community*. New York: Simon and Schuster.

Ramirez, Johnny, and Edwin I. Hernández. 2003. *Avance: A Vision of a New Mañana*. Loma Linda, CA: Loma Linda University Press.

Rausch, Thomas P., ed. 2004. *Evangelizing America*. New York. Paulist Press.

Richards, P. Scott, and Allen E. Bergin, eds. 2002. *Handbook of Psychotherapy and Religious Diversity*. Washington, DC: American Psychological Association.

Rodriguez, Clara. 2000. *Changing Race: Latinos, the Census and the History of Ethnicity*. New York: New York University Press.

Rodriguez, David. 2002. *Latino National Political Coalitions: Struggles and Challenges*. New York: Routledge.

Rodriguez, Richard. 2002. *Brown: The Last Discovery of America*. New York: Viking Penguin.

Rudolph, Susanne Hoeber, and James Piscatori. 1997. *Transnational Religion and Fading States*. Boulder: Westview Press.

Ruiz, Vicki L. 1998. *From out of the Shadows: Mexican Women in Twentieth-Century America*. New York: Oxford University Press.

Selznick, Philip. 2002. *The Communitarian Persuasion*. Baltimore: The John Hopkins University Press.

Shaull, Richard, and Waldo A. Cesar. 2000. *Pentecostalism and the Future of the Christian Churches: Promises, Limitations, Challenges*. Grand Rapids, MI: Eerdmans.

Smidt, Corwin, ed. 2003. *Religion As Social Capital: Producing the Common Good*. Waco, TX: Baylor University Press.

Smith, Christine M., ed. 1998. *Preaching Justice: Ethnic and Cultural Perspectives*. Cleveland: United Church Press.

Smith, Michael P., and Luis Eduardo Guarnizo, eds. 1998. *Transnationalism from Below*. New Brunswick, NJ: Transaction Publishers.

Spickard, James V., J. Shawn Landres, and Meredith B. McGuire, eds. 2002. *Personal Knowledge and Beyond Reshaping the Ethnography of Religion*. New York: New York University Press.

Suárez-Orozco, Marcelo M., ed. 1998. *Crossings: Mexican Immigration in Interdisciplinary Perspective.* Cambridge, MA: Harvard University Press.

Suárez-Orozco, Marcelo M., and Mariela Paez. 2002. *Latinos Remaking America.* Berkeley, CA: University of California Press.

Synan, Vinson. 1997 *The Holiness-Pentecostal Tradition: Charismatic Movements in the 20th century.* Grand Rapids, MI: Eerdmans.

Szasz, Ferenc M., and Richard W. Etulain, eds. 1997. *Religion in Modern New Mexico.* Albuquerque, NM: University of New Mexico Press.

Torres, Andrés, and José E. Velázquez, eds. 1998. *The Puerto Rican Movement: Voices From the Diaspora.* Philadelphia: Temple University Press.

Torres, Rodolfo D., and George Katsiaficas, eds. 1999. *Latino Social Movements: Historical and Theoretical Perspectives.* New York: Routledge.

Tripole, Martin R., ed. 1999. *Promise Renewed: Jesuit Higher Education for a New Millennium.* Chicago: Loyola Press.

Trueba, Enrique T. 1999. *Latinos Unidos: From Cultural Diversity to the Politics of Solidarity.* Lanham, MD: Rowman and Littlefeld Publishers.

Tweed, Thomas. 1997. *Our Lady of the Exile: Diasporic Religion at a Cuban Catholic Shrine in Miami.* Oxford: Oxford University Press.

Vento, Arnoldo Carlos. 1998. *Mestizo: the History, Culture and Politics of the Mexican and the Chicano: the Emerging Mestizo-Americans.* Lanham, MD: U. Press of America.

Walsh, Froma, ed. 1999. *Spiritual Resources in Family Therapy.* New York: Guilford Press.

Warner, Stephen R., and Judith Wittner, eds. 1999. *Gatherings in Diaspora: Religious Communities and the New Immigration.* Philadelphia: Temple University Press.

Warren, Mark R. 2001. *Dry Bones Rattling: Community Building to Revitalize American Democracy.* Princeton: Princeton University Press.

Warren, Mark R., and Richard L. Wood. 2001. *Faith-Based Community Organizing: The State of the Field.* Jericho, NY: Interfaith Funders.

Weaver, Mary Jo, ed. 1999. *What's left?* Bloomington, IN: Indiana University Press.

Wilkerson, Barbara, ed. 1997. *Multicultural Religious Education.* Birmingham, AL: Religious Education Press.

Wood, Richard L. 2002. *Faith in Action: Religion, Race, and Democratic Organizing in America.* Chicago, IL: University of Chicago Press.

Yohn, Susan M. 1995. *A Contest of Faiths: Missionary Women and Pluralism in the American Southwest.* Ithaca, NY: Cornell University Press.

Mongraphs and Dissertations

Aponte, Edwin David. 1998. "Latino Protestant Identity and Empowerment: Hispanic Religion, Community, Rhetoric, and Action in a Philadelphia Case Study." Ph.D. dissertation, Temple University.

Astacio, Victor. 1999. "Marital Satisfaction, Religious Problem-Solving Style and Coping with a Hispanic Sample." Ph.D. dissertation, Caribbean Center for Advanced Studies, Miami Institute of Psychology.

Austin, Stephen R. 2000. "'Love the Alien As Yourself, for you Were Aliens': Developing a Model for the Impact Church of Christ's Response to the Needs of Undocumented Hispanic Persons." D.Min dissertation, Abilene Christian University.

Baker, Jill Annette Harris. 2003. "Long-Term Responses to Childhood Sexual Abuse: Life Histories of Hispanic Women in Midlife." Ph.D. dissertation, Case Western Reserve University.

Benavides, Luis Enrique. 2000. "North American Hispanic Theologies: A Tillichian Revisioning." Th.D. dissertation, Gordon Conwell Theological Seminary.

Byrd, Mark. 2004. "Developing a Strategy for Calvary Baptist Church to Plant an Hispanic Congregation in Waynesboro, Mississippi." D.Min. dissertation, New Orleans Baptist Theological Seminary.

Cowden, Clark. 2001. "How the Presbyterian Church (USA) Can Develop a Meaningful Hispanic Ministry." D. Min. dissertation, Covenant Theological Seminary.

Cuellar, Rolando Wilfredo. 2002. "The influence of spiritual and educational formation on the missionary vision and programs of four Hispanic churches in the United States of America." Ph.D. dissertation, Trinity Evangelical Divinity School.

Davis, Brian K. 2003. "Preparing Anglo Adults to Teach Children in a Hispanic Sunday School." D.Min. dissertation, Erskine Theological Seminary.

Felipe, Roger. 2003. "Connecting Postmodern Hispanic Teenagers to the Church: Principles and Strategies for Reaching and Keeping High School Kids in the Community of Faith." D.Min. dissertation, Gordon Conwell Theological Seminary.

Fils-Aime Wentler, Alicia. 2003. "A Church Response to Latina Women With Mental Illness." D.Min. dissertation, Theological School, Drew University.

Gallo, Ana-Maria. 2003. "The Lived Experience of Latina Women Giving Birth in the United States." Ph.D. dissertation, University of San Diego.

Galvez, Alyshia. 2004. "In the Name of Guadalupe: Religion, Politics and Citizenship Among Mexicans in New York." Ph.D. dissertation, Dept. of Anthropology, New York University.

García, Ricardo. 2001. "Obtaining Consent and Establishing Competence For Marriage Nullity Cases Involving Hispanic Immigrants who Live in the United States." J.C.L., The Catholic University of America.

Gerrault, Joe. 2002. "Training Hispanic Church Leaders For Basic Youth Ministry." D. Min. dissertation, Southwestern Baptist Theological Seminary.

Guel, David N. 2003. "Developing an Awareness Strategy for Intentional Ministry to Undocumented Hispanics in South Texas." D.Min. dissertation, Southwestern Baptist Theological Seminary.

Guerrero-Avila, Juan Bautista. 1999. "The Hispanic Experience in Higher Education Mexican Southern Baptists' Attitudes Toward Higher Education." Ph.D. dissertation, School of Intercultural Studies, Biola University.

Guzman, Lucy. 2002. "A Strategy for Hispanic Leadership Development for Spanish Churches in the United States." A Ministry Focus Paper, School of Theology, Fuller Theological Seminary.

Hatcher, Denise Leigh. 2003. "Lessons Learned While Suspended Between Two Cultures: the Life History of a Latina Adult Educator." Ph.D. dissertation, Northern Illinois University.

Holliday, Karen Veronica. 2003. "Saints as Sinners: Healing and Hegemony in Southern California Botanicas." Ph.D. dissertation, University of California, Irvine.

Kozart, Michael Frederick. 1999. "Practice, Meaning and Belief in Latino Pentecostalism: a Study in the Dynamics of Religious Healing, Theology and Social Order." Ph.D. dissertation, Medical Anthropology, University of California, Berkeley.

Lastra, Juan C. 2004. "Single-Subject Experiental Design Using Melodic Intonation Therapy with an Adult Hispanic Male: A Case Study." Psy.D. dissertation, Wheaton College Graduate School.

Lay, Syndey. 2003. "Spirituality and Depression among Elderly Asian and Latino Americans." M.S.W. dissertation, California State University, Long Beach.

Lema, David R. 1997. "Development of a Church-Based Model of Ministry Designed to Meet the Needs of Hispanic Refugees in Hialeah, Fla. Through a Select Group of Leaders of the Iglesia Bautista West Hialeah." D.Min. dissertation, New Orleans Baptist Theological Seminary.

Lin, Irene Ching-Ting. 2000. "Protestant strategies: A study of assimilation modes in three Hispanic Protestant churches in downtown Los Angeles (California)." Ph.D. dissertation, University of Southern California.

Machado, Frederick. 1999. "Resourcing San Diego Hispanic Churches through Internet Development." D. Min. dissertation, Bethel Theological Seminary.

Marquez Maymir, Raquel. 1998. "Religiousness, Coping, and Mental Health Among Hispanic Individuals." Ph.D. dissertation, University of Cincinnati.

McCarthy, Malachy Richard. 2002. "Which Christ Came to Chicago: Catholic and Protestant Programs to Evangelize, Socialize and Americanize the Mexican Immigrant, 1900–1940." Ph.D. dissertation, Loyola University of Chicago.

Medina, Lara. 1998. "LAS HERMANAS: Chicana/Latina Religious-Political Activism, 1971–1997." Ph.D. dissertation, Claremont Graduate School.

Moitinho, Elias Santos Lopes. 2000. "The Effects of Marriage Enrichment Conferences of Marital Satisfaction of English-Speaking Hispanic Married Couples." Ph.D. dissertation, Department of Psychology and Counseling, Southwestern Baptist Theological Seminary.

Orozco, Eleazar. 2004. "Narrative Hermeneutics and Homiletics and the Hispanic Culture." D. Min. dissertation, Truett Theological Seminary.

Owen-Gemoets, Sara. 1997. "Hispanic Ministry: Strategies for Enabling an Established Congregation to Minister Effectively in an Inner-City Poverty Area." D. Min. dissertation, Drew University.

Palacios, Joseph Martin. 2001. "Locating the Social in Social Justice: Social Justice Teaching and Practice in the American and Mexican Catholic Churches." Ph.D. dissertation, Graduate Division, University of California, Berkeley.

Pantoja, Segundo. 1999. "Religion and Parental Involvement in the Education of Hispanics." Ph.D. dissertation, City University of New York.

Pitti, Gina Marie. 2003. "To 'Hear About God in Spanish': Ethnicity, Church, and Community Activism in the San Francisco Archdiocese's Mexican American Colonias, 1942–1965." Ph.D. dissertation, Department of History, Stanford University.

Prather, Craig M. 1999. "The Hispanic American 'Man of the House': Analysis and Comparison of Cultural Machismo with the Servant Lifestyle of Biblical Manhood." D. Min. dissertation, Dallas Theological Seminary.

Quiñones, Luis R. 2004. "House for Everyone: A Homeownership Training for the Hispanic Community in Philadelphia." D.Min. dissertation, Theological School, Drew University.

Ramon, Carmen Elisa. 2001. "A Study of Help-Seeking Behaviors and Perceptions of Mental Health Utilization Among Latinos." M.S.W. dissertation, Department of Social Work, California State University, Long Beach.

Reed-Bouley, Jennifer. 1998. "Guiding Moral Action: A Study of the United Farm Workers' Use of Catholic Social Teaching and Religious Symbols." Ph.D. dissertation, Loyola University, Chicago.

Ruiz-Balsara, Silvia Natasha. 2002. "Gender Belief Systems and Culture: The Endorsement of Machismo and Marianismo by Hispanics/Latinos across Gender, Acculturation, Education, Socioeconomic, and Religion Categories." Ph.D. dissertation, University of Arkansas.

Russell, Bradley T. 2002. "El Proyecto para Escuchar Moving Towards Mutuality in Hispanic-Anglo Mission." D.Min. dissertation, Austin Presbyterian Theological Seminary.

Solís, Jocelyn. 2002. "The Transformation of Illegality as an Identity: A Study of the Organization of Undocumented Mexican Immigrants and Their Children in New York City." Ph.D. dissertation, City University of New York.

Vasquez, Manuel A. 2001. "Saving Souls Transnationally: Pentecostalism and Gangs in El Salvador and the United States." Working paper, The Project on Lived Theology. The University of Virginia, Charlottesville, VA, http://www.livedtheology.org/pdfs/MVasquez.pdf

Webber, Malcolm. 2000. "A Comparison of Hofstede's Power Distance Index Between Mexican and Anglo-American Christians: The Influence of Culture on Preference for Decision-Making Structures and Leadership Styles in American Churches." Ph.D. dissertation, Center for Leadership Studies, Regent University.

Wilson, Catherine Evans. 2003. "A Different Kind of Mandate: Latino Faith-Based organizations and the Communitarian Impulse." Ph.D. Dissertation, University of Pennsylvania.

Wood, Robert W. 1999. "Making Disciples Through Hispanic Home Cell Groups." D. Min. dissertation, Southwestern Baptist Theological Seminary.

Zone-Andrews, Enrique. 1997. "Suggested Competencies for the Hispanic Protestant Church Leader of the Future." Ph.D. dissertation, Graduate School of Education and Psychology, Pepperdine University.

INDEX